The Courage
to Change

From Insight
to Self-Innovation

The Courage to Change

From Insight to Self-Innovation

by
EDRITA FRIED, Ph.D.

Grove Press, Inc., New York

First Evergreen Edition 1981
First Printing 1981
ISBN: 0-394-17935-8
Library of Congress Catalog Card Number: 81-47633

Library of Congress Cataloging in Publication Data

Fried, Edrita.
    The courage to change.

    Bibliography: p. 232.
    Includes index.
    1. Personality change.   2. Psychotherapy.
3. Ego strength.   4. Insight in psychotherapy.
I. Title.
RC480.5.F75   1981   616.89'14   81-47633
ISBN 0-394-17935-8 (pbk.)   AACR2

Manufactured in the United States of America
GROVE PRESS, INC., 196 West Houston Street,
New York, N.Y. 10014

Contents

Introduction

For several decades psychotherapy, an offshoot of psychoanalysis, has been preoccupied with particular diagnostic questions. The special emphasis was on the causes, and especially on the unconscious roots of the problems with which patients struggled. Moreover, most difficulties were conceived of as the result of conflicts between various layers or departments of the psyche, namely the id, ego, and superego. The assumption underlying the interest in the genesis of conflicts was that an individual who could comprehend all sides of a conflict, could understand which cast of characters had been responsible for that conflict, and could come to grips with its genesis, would recover from psychological handicaps. Tenacious repressions would be lifted, psychological energies freed, and the psychic system would resume full functioning, for it was thought that functioning lay merely dormant in personality disorders while conflicts held sway.

The stress, then, was on insight into the past. Indeed, so important was the emphasis on self-understanding that many persons became their own diagnosticians. They proved fully informed of the genesis of the disturbances from which they suffered. But what steps to take in order to find relief they frequently did not know.

Today, dynamic psychotherapy values genetic insight greatly, but it is equally concerned with the traces, stamps, markings which the past has left on the present-day psychic structures. Individuals who suffered damages in the past function under handicaps in the present which are the direct results of past injuries. Their psychic structures have remained primitive in many spots. They proceed under the umbrella of psychic organizing principles that are suited to a child but not an adult life: narcissistic inaccessibility, dependency, hostile passivity are among such primitive principles. By contrast, other leitmotifs such as genuine interest in others, independence, and directness are largely absent. The ego and many of its functions are arrested, and the self lacks authenticity.

These psychological disabilities in the present occur not only in borderline conditions but in very many so-called neurotic states as well. They are the result in the present of repeated interferences by the early environment with individual emotional, psychological, and cognitive development. While the injuries were occasioned in the past, the important fact is that they influence and affect the present. They have great impact on decisions made now, on moods, on the caliber of self-esteem, and on the all-important human relations with others. To examine the markings and vulnerabilities stamped by the past on the present psychic structures and, above all, to correct them through special forms of psychological learning, must become a principal goal.

This book aims to show that the possibilities for changing personality structures and correcting ego arrests exist and may take many different forms. The markings left by the past, primitive though they are, should not be compared to indelible scars. Rather, they resemble undeveloped musculature or an unsteady gait which can be improved by physiotherapy. Without stretching the analogy too far, psychotherapy can do the same for damaged psychic structures through the discovery and practice of innate strength and through development of greater familiarity with one's environment. Dynamic psychotherapy is constantly concerned with ridding persons of ego deficits and deformations by making them aware of hitherto undiscovered possibilities and by encouraging new types of functioning. Instead of dwelling exclusively on pathology, the emphasis is on "yes, I can" feelings. Hence, we shall have to stress psychological reorientation, the acquisition of ego *assets* where previously the personality was over-burdened by ego *liabilities,* and the connection with heretofore cut-off emotions. Such psychological, emotional, and cognitive enrichment is of primary importance for all problem ridden patients and not only for the so-called borderline conditions.

It is one of the primary purposes of this book to spell out the significance of ego arrests which are typically encountered in treatment and to describe psychoanalytically-anchored dynamic repair experiences that can become available. Among the areas of deficit functioning and explicit processes of repair discussed are these: the nature of narcissistic inaccessibility and its possible correction; distinctions between different functions which passivity fulfills and alternate routes leading to related healthy goals; unconscious aggression and, indeed, unconscious rage, and body clues alerting the individual to these emotions; transforming aggression into energy; the lack of specific self-representations and the gradual establishment of an adult self-image; the gradual development of self-esteem. A thorough application of psychoanalytic principles differentiates the learning experiences described in this volume from the learning that has been perfected by behavior therapy.

Especially important here is the fact that psychoanalytically based psychological learning takes place in and through the transference. In examining the possibilities of change, the role of reparatory experiences through and in the transference is greatly stressed. Reparatory experiences, it is shown, can be gained without necessarily requiring the detour of regressions to past expectations, fears, and submissions, to name but a few established psychological trends. The primary benefits of reparatory experiences derive from the ever clearer understanding that the therapist is a new object. With this in mind, the transference offers an opportunity to forge a relationship that is different from and superior to the damaging relations with others that occurred in the past. Here, in the ongoing transference with a non-punitive and understanding partner, fresh prototypes of relating can be envisaged and tried out. The carryover of such new prototype relations into everday life, whereupon greater freedom, enjoyment, and creativity ensue, is another major goal of therapy. It can be greatly facilitated through group treatment.

The process of "working through" which, in my opinion, has received far too little attention in the literature has a central bearing on the occurrence of change. Doing a good job with "working through" determines whether or not insights, once they are gained, are absorbed, by being actively used for the purpose of achieving alterations of psychic structures, and are applied towards the improvement of the quality of life. This implies that the insights be inspected from different angles; that the patient use newly gained insights in diverse situations and keep track of the results. When individuals are encouraged to "work something through," they feel anxious at first in making actual use of their widened self-understanding and allowing heretofore repressed feelings to surface. But some risks have to be taken in the pursuit of a cure.

The book deals with the fact that the "working through" process frequently requires that ego arrests be settled. Indeed, the "working through" process is seen as synonymous with ego enrichment. Only as the patient substitutes ego assets for ego arrests can insights be utilized. The main reason for filing the insights away instead of acting on them, as it frequently turns out, is the existence and stubbornness of some primitive aspect of the psychological structure. Thus, many persons can understand clearly that they are dependent or that they procrastinate; however, only after they acquire the capacity for first one and then another independent decision can they do something with their awareness of what the deficiency is. Only if a procrastinating person, to give another example, who uses the piling up of chores to obtain a feeling of fullness, gets the sense of being full in some other way can the guilt-provoking habit of postponing duties be abandoned.

Ego enrichment is achieved in many ways: by acknowledging and respecting one's own feelings regardless of whether others consider them to be right or wrong; by learning to accept the primitive features of one's psyche, even while wishing to change to higher levels of functioning; by becoming reconnected with our feelings, the semi-biological signposts that steer us through life and refresh us; by acquiring finely tuned ego skills. The basic ideas are simple but gigantic and were shown to us by Freud: to make friends with the archaic basic structure on which the psyche is based, while at the same time moving on to higher levels of development. These are abstract ideals that have to be carried out concretely if one is to feel the rewarding pleasures of full and joyous functioning.

ACKNOWLEDGEMENTS

In writing this book, I have been stimulated and helped, above all, by what I learned from my students and trainees and, of course, my patients. I wish to thank all of them for assisting me and, I do not hesitate to say, sometimes forcing me, to shape, to clarify, and to test my ideas about the process from problems to insight and from insight to change.

From among my collegues with whom I had fruitful discussions, I mention especially and with deep gratitude my esteemed friend of longstanding, Dr. Helen Durkin. I am also most grateful to my treasured collegue Dr. Marjorie Taggart White, with whom I have exchanged ideas for many years.

To Dr. Lewis R. Wolberg, Founder of the Postgraduate Center for Mental Health, whose rare combination of humanity, leadership and common sense has never ceased to amaze and strengthen me, to the Institute he created, and to my colleagues there goes my highest appreciation.

My daughter Jaqueline Fried Thomann, who has followed me in the profession, and my husband, who had the advantage of not belonging to the profession, patiently read various versions of sections of the book and gave me very valuable and much appreciated comments.

I cordially thank my long-time secretary Mrs. Ruth Marcus, who with great skill always found her way through a manuscript filled with insertions.

Edrita Fried

January, 1980

The Courage to Change

From Insight to Self-Innovation

1

Profiles
of Change

Individuals who are beset by psychological handicaps need not remain the captives of their problems. They can change significantly. More than that, they can relish the very changing process itself. This they accomplish by *gradually* opening themselves up to consecutive insights and to new, growth-furthering experiences. The human psyche, though highly complex, is essentially a *flexible* system if compared, for instance, with the instinctual equipment on which animal species have to rely in order to navigate safely through their environment. Although our instinctual equipment offers, in case of danger, a reliable and clear-cut warning and response system, it lacks the adaptability which allows the human psyche to grow. Our psychic system also possesses greater flexibility than our body system, even though modern medicine and rehabilitation research have found the body to be more susceptible to corrective influences than had been assumed.

The aim of dynamic psychotherapy is to bring about a number of profound transformations of the psychic structure and the psychic functions. Let us, to begin with, touch on a few of the most essential transformations.

3

1. A disturbed psyche is usually alienated from many of its own basic emotions. Those emotions have to be, and can be, recaptured. Having been, in early life, deemed "wrong" or bad, they became extinct, whether because they were repressed or because they never "saw the light of day" to begin with. They were considered so dangerous that they never were brought into contact with language and other forms of expression. They thus remained fuzzy and undelineated; consequently they were relegated to a state of incomplete consciousness, which is not the same as saying they were made unconscious. When emotions are discovered and rediscovered, the individual is reunited with basic affects and feels newly animated, richer and much more substantial. He or she possesses in the affects an important guide through the vagaries of life, for, in a manner that differs from our cognitive processes, the emotions attune us to what goes on inside our own self and in the outside world. They are the basis for instinctual perceptions that make use of clues which cognitive understanding misses. Our emotions guide us by picking up "hidden" events and the "hidden" significance of psychic and auditory expressions of others and ourselves. To tune in on one's emotions means to admit to oneself that something that is felt exists and deserves to be taken into account.

The question whether an emotion is right or wrong is secondary. The emotions represent bridges between the body and the mind, linking our instinctual inclinations with the mind and its rationality. If we connect with our emotions, we discover what we want. Thereupon, and only as a second step, we make contact with the rational mind to query whether or not to pursue our wants and by what means.

2. Another basic transformation occurs when the psychic structure is shored up and realigned, with its various portions brought into harmony with each other. The term *psychic structure* covers a big territory. Partly we designate by it the organizing principles which individuals have developed to scan and evaluate past and present experiences and to file them in their memory bank. These organizing principles determine the priority of our needs and of the experiences, life-style, and human connections we make to satisfy them. One per-

son equates the feeling of safety with financial safety and, therefore, focuses on the acquisition of wealth. Another gives high priority to the need for variety, etc.

Until we know much more about the ways in which neurological systems and behavior influence each other, we shall also use the term *psychic structures* to refer to differently functioning sub-structures in the psychic system: the administrative ego, the regulative superego, the instinctual id, and the interrelations between these subsystems. There is the assumption that the psychic structures produce the representations or images we have of the own self and of other human objects.

In any event, what we call psychic structure—and the term is used differently by different theorists—is influenced, reorganized and altered as part and parcel of the changing process. For example, a capable woman in her forties came, under the influence of a first psychotherapy, to regard the premature death of her mother to be the result of overwork imposed by the mother's hard-driving husband (the woman's father) and by social conditions. Partly as a result, she became very active in the feminist movement. However, under the impact of her second psychotherapy, the patient focused on the mother's masochistically caused reluctance to protest against pressures and the subsequent assault on her health. The perception altered the daughter's psychic structures by reshaping her organizing principles and mood structure. It led to changes in the patient's outlook and attitudes. While she continued her feminist work with even greater intensity, she went about her projects with greater optimism, which also profoundly affected her personal life. Having previously been seized by pessimistic moods of an inescapable fatalism, she now recognized that choices are available to both women and men, and above all that people have the freedom to seize existing opportunities.

3 Disturbed personalities invariably suffer from developmental arrest. During the most formative early years their psyche did not satisfactorily enter, pass through, and complete each developmental phase from narcissism, over symbiosis and individuation, to object constancy and the forerunners of peer feelings with adults. Instead, the prerequisites for growth and progression were ignored or even

obstructed by the environment. As a result, primary, healthy reorientations towards other human beings, towards the self, and towards the world do not come about because the individual remains stuck when major developmental phases have not been completed. Archaic prototype relationships and feelings linger on. If the narcissistic phase has not gone through full circle, the person will remain excessively self-preoccupied. If the young child has not enjoyed a full symbiotic phase, he or she will, as an adult, demand, often with seemingly inexplicable irritation, constant caretaking experiences, and thus be unable to reach full and generous independence. Such longings or their reverse, namely memories of excessive satiations, render the adult personality vulnerable and lacking in adaptive capacity. And ego skills, which are developed under facilitating conditions during the early life phases, are missing, deformed, or awkward, thus leaving the psyche impoverished.

As stated, developmental arrest is invariably due to failures of the environment to grant the necessary needs: that the narcissistic bubble be burst; that the symbiotic union between mother and child be gradually terminated; that needs for individuation and self-assertion be recognized and the individual permitted, indeed encouraged, to exercise them proudly; that object constancy be furthered by the environment and certain forerunners of parity between child and adults be recognized. When such developments occur, a sound basis for ego and self is formed. It is one of the goals of all psychotherapy and one of the prerequisites for change that such a basis be created belatedly and ego and self deficits be replaced by ego assets and strength.

Change, then, requires transformations of the ego and the self. Since there exists no complete agreement about the meaning of the two terms, especially about the extent of their overlap, we must at this point clarify their meaning as used in this book.

The term *ego* is a construct usefully implying the existence of psychological structures which are responsible for the practical conduct of life. The ego has many functions or capacities, such as perception, memory, thinking, anticipating, etc. (the forerunners of which were acquired in childhood and youth), that are being perfected and varied more or less continuously. The ego also evolves the defenses. Interestingly enough, analogies between physical and psychological behavior often determine the nature of specific defenses. For instance, detachment, a psychological defense, resembles physiological avoidance and flight. Psychological denial resembles physical hiding and gestures of sweeping something under the rug. The ego integrates various mental defenses and functions into larger strategies. It brings defenses and ego skills into harmony with other branches of the psyche, for instance with our wishes (referred to in Freudian context as the id) and our ideas and conscience (the superego). The ego constantly explores the physical and mental-emotional environment, issues warning signals against looming dangers, and chooses among potentially available defenses. It also carries out a myriad of other tasks.

If the psyche were to be compared with a government, then the ego resembles the administrative branch that sees to it that proper health care, welfare and education be carried out, that the economy be productive, and that the various governmental activities be properly integrated.

The self, as here conceived, is also a construct, which we use to explore various psychological phenomena, at the same time searching for new psychological and neurological data. It has the task of maintaining overall awareness of one's own individual existence. It accomplishes this, in part, by forming a clear self-representation (self-image) and by settling on certain goals which vary with time but cluster, in states of mental health, around steady nuclei.

In pathological states, the self-representation is fuzzy, built around an unstable core and derived from global imitation of and identification with others. In such cases we speak of a false self. By contrast, the healthy self is the outgrowth of selective identifications, ideas, and ideals that have been sifted and molded individually over a period of time. Such a self, because it is not rooted in borrowed conduct, produces continuity and does not function in spurts. Being an *authentic* self, it is the core of a sense of identity. The way in which the self is structured determines that all-important phenomenon, our self-esteem. In creating a true and genuine self, the individual consents to accept his or her personal characteristics, both physical and psychological. For instance, a person who is short and narrow-chested and thinks a good deal in images must learn to acknowledge these characteristics if there is to exist authenticity. At the same time, some physical and emotional-psychological attributes can and indeed need to be altered, for life is rich only if we stretch our body and mind within the potentialities. However, there exist limits to the degree to which aspects of the self—in brief, individual identity—can be bent and changed. As a result, human existence is subject to a duality of constancy and change. The healthy self swings back and forth, as appropriate for the individual, between the need for change and the need for a position of stillness.

When I speak of the necessity to make up for developmental arrest, and specifically the need to replace ego and self deficits by ego and self assets, I refer to forms of ego and self reconstruction which are considered essential in the treatment of any person with serious problems. The treatment might reveal a host of problems: malformations of character structure that lead to marital failures; recurring symptoms such as phobias or anxiety states; mood problems, such as lingering depression and a concomitant need to lie low for fear of either failure or success; or experiences of depersonalization. The important point is that ego and self arrest play a serious role in all symptomatology, not just in borderline cases and other so-called severe psychopathology (Stolorow, 1978; Piaget, 1970). Indeed, defects of the psychological structures and of ego functions render many insights useless. Many so-called neurotics and persons with character disorders work long and hard until they recognize and admit their own shortcomings. But all their insights, hard as they were to come by, do little or nothing by way of a cure. The reason is that existing ego deficits make it impossible for them to translate the insights into practice. Until the ego arrests are relieved and ego assets are developed in their stead, the patients cannot complete what is called the "working through" process.

A typical example was a writers' agent who found herself unable to confront the authors, publishers, and public relations firms that she dealt with. Nor, indeed, could she stand up to her young daughter. This woman was aware of the grave disadvantages caused by this inability to assert herself. However, it was only when she became able to uncover her violent aggression, to express it in the safe laboratory of therapy, and finally to convert rage into assertiveness that she was able to use her insight and face confrontations.

The liabilities of her ego and her self had to be transformed into assets before insight could produce behavioral change.

All persons with lingering difficulties have ego and self flaws. While there do, indeed, exist differences between the so-called neurotic personality on the one hand and the borderline condition and psychotic disturbances on the other, it is erroneous to assume that the many difficulties in loving, working and living faced by the neurotic personality are exclusively the result of conflicts. *Rather, the underlying ego structures and functions are not adequate to resolve the conflicts,* even after the patient has become convinced that solutions and resolutions are necessary.

DYNAMIC PSYCHOTHERAPY — A SPECIFIC LEARNING SYSTEM

Psychoanalysis, as the late Ernst Kris observed, is a theory of learning (Kris, personal communication, 1949). Its offshoot, dynamic psychotherapy, consists in large measure of learning, enriching, and building experiences. These lead to reorientation as far as relations to others and the self are concerned. The learning experiences gained through dynamic psychotherapy also relieve ego and self of acquired deformations and make up for existing gaps in development. We may say that, in large measure, personal change occurs when the psychic structure, especially the ego, grows and gets rid of the deformities into which it was forced, and acquires the shape and functions it would have developed under more fortunate environmental circumstances. It changes as a result of discovering and trying out the potentialities to which, as an immensely inventive and flexible organ, it has access. It develops, furthermore, by learning that emotions, in and by themselves, are not judged by standards of right and wrong. Whatever is felt by an individual is acknowledged in dynamic psychotherapy simply because it exists and not because it is good or bad. As to the discovery of new possibilities, the focus is particularly on new variations in object relations as these emerge in the therapeutic setting. Whenever a narcissistic person, who characteristically "feels nothing," leaves a session, or any other encounter, sad or angry, this is a sign of progress. It shows that his encapsulating cocoon has been punctured.

Divergent schools of psychotherapy fasten on to different prob-

lems, concentrate on different levels of depth, and tend to put dif-
fering emphasis on specific problems and symptoms. Hence, they
recommend varying methods of cure. The therapist's concepts about
the nature of the psychopathology determine to a large degree what
crises in the life history will receive prime attention and what
methods of change will be proposed (Kauff, 1979). But amongst the
goals of all psychotherapies one stands out invariably: to discover
maladaptive behavior patterns and to replace them by adaptive
forms of conduct.

To illustrate, let us look at the kind of learning that takes place in
dynamic psychotherapy, which differs, for instance, considerably
from behavior modification, despite certain convergences. One of
the differences is the way in which insight and learning are combined. Dynamic psychotherapy holds that at times insight can only
occur *after* change has taken place (Fried, 1961). If psychotherapy is
dynamic, it is not overly concerned with the *genesis of maladaptive,
rigid and unhealthy behavior*. We do not restrict ourselves to studying
how primary figures in the childhood environment interfered with
the expression of emotions and with healthy development. It is
equally important that the disturbed person discover *in what ways
long-practiced behavior and feeling patterns have ceased to be functional in the
present-day circumstances*.

The next question is how nonfunctional, traditional patterns that
should have been abandoned can be given up, and what changes in
ego orientation, ego functions and the self structure are required to
make the acquisition of fresh approaches possible and their practice
continuous. The old and obstructive ego orientations, ego functions
and self-representations are sometimes pointed out directly to the
person. However, the need for authenticity and for the emergence of
a sense of independence on the part of the patient calls more often
for another process: that the old obstructions, rigidities and limitations of ego and self be perceived in the way the patient interprets
and shapes the therapeutic setting. When non-functional, outmoded
bits of behavior are identified in the transference, new prototypes of
relating eventually surface. This is so either because they were there,
ready to be released through a catalytic experience, or because the
patient makes an effort to take off in new directions. By continuous
connections between the past and the present, the person is helped to

become really aware of existing deficits, and this serves as a prelude to altered behavior. Furthermore, the unique setting of the patient-therapist relationship is utilized to provide reparatory experiences. These experiences 'are varied, depending on the particular pathology. It may be added that not all reparatory experiences are limited to assurances of affection or to unselective support.

At the same time, it depends on the patient whether or not therapeutic and reparatory opportunities are being used. The only remedy against the patient's frequent unwillingness to learn to live is the removal of resistances—which is what psychotherapy amounts to.

The overcoming of resistance is one of the acid tests of every form of psychotherapy. One method is to point out repeatedly and explicitly the evasions, purposeful misunderstandings, hairsplitting devices, etc. which are used in order to escape the truth. This "frontal attack" method requires long, drawn-out efforts and can become exasperating and overly intellectual. *The process can be shortened by bypassing the resistance in various ways.* One method is to induce the patient to anticipate the consequences, crises and conflicts that are shunned by remaining resistant. Instead of exploring the strategies employed by the patient for the sake of evasion, the patient-therapist team pursues the ticklish psychological issues that are being avoided. The patient is asked to "take the problem further." The individual subsequently envisions what he considers to be the likely consequences of his internal feelings and plans. Almost invariably it is found, when pursuit rather than avoidance of a thought or feeling is contemplated, that the dangers anticipated in the case of pursuit 1) are being seen as too formidable, and 2) can be overcome when reduced to their real proportions. This makes resistance dispensable. Moreover, the forms which resistances are likely to take, and with which the patient should become familiar since they constitute an important aspect of the character structure, can be explained at some later point when tensions and conflicts have lessened and the urgency to evade has become less prominent.

A married woman, Sarah, had come to treatment because of frequent experiences of depersonalization, depressive episodes and an empty marriage. She respected her husband and wished to remain married to him, but could not find the strength to discontinue a love affair that gave her many narcissistic satisfactions. In therapy, whenever Sarah discussed her marital difficulties she soon dropped the subject and resumed talking about her lover. Since one of her purposes in coming to treatment was the sincere desire to improve her marital situation, such diversive tactics obviously presented a resistance.

After pointing out to Sarah a few times how she resisted facing one of her major problems, I took another turn. When her attention wandered from husband to lover I asked her what would happen if she tackled a specific marital problem, for instance her inability to counter the continual criticisms which the otherwise loving husband directed her way. Her response was that her husband would walk out on her should she protest what she called his "beloved" exhortations. I countered by asking Sarah why she feared the real consequences—not a desertion but a series of confrontations with her husband. The answer revealed expectations of a formidable encounter: "I will spit at my husband." "I might want to strangle Robert." "I'll knock down his mother, whose fault it all is."

What matters in this context is that bypassing the resistance accelerated the patient's progress. One of the issues that was emphasized throughout the treatment of this woman was her flight patterns and the fears of sudden abandonment and intense aggression which flight was expected to avoid. By contrast, behavior therapy works on different principles. It provides primarily opportunities for the learning of problem-solving behavior that is devised by the therapist rather than discovered through teamwork between patient and therapist. The therapist's prime function is to be a teacher of specific behavioral skills. There is little or no emphasis on gradually altering the underlying internal psychic structures, on connecting the emotions with the cognitive functions, and on providing a system of extended and personalized reparatory experiences.

Among the basic propositions of Freudian psychoanalysis, none is more central than the idea that unconscious conflicts are the cause of psychopathology, especially conflicts between the different psychic departments—for instance, between the rational ego and the biologically founded id. Freud and his immediate followers assumed that the answer to conflict and the promotion of conflict solution lay in *full self-understanding*. When the individual acknowledges both types of forces that underlie a conflict, the conscious and the unconscious ones, then, so Freud assumed, personal integration and restoration of full measure of energy will occur.

More recently, through the work of the ego psychologists (Mahler, 1968; Spitz, 1965), the emphasis has shifted significantly. We have come to understand that the troubled psyche is on shaky ground not only because some of its important processes have been made unconscious through the defenses and have been condemned to obscurity, but also because the very form and structure of the ego are lacerated and have become arrested, weak and incomplete. In these circumstances, observed mainly in borderline cases (Kohut, 1977; Kernberg, 1976), it is found that the many aspects of the ego itself, not merely the defense system, have to be changed. To this has been added the concept that beyond the ego there is another structure, the self, which needs alteration and repair for basic changes to come about in the individual. As mentioned, such ego and self changes are required in many people who are not classifiable as borderline or schizophrenic (the ego is not disintegrated into many ego nuclei, nor is splitting the chief defense) and who function well socially and occupationally. They exhibit ego deformations, arrests, and self-damage in mild doses rather than in the more obvious manifestations which are found in the more serious disturbances, as Loewald suggested (Loewald, 1960).

We shall discuss in the following chapters many forms of ego and self repair, achievable by adopting new organizing principles: making contact with the emotions; rendering the self more authentic as well as stretching it towards new frontiers; developing competent skills to replace archaic and misshaped ones. These tasks call not only for insights, but more importantly for learning and building techniques and experiences that are remedial.

Diagnosis, though indispensable for guiding the therapist towards selection and application of the appropriate curative steps, for instance in making room for the right remedial experiences, is in and of itself not curative. This fact can be overrated. The idea remains too often entrenched that labeling certain psychological defects by attaching a diagnostic term to them has value in itself. It seems that the popularization of the terms *narcissism* and *narcissistic* has had some undesirable effects. People are told that they are narcissistic, implying that something is seriously wrong with them. But apart from the application of the diagnosis, no specific measures are advised or taken to cure the condition. The individual so labeled is not shown a way out. Frequently there is a paralyzing effect on the patient if he or she learns the diagnosis without simultaneously or soon thereafter embarking in the direction of change. An example is a man in his forties whose son died suddenly. Soon thereafter the man was seized by sensations of trembling and feelings that the ground beneath him was not safe. When he was told by someone that he was suffering from an anxiety neurosis, he was at first relieved to have a diagnosis. But eventually, just settling for the new term had a paralyzing effect on him. Not having been advised how to embark on a course of change left him stuck in a frightening condition for which he had a name but which he could not cure. By contrast, persons who, far from remaining stuck only with the diagnosis, are helped to discover the processes of change find the cure exhilarating, especially to the degree that it calls for their own participation. As a patient said to me on one occasion: "I do not want to be in therapy forever. But these processes I am discovering and beginning to use I want to keep and vary all my life."

Neurotic adults, who by definition are partly stuck in or have regressed to infantile modalities of feeling and behaving, invariably want to get by on a "no fault" psychology. The implication is that the adult who messes up his or her life is not responsible for the pathology which lies at the root of all problems and which the parents and educators encouraged or made necessary. The answer to this position is that it is not relevant who *caused* the psyche to be inadequate. Nothing is gained by knowing whose fault it was. What is pertinent is to change the present and the future of the individual—the strengthening and enrichment of the psyche are the present-day responsibility of the person. Disclaimed action, action not acknowledged as self-originated, is a form of resistance. Less disclaimed action means that the patient acts and feels as though he or she has a hand in what goes on (Schafer, 1976).

Change, signifying *psychological progression as distinguished from regression* and a willingness to work out problems rather than relishing them masochistically, demands a change of outlook: *The would-be changer shifts from a problem outlook to a solution outlook.* For every stop before the appropriate turns of development are taken, for every suspension in activeness (Fried, 1970), we need a go-ahead signal that denotes courageous, forward-directed procedures which are steeped in information, energy, and wisdom about life and which do not shrink from risk-taking. Some dynamic psychotherapy has been too problem-oriented. While it has contributed much to the skills of self-understanding and to the grasp of pathology to the point where many patients have become semi-experts, emphasis is needed on processes which facilitate growth in special problem areas and of the whole person. As far as change is concerned, there has been too much exclusive emphasis on pathology and the distinctions between neurosis, borderline phenomena, and psychosis. We do need to understand many disturbances more fully—for instance, in terms of the neurological correlates that are connected with them. But the explorations of the ego psychologists and of Piaget (1952), some aspects of the human potential movement, and behavior therapy (much as one may disagree with specifics of the latter) change the emphasis and the major direction of technique. As we now have new frontiers because of a thorough familiarity with the phases of human growth and a knowledge of the healthy stages of human development, we are able to help patients seek out those insights and those corrective experiences which bring solutions more quickly and safely into reach.

THE NECESSITY FOR CHANGE

Not only is change possible on an emotional and on a cognitive basis, as a variety of observations from widely divergent fields of study attest, but it is often exhilarating. Though we fear change in some measure and resist it as though it could be painful or even dangerous, we must undergo periodic alterations and transformations of ego, self, and indeed the entire psyche in order to stay optimistic and well. Many a status quo existence of the mind, designed to avoid change, seems reassuring at first, but leads in the long run to the dead-end condition of paralysis, passivity and chronic depression.

Absence of change comes to feel like gradual death. We have to move about as psychological beings in order to stay in shape, much as the body must be exercised and put through diverse uses of muscles if it is to remain resilient and healthy. Change consists of exposing oneself to new stimulation, undertaking fresh human contacts, developing the psychological functions, and getting hold of and expressing emotions. Even if external circumstances stay the same, it is essential to produce varying and fresh psychological responses. In Thoreau's words, "To affect the quality of the day, that is the highest art." It is up to each person to discover ways of widening the sphere of his or her sensibility.

To stay alert, to fill the mind with perceptions and thoughts and the entire mind-body unit with emotions, we tolerate and indeed seek out transformations that in turn call on energy and imagination. This process keeps flexibility alive—one of the greatest of human assets and indeed one of the chief distinctions between inanimate objects and living species—and avoids boredom. Boredom is not just a nuisance, as is too often assumed, but a serious affliction which contributes importantly to the suspension of the life processes. It is similarly hazardous to permit too much automaticity, even though it may be needed to permit minimum expenditures of energy on repetitive and purely technical tasks. A predominance of automaticity and an inclination towards fixed and impenetrable ego boundaries lead eventually to decay, as we shall discuss.

Change is a prerequisite for activeness which, though not synonymous with activity, denotes an active state of mind that gathers new perceptions, encourages the emergence of vivid and fresh emotions and the exercise of psychological competence (Fried, 1970). Activeness and psychological competence are needed to extinguish depressions in their initial and milder stages. Depressions are part of life and remain manageable as long as the person has the activeness, energy, and power to overcome them at or near the onset. It is not the absence of depression that separates the healthier person from the disturbed one, but the ability to stem these low periods when they occur on the heels of failure and loss.

The idea that change inevitably entails stress is elaborated by Selye (1974), who speaks of tolerable stress as a spice of life. Stress theory, which reserves the term *eustress* for tolerable and, indeed, stimulating stress, emphasizes that eustress accelerates physiological changes to which the body and mind have to adjust, within limits. Such stress changes the endocrine balance by arousing hormone production, moves the respiratory system to inhale more oxygen, raises the level of blood sugar production, and prepares the entire physiological system for responding to dangers, emergencies, and other unforeseen developments.

The importance of change and self-alteration has been investigated by general systems theory, which traces how living systems fare both individually and in interaction with one another (Bertalanffy, 1968). Since human beings are living systems which are connected with one another, the investigations of general systems theory have become interesting to psychotherapists who apply some of the findings to their own field of study and work (Levenson, 1978).

General systems theory has found that in order to avoid entropy, which is to say chaos, and to preserve their own organization, living systems must remain in states of flux; they must especially make sure that their boundaries remain permeable so that new information and new energy can penetrate and register. The boundaries of living systems can be likened to the ego boundaries of man in the sense that the ego boundary is thought of as a psychological condition or delineation that controls the amount of stimulation that is admitted and determines the emotional consistency which is deemed tolerable. If too much stimulation is admitted, certain personalities are overtaxed by the burden of processing that information, and a state of confusion and fatigue sets in. If the emotional charge becomes too high, there occurs a condition which makes it hard to sustain ego organization and which feels subjectively highly uncomfortable, as though the whole psyche were bogged down, weakened, mushy, and in a state of partial dissolution. If, on the other hand, too little stimulation or emotion is admitted, say out of defensiveness against overload, then the emotional-cognitive state is also dangerously pathological. The answer is that living systems and human beings need to gauge what the proper degree of permeability should be for a harmonic and tranquil state of change and exchange to occur, thus avoiding the danger of entropic disorganization. In no event does the answer lie in the complete avoidance of change.

Recent studies of retirement and old age highlight the fact that without the opportunity for participation in the life of the community and in some form of productivity, people tend to disintegrate. To survive and survive well, human beings have to stay in motion,

direct themselves to tasks which involve work, some risk and inevitable change, and retain a forward-directed outlook which is
hopeful.* Such projects keep individuals away from changeless
apathy and induce them to move, to summon energy, and to draw
on their capacities, thus remaining in a state of flux. Nothing is
worse than perpetual rest. It is all right to take a psychological sab-
batical, but it should not deteriorate into an interminable leave of
absence.

SPECIFIC STEPS THAT LEAD TO SELF-CHANGE

The changes we are discussing here are always changes of internal
psychic structures and functions. Patients who aim at them are first
helped to understand which of the structures and functions on which
they rely are self-defeating or otherwise defunct; then, they are
helped to overhaul, develop, rebuild, and enrich the ego and self
structures. It happens frequently that an important internal change
leads to a clear conviction that in order to function fully, freely, com-
petently, and joyously, the patient must indeed seek out external
(environmental) changes, perhaps by dissolving a marriage or
another relationship, by moving out of the parental home if the
dissolution of a symbiosis is to be on totally secure footing, or by
changing occupation or training if required by the change in self-
image. In these circumstances, the determination and ability to
change the external conditions are secondary to the change and
growth of ego and self. Self-change bears some relationship to education or reeducation and to rehabilitation. Drugs are largely dispensable except as occasional fortifiers on the therapeutic road.

In this study, emphasis lies primarily on *conditions* that are con-
ducive to self-transformation. Specific types of change made possible
are so manifold that only a partial listing can be brought in and
discussed as they serve to illustrate circumstances which facilitate
revisions of psychological structures, functions, and processes. Some
of the many possibilities for thoroughgoing alterations in the per-

---

*A very readable book, Olga Knopf's *Successful Aging*, written by a woman psychiatrist who
accomplished just that at an advanced age, stresses the importance of being engaged in a project that points to the future and has duration.

sonality structure will, however, be briefly mentioned in this section just to show what is meant by specific types of changes.

A specific form of change is like a second chance. It allows one to make a new turn, to discover and tread a new alleyway, to reach broad overall goals of maturity, competence, and heightened energy level, to foster an ability to delight in relations with other human objects instead of drawing back. In nearly every instance, the specific changes mean that patients get the past out of their systems as it proves detrimental to the conduct of the present and the shaping of the future. In shedding large chunks of the past and the arrestations that are, for example, implied in the pursuit of transference and persistence of ego and self malformations, individuals acquire many new capacities. Instead of remaining narcissistically self-preoccupied, they turn into caring and loving human beings. Self-esteem, a substantial base for inner safety and subjective happiness, is gradually established. Genuine, authentic identity that derives organically from acceptance of the the very roots of the individual's being moves into the place of the previously wavering and false self-image that was the product of defensive identifications with aggressors and of symbiotic experiences. Essential also for the construction of self-esteem and a solid self-image is the acquisition of such ego functions as anticipation, clear thinking, objective judgment, and integrative capacity (Fried, 1955).

Among specific steps that lead to a revision of the self-image and an enrichment of self-esteem is the adult patient's progression from the illusion that he or she is still a child, at least in part, to the experience of oneself as an adult. From a psychoanalytic point of view, which calls for a true "working through," this means the ability to renounce any hidden or conscious yearnings for dependency and to exchange them for an acceptance of the need to conduct an independent existence. This does not arouse as much anxiety as is often forecast, but some anxiety is inevitable. People fear that they will be punished for their presumptuous claim to the adult position. Or they anticipate that they will be ridiculed for being so ambitious, these being misgivings that have been carried over from childhood. The capacity for making decisions which is part and parcel of all ego-building—it has become a focal point of some present-day branches of therapy (Goulding and Goulding, 1979)—can be acquired through the analysis and change of the transference. Decision-making, along with the making of choices, furthers experiencing oneself as an adult. Indeed, when other functions and capacities are perfected, such as independent reasoning or objective judgment, they are all used in the service of establishing the image of the adult where previously the child image lingered for much too long.

In order to build up an adequate self-representation, which is an essential prelude to self-change, it is necessary to give up all or most tendencies to submit, to found one's behavior on identifications, for example, with the aggressor, and on habits that are derived from the symbiotic position. In the words of Chekhov, "we have to squeeze the serf out of our souls, no matter how he got to settle there." Again, the transference situations in dynamic psychotherapy offer many opportunities both to draw the patient's attention to his or her repeated attempts to agree with and defer to the therapist and to encourage instead whatever genuine disagreements and assertions of self the patient can muster. It can easily be observed that patients are especially inclined to squelch dissent or rebellion when they are angry or believe, often on account of projection, that the therapist is angry. Face-to-face with what they believe to be the aggressor or the deserting symbiotic figure, they settle into renewed identifications and submissions.

The above-mentioned steps in the direction of self-change not only entail positively colored alterations in self-image (self-representation) and self-esteem, but also lead inevitably to revisions in the way persons relate to human objects. Indeed, most changes of self and ego eventually have an important impact on human relationships which are a function of the ego and the self and which every aspect of psychotherapy is bound to affect. As the individual corrects, through psychotherapy, the malformations to which his or her ego and self were subjected when the developmental phases were not properly completed, new capacities, functions, and structures are acquired which, in turn, deeply affect what is closest and most important to each individual: the nature of relationships with other human beings.

In every treatment, not merely that of the borderline personality, a gradual outgrowth of the narcissistic phase and narcissistic inaccessibility takes shape. The person discovers that it is a narcissistic error to assume that everyone is like oneself or that only duplicates of self are lovable (Freud, 1959). The individuality of other persons becomes more interesting and is taken into account as people learn quite literally to listen and to direct attention to others.

The therapist in many instances is the experimental object with whom these discoveries are made. The patient gradually learns to use in other situations what he learned in treatment. One of the important consequences of every treatment should be the discovery that one never need be without human objects and the precious relationship to them, "A normal person will at once begin looking about for a substitute for the lost attachment" (Freud, 1959d). While substitutions are perceived to be betrayals in some moral systems and cultures, they are considered as necessary for the reestablishment of emotional and general psychological balance within the physiological-psychological framework of psychoanalysis—provided time has been allowed for due processes of mourning. The mourning process does not mean that the human object that has been lost is forgotten; rather it signifies that the internal representations which are the leftovers from the old relationship are replaced by memories and that the person who left us is forgiven finally after inner rage has subsided. Thereupon the psyche comes together in new form and can make new attachments. This is another illustration of the fact that psychoanalysis and psychotherapy are meant to deal with psychological processes as a starting point for making psychological repairs. They are not approaches primarily concerned with moral issues per se.

Every effort at self-change by disturbed persons calls specifically for gradual discarding of negativism and arbitrary opposition and the gradual acquisition of patterns of cooperation. Negativism and opposition, though the product of many pathological currents, usually are firmly rooted in early mishaps during the phase of separation and individuation. Parents (particularly mothers) who have the need to hold on to the symbiotic tie oppose their offsprings' attempts to establish independence and to express individuality, often by opposing parental demands. As a result, either open or hidden opposition becomes a way of life. The emerging negativism is frequently perpetuated into adult life to protect the individual against sliding back into a symbiotic, submissive position; similarly, ego boundaries are tightened so as to separate the self from the influence of the environment. To instill cooperative trends, therapy must encourage open displays of opposition and disagreement, especially in the transference situation; obstinate behavior, unless it is destructive, has to be sanctioned as a necessary and healthy phase of passage towards independence. The reparatory experiences in these instances consist of encouraging open and courageous opposition. Moreover, patients benefit greatly if we help them to stop blaming others, especially the figures closest to them such as parents, spouses, or friends.

As individuals grasp that authority figures and supposed antagonists are powerful mainly in the eyes of beholders who, still feeling like dominated children, assign to them their supposedly exalted position and coercive intents, they not only stop deferring, but they also make fresh evaluations. Instead of perceiving an authority figure as indomitable and ill intentioned, the patient begins to perceive existing weaknesses. He is ready to recognize that more often than not the authority or supposed antagonist is rigid, has a closed mind, and holds absurd convictions rather than being invincible or evil. Abandoning the previous childhood absolutes denotes a form of maturity (Schafer, 1977b). Interestingly, this type of maturity is often found in the arena of politics, where those who are successful have realized that there are no authorities, only peers who can be persuaded and led, often by twisting their arms. The individual who uses and obtains power is frequently a person who in some measure has come to realize that there are no people with absolute power. This does not mean that full maturity has been achieved, but only that one specific truth has been recognized.

The second chance at conducting life on a higher and more effective level which therapy gives to those who want to change their own self does not mean—as some persons would like to think—that everything that has been done and all the psychological errors that have been committed can be rectified. This is true only in the sense that the internal, false, and dysfunctional realities that neurosis and other disturbances have created can be altered. Everybody who tries prudently can obtain more self-esteem, a more workable and realistic self-representation, more competent ego functions etc. But we cannot excise pieces of past conduct. Dynamic psychotherapy provides insights into the deleterious effect of past conduct at the price of demanding that these insights remain free of abuse. The lamentations, "If I only had done this or that differently," constitute a serious waste of self-understanding. The "if only I had" outlook matches "as if" behavior in the gravity with which it obstructs gradual change, which is the only genuine and lasting form of psychological reconstruction. Swift experiences of conversion and regeneration appear in legends and in folk tales, but not in everyday life.

A troubled 50-year-old mother who had reared a schizophrenic son, for whose disturbances and failures she considered herself responsible, was obsessed by the wish to "bring up Lawrence all over again." When Lawrence, her oldest son, was born, she was a highly anxious person, dependent on her husband, a steadfast man, and she behaved, as she recognized in retrospect, like a passive and erratic child. Finally, this woman made peace with and eventually overcame the archaic features of her psyche. She stopped being ashamed of the primitive streaks in herself. Only then was she able to part with regrets over the behavior in bygone days, and only then did she turn to the project of thorough self-change. She became a rather humorous person, and the relationship with the son became both firmer and better.

IF CHANGE IS EXHILARATING AND NECESSARY, WHY DO WE RESIST IT?

Self-examination and self-change are fascinating undertakings. Many persons who pursue a course of therapy and anticipate the effort and pain of self-discovery and self-development with misgivings find self-search and attempts at transformation absorbing. They discover the involvement in treatment to be more intense and many stretches of therapy to be more gratifying than, say, attendance at a spectator sport. Though anxieties weave in and out, many a good therapeutic hour can be more absorbing than a football game on television.

Yet, fascinating though therapy becomes, the desire to discover and apply new ways of feeling, loving, working, and living is often sharply opposed by tugs in the opposite direction. Many persons who want to be cured, who realize that their marriages, relationships

to their children, and ability to work effectively are in danger if they
do not change their feelings and behavior, nevertheless have one foot
in the camp of resistance. They have misgivings about letting go of
established habits, functions, and modes of relating, unsatisfactory
though they have proved, for fear that there will remain nothing but
an empty gap or else that a replacement will lead to something unfamiliar and hence suspect. Equally often, however, patients balk, at
least at certain points in treatment, because they feel and indeed are
threatened or confused by a particular direction or specific procedure adopted in therapy.

In such instances, responsibility for the standstill lies with the
therapist, who will have to design and apply adjustments,
realignments, and shifts in approach. One of the corrections that
helps and puts an end to resistance, at times within one session, is to
add to the *problem outlook* a *solution outlook*. No one is strong enough to
deal continuously with personal problems, defenses, and deficits. A
variety of patient conditions call for this shift in therapeutic approach toward the solution outlook, for example when persons in
treatment uncover beneath defenses (that have become conscious)
hitherto warded off intense aggressions but do not yet foresee any
alternative to the expression or expiation of aggression except
through rage.

Therapeutic shift is indicated by yet other conditions: when the
individual cannot as yet envisage ways to enrich and rebuild the
weak ego and unintegrated, shaky self which he or she has
discovered to be all the equipment available to navigate the seas of
life; when the patient cannot yet envisage that frustrations can be
approached not only with rage but much more effectively by expression of hitherto repressed or otherwise unacknowledged needs; when
he or she does not yet know or, better still, sense that safety and
hence the cessation of the seemingly endless frustration-aggression
sequences are achieved by gradually revisioning the perception of
the environment as totally hostile and by obtaining slowly growing
competence and mastery; in sum, when it is felt in the absence of a
positive vision of the future that an escape cannot be found from the
tiring and frightening alternations between seemingly unavoidable
frustrations and dangers on the one hand and aggression on the
other. In such situations of great and prolonged stress, which are

partly the result of emotionally and cognitively determined lack of vision and hope, it is necessary to muster on behalf of the patient various forms of support. These derive from getting closer to future possibilities. In this case we shift from a problem-centered approach to a solution-centered one.

1. It is often necessary to work on several issues at once so that the territory under investigation becomes broad enough to allow fuller vistas which include an emerging and growing awareness of potential strength.

2. The therapist, together with the candidate for change, needs to look for and articulate psychological assets. A woman in her forties, who was always gracious, mentioned that her father told her when she was a child and once screamed loudly that he wanted her never to scream again. His voice was "thundering." As a result she could not, as an adult, ask decisively for what she wanted, especially from a man. When the therapist reminded the woman that she could state firmly and sometimes loudly what she wanted in her professional life, and that she could probably use the same forcefulness in love situations, she smiled mischievously and said: "Maybe you have pointed at a potential I have felt it necessary to hide. I'll tell you what happened when I see you next time."

3. Some patients can move ahead without stalling only if very small and concrete pathological reactions and interactions have been examined, understood, and replaced by alternate, healthier ways of functioning. This helps particularly if it happens in the transference.

4. When patients have continued to experience comments as intolerable emphasis on deficits, the wording of explanations and interpretations has to be changed. To give a small illustration, it is often very helpful to stress the future rather than the past. Instead of saying, "You have often attributed ill intent to people who really have meant well," one finds the following formulation superior: "You will find that some people try to understand you better once you give them a chance to hear what you want."

5. When the patient has gone too fast, made too many changes, become too anxious over unfamiliar reactions, and needs to put on

the brakes, the therapist should indicate explicitly that it is necessary to slow down and take it easier.

6. Patients may come to a halt and resist because they are confused. They have not understood and have not been touched by explanations and interpretations that were offered but, eager to make a good impression or fearful of appearing dense, they do not reveal their confusion nor do they make up their own version of what is happening to the state of their inner world. Or they simply do not agree with what has been said and balk in protest. Communication here has broken down and must be reopened if the patient is to regain trust and hope.

7. People are invariably as fearful of succeeding as of failing. In fact, therapy must highlight and articulate existing fears of success. But the patient, though accepting this interpretation sincerely, may not know what psychological repairs to undertake in order to accept achievement; resistance is in itself a manifestation of existing misgivings about accomplishing something. Movement returns when the psychological ego- and self-building which must be accomplished is outlined in concrete steps (see Chapter 6).

The human personality is a living system, the parts of which interconnect. Therefore it is difficult, though possible, to change one part, one subsystem, or for that matter the entire system without making corresponding alterations elsewhere in the system. The situation resembles the reconstruction of a house. Any builder who takes out windows or stairs on the second floor and enlarges space has to wonder what effects such an alteration will have on the first floor and the basement. Often he has to make proper allowances for the change in balance. Similarly, a person who introduces one change must anticipate that this will necessitate other changes, some secondary, others primary. The entire order and context are shaken up. For instance, a woman who had been rather distant but became in her treatment more capable of intimacy had to realize that her particular advertising career no longer suited her new needs for heightened contact with reality. The changed modality of her relationships with human objects led to new professional interests.

For such reasons psychological movement and development must be slow, and caution is necessary. It follows that this is a delicate task, requiring a good deal of finesse and judgment, and sometimes a need for putting on the brakes. Certain steps to be taken by the patient need a good deal of preparation if the entire system is to continue holding together in altered form. There are many important occasions when resistance to change is the signal that the change, or its extent, is premature and that it is, indeed, dangerous to allow the present order of things to be rearranged and rebuilt in the rhythm and form that have been used.

"If change were too easy and mental structures too fluid, the result would be general instability, not quicker psychotherapy" (Guntrip, 1969). One might add that if change is too slow and the energies that sustain it are throttled for too long by intrusions from inside, then we have an enervating emptiness that makes for depression and apathy. Let us distrust the "good luck" of patients who seem to change with continuous rapidity. Yet, let us also seek new methods for the ones who seem to die on the vines of their treatments.

We should also remember that within the context of alternations between forward movement and resistance the presence and work of the will have an important place in therapy and life. For a long time the phenomenon of will appeared suspect to dynamic psychotherapists because voluntary effort was exercised on behalf of repression in accordance with turn-of-the-century morality—the reaction formations of false courtesy. Will was seen as serving as an underpinning for the total obedience demanded in the nursery and in schools. It was a kind of Victorian will (May, 1969) that was quite rightfully considered undesirable because it forbade the straight admission of what a person wanted. That kind of will acted against a free admission of feelings of aggression, love, sexuality, and the many other needs that vital and vigorous people have. It served resistance and kept the patient from becoming a deciding agent in important matters of his or her own life (Schafer, 1976). But when we regard other aspects of will such as endurance, a readiness to acknowledge that every accomplishment results from an expenditure of energy, that effort and sudden enlightenment are not mutually exclusive, and when we add to this concepts of being accountable

(Farber, 1966) and regarding oneself as responsible for the outcome of one's own life, then will fits into the therapeutic system. It is of a different order than free association but it counts equally in the successes for which patients try and which do not just happen in the way of "aha" experiences. There is room and need for many forms of experience.

THE SLOW PACE OF REAL CHANGE

To paraphrase a popular expression in economics, as far as change is concerned, slow is beautiful. For a profound, comprehensive, and genuine emotional-cognitive reorientation and restructuring to occur, the eager patient must be or become willing to work and to wait till the larger impact of many small changes is felt. While the sudden "aha" experiences occur, they are not the prime conveyances of progress. Both as patients and therapists we need to aim for a combination of "patience and passion." Moreover, it is important to stress that there exists no such thing as a completed treatment or a totally analyzed person. Although a high plateau of improvement can be reached, it is necessary to continue to grow as long as life lasts. Each of the two partners that make up the treatment team, the patient and the therapist, has to realize that some less desirable proclivities, for example, a gravitation under stress towards a fragility of ego boundaries, may be profoundly improved but will never disappear totally. The same is true about certain personal limitations. While psychoanalytically-oriented psychotherapy can help every person to become less rigid, more articulate, and more authentic, not everybody will reach a high level of artistic creativity. Many persons who believe that they suffer from an artistic block are not as talented as they wish to be. The realistic acceptance of creative, cognitive, and energy limitations is in fact "as basic to psychic maturity as active responses and adaptative mastery" (Zetzel, 1970).

Many mini-steps have to be envisaged, tried out, and repeated until they are assembled into an emotional-cognitive repertory which is integrated in the unique context of the individual's personality. As these small changes are adopted and combined, a few at a time, until the larger integrations occur which together yield the

far-reaching emotional and psychological overhaul or renewal, patients are not necessarily aware of the progress which occurs. While
such unawareness is partly the result of the low degree of consciousness that attaches to many healthy core processes of a
physiological and psychological nature—we are not usually aware of
our breathing as long as the heart and lungs are okay nor of being
optimistic unless we fall prey to depression—another phenomenon
plays a role which is neither natural nor healthy; rather it is noxious
and must be analyzed.

Residuals of narcissism, probably the most tenacious form of
pathology which holds human beings back from truly using and en-
joying their lives, create the expectation that through therapy one
can obtain spectacular and magic transformations in personality, demeanor, and life itself. Patients are inevitably disappointed who cannot distinguish genuine self-changes, which are the results of their
own efforts, from the unreal miracles which happen with lightning
speed in fairy tales and popular films. What they expected, it turns
out, was not a new level of existence, a gradual dissipation of longstanding anxieties and fears of persecution, the freeing of emotions
and forging of new life skills, but rather the emergence of an illusion
come true, of a mirage arising fresh in the arid sands of life.

As psychologists and psychotherapists, we know that the mind
tends to lean on synopsized images. Examples are the so-called
screen memories which in one brief episode embody and condense a
variety of similar events which actually occurred over a period of
time. In somewhat related fashion, the kind of anticipating and
thinking that is produced by the mind which is still gripped by the
narcissistic outlook nurtures the expectation of sleight-of-hand
changes. Patients who have become much more sociable through
treatment, more versatile, popular, and attractive are often
dissatisfied with the gains they have made because the held-over narcissistic outlook calls for infinitely more. In these numerous instances, often admitted only with great reluctance, clear interpretations and explanations are called for and will be reluctantly accepted
as to the ways in which the narcissistic position interferes with real
and deserved enjoyment. Only after parting with the false euphoria
built by narcissism will the patient perceive, relish, and make full
use of the changes he or she worked for.

As varying types of problems present varying symptoms and maladaptations, so they also demand not only varying treatment approaches but different lengths of therapy. Treatment of narcissism and the varying forms of disorders it invariably entails, both in the form of lasting wounds and a complex defense system against the pain that is felt, is time consuming. We have to help narcissistically disordered persons to deal with their wounds by convincing them that we are capable of giving them emotional attention so that the hurts and pains inflicted in infancy and early childhood gradually heal. And we have to make them aware of their many narcissistic defenses in the form of immense self-preoccupation, indifference to others, arrogance and contempt, and make them conscious of the global rather than selective identifications which are used by them. Any serious treatment strikes those who are narcissistically afflicted as most unreasonable since narcissism is experienced primarily as ego syntonic rather than ego alien. It is necessary to make clear to the patient the length and extent to which treatment will have to go.

On the other hand, many dramatic and bizarre symptoms are removable in relatively short spans of time although the character disorders that invariably go with the symptoms call for prolonged treatment. While it proves generally very helpful to explain that treatment is going to take much time, roughly speaking, and what some of the roots of the problems are, it is most inadvisable to label the psychological disorders. Labels frighten; they are often misused by patients, as well as by the profession. It is still much too customary to assume that the treatment of a borderline case or schizophrenic will take much longer and present a far more serious problem than, say, an obsessive rigid character structure.

In a study which compared the rate of change in three patients of approximately the same age who had been accepted as patients on the same day, it was shown that the borderline patient made the most conspicuous progress and in the shortest space of time, even though the psychoanalytic therapy used in all three cases by the same therapist was not of a short-term nature (Fried, 1952). At the time of publication it was not mentioned that the closest friend of the borderline patient was treated in the same setting but by a therapist who, along with the fashion of that time, regarded a borderline constellation with a great deal of therapeutic pessimism. That patient never recovered, a fact to which the therapist's pessimism may have contributed. Anxiety is likely to bring about the very things it fears (Bateson, 1958). It creates its own disasters. Optimism in both patient and therapist, on the other hand, is an excellent ally of recovery, provided it is true optimism and not wishful, narcissistic thinking.

2

Insight

For all the great emphasis on insight* which has developed over the years many important differentiations remain obscure. There exist many different forms of insight, depending on distinctions such as these: Is insight (namely the understanding of certain truths about the self) employed in the service of change or merely prompted by intellectual curiosity and the desire to be amused by penetrating into previously hidden layers of the self? Are only those insights sought after that tell the person about the unfolding of his or her earlier past or do we pursue those more painful truths concerning present-day life that are equally important, if not more so? Is insight in and by itself valued, or are relief and change forthcoming through the conflux of the patient's insight with the therapist's understanding—made possible because the patient found the courage to discuss feelings and behavior in an idiosyncratic, subjectively true way, previously shunned for fear of censorship?

---

*The term *insight* as we now use it was first employed by German Gestalt psychologist Wolfgang Koehler.

In this context, we will examine insights whose purpose is to enable change to occur, not to satisfy personal curiosities about depth psychology.

The pursuit of insight can be overdone. When this happens, insights frequently are used for the purpose of resisting change, the underlying notion being that the difficult job of self-change will be accomplished once full self-understanding is achieved. Individuals in these circumstances pursue the genetic fallacy (Helen Durkin, personal communication). The facile idea is: if one understands when, how and through whose doings traumata were incurred, this will result in change. On the other hand, the truth becomes a magnificent tool in the hand of individuals who understand that while insight left untouched might further the self-limiting goals of narcissism, self-understanding combined with emotional and cognitive activeness is the first station on the road to change. *Active* insight allows for the recognition that many gains come as a result of undaunted striving and do not occur just out of the blue; safety and self-enrichment come, like freedom, when you exercise them and not because you desire these states. If patients set out to apply their uncoverings and explorations rather than merely discussing them at length or viewing them with interest, insight then becomes integrated into life as it is lived. Its ultimate purpose is more than the admittedly considerable gratification of realizing that it is heard by others, especially the therapist. It is to stimulate the psyche to voluntarily employ its defenses more sparingly and thus stay closer to the truth. Above all, insights are the prime movers towards building a sound and complete ego and a genuine self.*

Active insight is used by the individual to determine what behavior flows from the false and what from the authentic self; when stalemates replace the flow of life; what emotional and cognitive approaches and functions are archaic and have to be replaced by psychological innovations, and so on. It is fruitless to bemoan the fate supposedly allocated by an unfair environment. I assume that one of the gratifying directions in which life needs to proceed is the

---

*The *ego* is here considered to be the integrated totality of executive functions through which the individual pursues daily activities and life itself. The *self* represents the individual's awareness of existing directions, either innately given or chosen.

more or less continuous progression, on varying levels of behavior, from initial *narcissism* (personal isolation and inaccessibility) to *dependence* (one-sided connectedness and communication with a life-supporting person) to *autonomy* (gradual completion of the ego and self as independent systems) to *love* (mutual connectedness and communication with others). Against this background of desirable attainments, the act of relating to other individuals via submissiveness and identification is always felt to be archaic. It has to be replaced by the ability to relate as an autonomous, self-motivated, concerned, and loving person. This worthy intent is achieved through a merging of active insight with ego and self-growth achieved through psychological work and reparatory experiences.*

A predominance of *spectator* insight in dynamic psychotherapy is a sign of dilettantism. It is a counterfeit process produced by persons who merely stand by, passive and static, and hoard self-discoveries as if they were collectibles that belong in a showcase, to be used for escape or as conversation pieces. We abuse the precious medium of psychotherapy if we merely ruminate instead of fusing insight with new feelings and actions, letting them filter down into daily life. While there is important room for contemplation at many points in psychotherapy, it must not remain the end-all of treatment during which many more approaches must be utilized in order to renew the psychological life.

It is one of the historic merits of psychoanalysis to have demonstrated the crucial connections which exist between past and present. When we know what happened when we were very young, our perspective widens and we may be able to shed guilt by becoming aware that we have been shaped by events "beyond our control." But if we are not also aware of our own responsibility in shaping the present and the future, then knowing the impact of the past can lead to dangerously fatalistic attitudes. Psychological fatalists are infatuated by the power of history and neglect the potential strength of the living person. They are stuck, unwittingly or not, with but one of several divergent observations made by Freud, whose world view alternated between the poles of pessimism and op-

---

*Reparatory experiences come about through growth in the interaction with the therapist. See Chapters 5, 6, and 7.

timism. His pessimistic statement that man is the victim of his reminiscences (Freud and Breuer, 1959) was counterbalanced by the optimistic idea that the fatal and seemingly closed circle of repetition to which unconscious motivations subject man can be broken by therapeutic interpretations.

In sum, Freud's own teachings and experiences encourage the more optimistic view that the potential for change exists. Therapy offers us the means not only for self-understanding but also for self-change if we seize opportunities for resuming developmental trends that were interrupted in the past. New directions can be discovered, envisioned, and, above all, actually tried out, especially in the transference situation. Present- and future-oriented therapy studies the imprints of the past, to be sure, but never without including the chief purpose of discovering new destinations and the means of reaching them. It is the purpose of activist search that human beings recognize their own contributions to existing problem situations and correct their behavior.

Sarah, the previously mentioned married woman, had come to therapy shortly after her thirtieth birthday in order to get rid of feelings of depersonalization, depressive moods, and suspicions about everybody, especially her parents. She wished to have a baby but did not want to pass on to a child her worries and fears, which she readily recognized as irrational. In an early session, the patient mentioned that both parents, themselves a closely knit symbiotic couple, cared little about her; she felt no warmth coming from them even though she loved both mother and father. When asked what *she had contributed* to her parents' apparent neglect, she fell silent and finally said that there was nothing she could put her finger on.

When this patient returned to her next session, she talked first about an interesting work assignment and then said eagerly, "Hey, I found out that it was I who got my parents started on what looks like their disinterest. Mother used to be so overprotective that when I moved away from home she called two or three times a day. My monosyllabic conversation got her to stop that. Amazing how I turn things around. I called her and she was again too concerned. I'll have to stop her less abruptly." Although clinically this hardly signaled a great improvement in a fairly paranoid character structure, it showed a grasp of the principle that self-understanding is not a "don't touch possession" but a plan for action to be built into the living world. Whether the patient's report sprang from a wish to please me or came genuinely from within, what matters here is that she had obtained a feel for the need to make insight and life congruent and to assume responsibility for her own contribution to her problems.

If treatment is to accomplish real life changes rather than mere abstract comprehensions, then the first transformations should occur in the transference, which is the life situation that the patient sets up with the therapist. What counts is not a *mere understanding* that automatically and unconsciously the therapist is perceived as though he or she were some important authority figure from the past, but rather that patients begin and continue *to behave differently*. They have to revise their expectations, develop feelings that fit the new human reality, and behave more in ways that take into account the person of the therapist and the context of treatment. The just-mentioned patient, Sarah, wanted persons whom she found interesting and attractive to fit into her category of "terrific people." In case a person had a selfish, cruel, or otherwise unlikable character trait, she made him or her over. "With the exception of my parents, I am a people converter," this narcissistic woman would say in reference to her coterie of friends. As it happened, she usually placed the therapist in the category of "terrific people," quickly retouching any flaw that she saw in the therapist's image. Quick to learn, Sarah soon perceived how she converted the therapist and, more important, altered her long-established stance and voiced questions and criticisms. Eventually this changed transference behavior was paralleled by changes vis-à-vis husband and friends. For example, Sarah broke with her oldest pal, a woman who had betrayed her repeatedly. As a result, she felt that she was planting her feet on the ground and hence she was beginning to know what strength is like. A perturbing sense of confusion started to give way to clarity.

The purpose of insight is to undo the continuing influence of past events on the psychic structures, on the ego functions, and on the sense of self. Persons who use their insights actively to experience new feelings and develop improved capacities attain a new self-image. Unless this happens, psychotherapists and patients become psychological historians or archeologists who merely record what happened and get lost in digging expeditions (May, 1953). Instead, they need to be planners and doers.

To be sure, it is essential to help a person realize and remember what kind of repeated frustrations—the one time trauma is no longer considered the all-important hazard—were inflicted by close family figures in early childhood and the still tender years of adolescence. Such reviews of the past fulfill many purposes: the person who looks back usually recovers important memories which establish links between heretofore disconnected processes. The previously mentioned patient, Sarah, who was fearful of making waves in her marriage, discovered that whenever her own mother opposed her father he declared that his marital years had been nothing but a waste. Small wonder that she was reluctant to disagree even moderately with her own husband. Moreover, persons who reflect back on the past gain in their own estimation of their personality structure, for they discover that psychological imbalances and destructive behavior habits which they acquired in the past started out as rather ingenious ways of adapting to highly unfavorable circumstances and to frustrating family members.

Despite these and some other obvious gains, it is necessary to go beyond the recovery of lost memories and the grasp of maladaptations that started out as imaginative adaptations. What is called for are dynamic solutions and a future-oriented approach. These dispense gradually with guilt and revenge feelings, two kinds of past-oriented affects which are rooted in both omnipotence and self-deception. Guilt preserves the illusion that one could have proceeded differently and successfully had circumstances been different. Revenge feelings imply that the individual has special claims to love and safety by eliminating detractors. Both categories of feeling serve the purpose of circumventing acceptance of the reality principle which tells us that the frustrations of life are many and must be borne with fortitude.

What we need in terms of historical vs. contemporary insights is a mix. The historical part of the mix should aim at discovering not just the facts as to *what member* of the primary family inflicted *what frustrations*. Above all, the historical and genetic inquiries must make clear *what functions were fulfilled* by adopting, under the pressure of former frustrations, the old and seemingly destructive feelings, twists of personality and behavior. Historical explorations are the more valuable to the extent that they elucidate *for what purpose* affective psychic structuring and ego and self-growth were sacrificed. By contrast, the question of who was responsible for development being suspended is far less likely to promote new growth. We want to know, for instance, what functions passive-hostile standstills served rather than to dwell extensively on the question of which parent interfered with the achievement of individuation. Or, we wish to find out *what ends were served* by adopting a yielding, artificial, pretend self rather than one that is genuine and strong (Winnicott, 1965).

The contemporary portion of the insight mix deals with questions such as these: What is amiss in the present-day psychic structures? Does a person have to spend more energy on revenge ideas than on living for the attainment of love? Does the individual in question possess some vision of what happiness means to him? Does he keep repressing aggression because he does not know how to convert rage into firmness and how to use the latter to make human contacts? Will it help to teach the subsequent steps that convert aggression into energy: 1) becoming aware of body signals which are a clue that rage is aroused; 2) expressing anger in a safe environment, for instance the therapeutic setting; 3) asking for what the individual wants and rearranging the inner and outer life so that it can be had?

Unless we combine historical and genetic inquiries with insight into the condition of the existing psychic structure and undertake imaginative rebuilding of the ego and the self, the result is to throw the patient into a resistant frame of mind, in which narrations and masochistic-nostalgic preoccupations with the past can be used to defeat change. Admittedly, the making of the proper mix is difficult. The more disturbed some persons are, the more disillusioned they become with the past; others practically live in the old days. Some therapies give overwhelming preference to the past and settle for spectator insights. But early in treatment, historical reviews and recollections are more necessary than at a later time.

Narcissistically damaged personalities, whose numbers are abundant since narcissism is a central aspect of all disturbed development, and whose problems have been illuminated through important recent contributions (Kohut, 1977; Kernberg, 1976) need clearly *a special combination of historical inquiry with on-the-spot reconstruction.*

In these disorders, the emotional attention (empathic listening) paid by the therapist to *old injuries* inflicted by emotionally inattentive, narcissistic, absentee mothers constitutes an important reparatory experience. On the other hand, the well-known *narcissistic defenses,* such as self-absorption, grandiosity, and role-playing, do not profit from empathy. Rather, the person who uses such defenses must become aware of their injurious effect: they intensify alienation and increase the already-existing inclination towards boredom. Hence, different forms of self-protection must be envisaged and tried out in the transference. As a narcissistic man said: "I have found that the love I crave comes my way when I let people see that I am hurt and not when I hide behind arrogance. As long as I flaunted my brilliance I drove people away."

I would like to mention at this point that psychic structures based broadly on narcissism do not work. *This is an insight which our present-day society needs.* Both the unhealed narcissistic wounds and the seemingly clever defenses like arrogance and avoidance of commitment promote such a degree of inner emptiness and unreality that eventually the entire narcissistic structure caves in.

Often in the history of mankind certain social regulations and practices previously considered indispensable are found to have outgrown their usefulness and are discarded. This happens at pivotal points when simpler, more direct, more functional solutions are found for tasks heretofore performed rather clumsily. The same holds true for the psyche. When adults look over their childhood habits, many of which have been unwittingly retained, their adult, more skillful, stronger, and more daring psyche devises approaches that are less roundabout, less tentative, and less energy consuming. Adults who are capable of activist insight can be encouraged to ask themselves on such occasions for what special, though not readily evident, reasons they have long behaved oddly and with much wasted effort. What function does a certain kind of cumbersome conduct serve? Can not the end results be accomplished in ways that are more direct, more enjoyable, easier, and actually safer? If therapist and patient really probe, it becomes possible to dispense with all kinds of neurotic frills and restrictive behaviors.

Monty, recently married to the girl with whom he had lived

quite happily for two years, was startled and eventually shock-
ed to discover that he pulled away from his new wife although
he longed to embrace her. He developed an intense desire for
privacy and looked forward throughout the week to a Thursday
lecture which he gave out of town. Regularly, before the lecture, he would eat by himself in a dark little restaurant, sitting
at a small table, pulling out a newspaper and holding it in such
a way that the waitress could not read the headlines or catch a
glimpse of the pictures. As he gave orders for a five-course dinner—an extraordinarily big meal for this usually poor
eater—he would demand regularly that the waitress put the second and third course simultaneously on the table exactly in
front of him so that he could view both dishes. In therapy it was
pointed out that Monty behaved in this manner so as to make
sure that nothing could be taken away from him.

A few nights after this remark, the patient, whose wedding
had taken place in Italy during a vacation, dreamt that he was
in a room with a bathtub filled with spaghetti several yards
long. His brother, always the preferred child who was spoiled
by a rich aunt and by a grandmother, was about to grab the
spaghetti away from him, but Monty threw him out of the
room. The patient and therapist concluded that Monty, who
during treatment had allowed many previously repressed or
concealed desires to break through, and whose marriage
represented for him the highest level of fulfillment, pulled away
from his wife out of fear. He did not allow himself to enjoy his
wife, especially to touch her skin which he loved, because he
was afraid that she would be pulled away from under his nose,
like the spaghetti. He wanted the newspaper all to himself, the
five-course dinner and courses two and three planted in front of
his eyes, the newpaper headlines unseen by other eyes in order
to protect the high level of possession he had achieved. The
spoiled brother and other go-getters, especially the father, were
not to deprive the patient any longer.

In discussing Monty's self-imposed abstinence with his wife
and the stealth with which he warded off competition, I suggested that he could guarantee his safety by more direct means.
He could proceed in directions harmonious with the healthy
aspects of his personality. Why continue to invite the basically
distrusted brother to his house, instead of taking a trip to the
West Coast where the brother lived and renting an apartment
by the sea for a vacation? Why not spend hours fondling his
wife whose skin he loved rather than pressing immediately for
intercourse? And, after all, instead of breaking off his treat-

ment session a few minutes before time was up, as had been Monty's custom to protect himself against the announcement that time was up, he could find some better solution. Indeed, this is just what happened when the patient brought along a clock with an extra large dial, informing me that he himself would determine the end of the fifty-minute hour.

This patient's self-deprivation, glaringly apparent soon after his marriage, had in one form or another overshadowed his entire life. What he discovered in treatment was not only the extent and the specific ways of shortchanging himself in order to avoid rejection, but above all, through active insight, satisfactory solutions. He taught himself to preserve and protect his rights as a husband in much more direct and pleasurable ways. One day he reported proudly that he had let his wife know in three different ways the previous evening that he loved her a lot.

Just as insight may precede change, so may change precede insight. This is known to travelers who return from trips to their home settings, to mates who are reunited after long separations, and to students who have had prolonged exposure to new academic and cultural environments. Persons who become thoroughly acquainted with settings where things are done differently, where novel personality structures are encountered, where new kinds of defenses are employed and priorities ordered differently, look with new eyes upon old familiar arrangements to which they return. Having changed their angle of vision abruptly and significantly, they no longer fall into habitual and automatized routines of perceiving the old world and performing old chores. New insights force their way into the previously mechanical view of the world. Circumstances permitting, a variety of changes are made before the old perceptions take over again. In treatment situations, behavior therapy has utilized this phenomenon and there is no reason why it could not also be utilized in one form or another within a setting of dynamic psychotherapy.

FROM WHO WE ARE TO WHO WE CAN BE

The emphasis is no longer on the notion that the insights most helpful for setting in motion the wheels of change are the "aha!" experiences which consist of sudden flashes of memory and comprehension. While it holds true that genuine insights, which connect previously separate experiences and integrate them in more meaningful contexts (Horney, 1939), occur often in the wake of emotions, suddenness is not the prime feature. More important is the fact that such kinds of understanding are rarely the result of compulsive, logical thinking that focuses on some section of the problem (Martin, 1952). Genuinely creative and integrative insights occur more readily in loose states of consciousness. They are not "willed" but "found," much as one chances upon a four-leaf clover. The fixed, hemmed-in state of consciousness is not of help when it comes to making discoveries of connections, meanings and possibilities. Hence it is not so much suddenness as openness that brings the genuine understanding that can be applied in an activist fashion.*

To relieve the character and mood disorders rather than the isolated symptoms many different insights are needed which *happen* to persons who are or become receptive, and *remain* with personalities who are or become active. However, this does not imply that the gained understanding is applied automatically and directly towards a changed conduct of life. A good many patients need at least a partial overhaul of emotions and personality structure because they suffer from disorders of the ego and the self as a result of developmental arrests (Lachman and Stolorow, in press). The ego and the self have not had the opportunity to pass without distur-

---

*The more sudden "aha" type of discoveries, where they do indeed occur, can be variable in the treatment of the symptom neurosis. In this disorder, which was seen more frequently around the turn of the century in Western society, seemingly bizarre blockages of functioning occur. It was discovered that such symptoms as not being able to walk, being tortured by a seemingly inexplicable phobia or forced into a compulsive washing ritual can be the outcome of repressions. Growing up in a Victorian society with its strong inhibitions of basic psychological-biological needs of a sexual, aggressive, or anal nature, the afflicted persons inhibited such needs by bringing to a standstill neural connections commonly used to satisfy these supposedly infamous desires. An illustration is the woman who, desirous of extramarital sex, immobilizes her own legs lest she approach the man with whom she wishes to be intimate. Such patients are rare in our contemporary liberal society, but in Nepal I was able to see a number of women with hysterical paralysis. In cases of the symptom neurosis which Freud treated, studied, and often cured, the discovery of the repressed impulse constituted indeed that form of insight which proved crucial in the dissolution of the disabling symptom. But aha experiences, even at that time, did not change the pathological character structures. Nor did they alleviate depressions that stemmed from far-reaching dissatisfactions because the incomplete and damaged psyche did not permit a full range of emotions, the enjoyment of a healthy self, and good relations with other people.

bance through one or several or, as is most often the case, all of the developmental phases that are needed to round out the shape and capacities of a mature, fully-equipped psyche. While insight alone does not suffice to lay new foundations, self-understanding remains a high priority in helping patients to become active, willing, involved partners in the therapeutic enterprise. A great deal of revision and entirely new psychological building *begins* with insight, though it *cannot stop* at revelations alone.

Many seek help because they suffer from more or less continuous depressions, which register as a comprehensive feeling of listlessness, pessimism, and psychophysiological malaise. They want to change because they have become aware that they walk about with anxiety. As a woman said, "I feel that I have to run in place because I am afraid to step outside. Outside my door there are no steps that lead to a passage, a street, or a garden. I am afraid to move about. And always the churning and knotting in my stomach!" In today's fluid society where mere manners and courtesies no longer suffice to carry people along, there is an awareness that the ego and the self have to be put on the line. An incompetent ego and false and synthetic self cannot do the job; real capacities are needed. In many instances it is just those structures which psychotherapy helps to build—a complete ego and a real and authentic self (Winnicott, 1965)—that can endure turmoil and, under pressure, continual social change and bombardment by advertising and magazines which tell us, rather than ask us, how to live.

In this context, insight cannot mean primarily the discovery and the dissolution of repressions. It is more like a process of learning to understand one's own make-up. Thus, to find insight is to strive for those alterations that are necessary to complete a personality which has skipped certain phases of development, dwelled too long on others, and not made the best use of its own forces. A man or woman who perpetually seeks romantic love might never have had the privilege of a satisfactory symbiosis. Another person who continuously tends to overrate people of importance and hang on to them as if they were omniscient may have had so prolonged a symbiosis that the craving for more cannot be given up. And someone who trusts nobody and merely navigates marginally on the outside of things may have been exposed to so many double binds and been so afraid of threatening though veiled signals that the self has never dared to develop its own solid outlines. Of course, *it is not the occasional deprivation, overindulgence, disguised threat, or negation of eventual autonomy that misshapes the personality, but rather habitual infringements by parents, other nurturers, schools, and societal regulations,* all of them interfering with development not out of ill will but because of inability to understand or to satisfy the needs of the very young. For the needs of the elders are pressing, often remain unrecognized, and interfere habitually with the needs of the younger generations, though not always to the point of chronic psychological malformation.

The ever more specific findings of ego psychology, described by such innovative thinkers as Rene Spitz, Edith Jacobson, Margaret Mahler, Heinz Hartmann, and Gertrude and Rubin Blanck, make it much more possible to identify the kinds of gaps and mishaps that may occur in the phases of individual development. These observers and theorists have described what to expect as each human season arrives and passes, what fruit to anticipate, and what blights to stem. How did the mother and father help the baby to get out of the narcissistic cocoon that envelopes the small child, how did they regulate the needs for nurture and symbiosis, and how much or little help was given when the time came to claim autonomy, to individuate, and exercise will and independence? These are the questions that patient and therapist have uppermost in their minds and into which insight has to be gained.

In order to make sure that the insight which is gained furthers the resumption of ego and self-development, and in order to go about our investigations somewhat economically, the problem arises as to which of the many factors that have shaped the individual's life deserve particular attention. Let us say that there are five categories of information among which priorities have to be established:

1) Which parent or relative threw up the big roadblocks?
2) What caused the scarcity of satisfactions and the hindrances to forward movement?
3) In what ways and by which means did those in charge of caretaking make their wishes felt, so that conflicts were created with the child's natural needs?
4) If we accept the phases of development outlined by ego

psychologists as the narcissistic stage, the symbiotic stage, the phase of individuation and separation, with the oedipal period and, eventually, adolescence following in tow, what particular phases were subjected to interference or given the right kind of support?

5) Finally, what psychological scars, or, conversely, assets are still in evidence in the adult personality? These scars, unfunctional styles of acting habits that belong only to the past when they served some restrictive or regulatory needs, now hamper free and fruitful conduct.

Personalities who are taking stock of their lives will want to do some free roaming and consider the primary persons who helped or hurt them and the reasons why they behaved the way they did. But it needs to be made clear in therapy that *impact insights* should be given big weight. Impact insights focus on the leftover, still active, still festering wounds that were made. Above anything else, patients should be occupied with points 4 and 5 above. Which classes in the school of life was the patient not encouraged to experience happily and to complete, thus being prevented from gathering and stocking up on the psychological inventory that grows out of that phase of development? And what scars, gaps, and malformations have resulted that disturb the mental structure with which life is to be approached?

It stands firmly established that the past and the present are intimately connected, and if we do not sort out and modernize emotional and mental inventories, the future might be a replica of what has gone on before. But, although there can be no doubt that the past has a direct and powerful impact on the present (Spitz, 1965), this does not mean that the genetic point of view comes first (Rapaport 1967) nor should it overshadow other vantage points from which to reconnoiter life as it stretches from the then into the now. Since practical limitations force psychotherapy to be selective and to steer attention to essentials, insight should dwell on the present-day impact which childhood environment still adversely exercises on adult functioning. And we must be sure to take note of both the scars and the glow which the past has left us with, so as to make corrections or utilizations. Neither the importance of the "here-and-now" (Perls, 1973) nor the impact of the past can be questioned. The essence is that the two fields of life have to be continuously connected. Therapists and patients are not expected, for the sake of pure scientific interest, to explore other eras. Rather, they are active human investigators who, while respecting the past and realizing that knowledge of its continuing influence reduces feelings of shame and guilt and confusion, make their searches in order to remove unwelcome traces from the present. The purpose is always *to eradicate impacts* that are automatic, habitual, and harmful.

Maximilian, a psychologist who had difficulties in letting others take a good look at his talents and his stock of solid knowledge, always spoke very briefly and in a hurried staccato. Trying to discover what events in his rather traumatic childhood could account for both his timidity and his hurried speech, he touched on the still continuing behavior of his mother. "She acts like Billie Bird, the comedienne who never had the patience to stop long enough to hear what somebody had to say. She is a kind of birdbrain, never quite there, preoccupied with herself. I seem to take it for granted that other people are the same way." "Did you notice that I listen quite carefully and that I remember most of what you tell me?" I asked Maximilian, who answered: "Do you really? I never noticed." "Well, start noticing now," I proposed, "and also watch how carefully your friend, Hughey, takes note of what you tell him. You mentioned something only last week that you had discussed and that he referred to." "Well, for goodness sake," said Maximilian, "so I do it to lots of people. I expect they won't listen, so I never say anything I care about. I wonder whether that's why I rush to get the words out, trying to get something in edgewise before the switches are turned off?" Maximilian's response shows him discovering present-day impact, welcoming the discovery, and seemingly taking to heart the fact that he deprives himself of attention in the present by assuming automatically that it is not available, just as it had not been in the past, and neither asking for it nor detecting when the present is indeed different.

It is the mission of psychotherapy to discover through impact insight the wheels that got stuck and to set them in motion through a combination of understanding and new therapeutic discoveries and experiences. As one author stated it, human beings are endowed with a potential for achieving levels of functioning that were formerly blocked (Bibring, 1937). If people run into deadlocks, this is so because of past interferences with their capacity for progression. We draw upon remembering not only for the sake of reconstruction but for resuming progression.

Several types of parental neglect result less from ill will than from human limitations. They vary with changing sociological structures and technological changes. For example, something new has been happening to child rearing that helps us understand the wounds, sufferings, and needs of psychopathic and sociopathic personalities which we find in large numbers among younger people. Gadgets have multiplied, and parents flock to them because they supposedly make many tasks easier, particularly the bringing up of kids. The extended family has largely disappeared, and there are no grandparents or aunts readily available for baby-sitting. Instead, there is a succession of frequently changing sitters or neighbors only marginally involved with the child.

All this has, of course, a serious effect on development, for instance on that very important aspect of human relations (object relations) which we refer to as loyalty or object constancy. The formation of lasting, clearly defined, and unselfish loyalties, in the form of object constancy, that can survive frustration is an inner process that has become difficult for a lot of people. How can it be otherwise when the caretaking figures are not part of a small, stable and intimate unit, but a changing repertory that disperses not only with each new season but every few weeks. How can anybody be humanly devoted to briefly satisfying pleasures such as chewing gum and other little goodies, and to the watching of television sets that blast forth with a deadening rhythm and loud voices that seem inhuman because they have a steady pitch rather than the natural cadences of a loving person. Because of the neglects that are the result of this age of gadgetry and undefined people passing through revolving doors, we observe the phenomenon that the inner images, the representations of other people, are blurred.

To gain understanding, patients and therapists must view what the results of absentee parents and gadget-oriented child rearing are. Love and hate, the prime emotions, become blurred because the targets change too quickly for feelings to become solidified. They spread all over, as it were, and bits and pieces of them are beamed temporarily to anybody. They remain generalized and blurred as they are perpetually diverted off target. Moreover, the transient gadgets offered—food goodies, artificially high temperatures, the presence of the monotonous television hum, and furniture conveniences made of plastics—are chosen not for loving preservation but for the purpose of quickly quieting the young so as to offer brief and transient satisfactions. As a result, there is little or no patience or tolerance for frustration. Instead, there exists a hunger that looks continuously for satiation since the satisfactions through obtainable gadgets and cheap goodies are never deep enough.

Locating the developmental phases and the interferences which occurred, often because of the parents' own problems, must not turn into a course of blaming the parents in the hope of healing the patient's wounds. While the emergence of rage during the search for the causes of childhood blemishes is inevitable and salutary, it is merely one step in the right direction. The parent-directed angers, having been duly uncovered and expressed, must be worked over and converted into energy to supply the ego and self eventually with the power needed to remedy the problem-beset personality. While the conduct of the parents is among the most important causations of disturbances, adult persons *must eventually regard themselves as their own caretakers,* responsible for healing their psychological scars.

It is neither parent blaming nor accidental and miraculous sudden enlightenment that gives insight the force and wallop to make the difference. Men and women change because self-understanding becomes applied to the skill of self-restoration and self-building. Insights into the past must alternate with visions of the future. Emerging awareness at the start of change must merge with the awareness that dawns when self-change is already under way. And insights, though invariably enriching, should eventually go beyond the kind of enjoyment gained when one has climbed a mountain and looks around at the ranges that have become visible. Patient and therapist teams need also to liken themselves to the foresters. After having achieved access to a previously undiscovered peak, they draw up maps of the region, and plan and make pathways that enable them and others to traverse the forests and master the territory.

Too large a percentage of individuals become aware of what is harmful but continue to go along in their old ways, for there is a "world of difference between gaining an insight and responding to it" (Angyal, 1973). Self-understanding then ceases to be therapeutic, and people remain too set and constricted, or else too loose and unaware. An insight is to be experienced like a privilege for which one must "do," "experiment," "practice." The reason insights remain unapplied is not necessarily because something has not been worked through in the mind; rather it results from a fear and unwillingness to make shifts to active, real life. The therapist who encounters such timidity and lethargy has to make careful decisions: Can the person really not move? Is is autocratic to interfere? Does the person not know what new steps to take? Or is the would-be patient-explorer too lazy to study and apply his or her findings? We should give those who want to change freedom of choice, but also assign to them the responsibility of following through. Otherwise, as Freud sometimes feared, "the psychoanalytic approach has a greater future as a means of learning about oneself than as a therapeutic method" (Freud, 1959c).

WHAT THE FULL RANGE OF EMOTIONS ACCOMPLISHES

To be psychologically vigorous and to find our way through the maze of stimuli and human reactions that abound in the environment, we need to be connected with our emotions. Our emotions are a vital source of energy and bounce which enriches the cognitive life, while also serving as fine interceptors of messages sent out, often unwittingly, by others who wish to conceal what goes on in their mind.

Governed by their own laws, emotions are anchored both in the body and in the mind; in fact, they probably serve as bridges between body and mind (Spitz, 1965). In disturbed personalities, the interplay is disrupted. To remedy this, the emotions must be stirred up again, whereupon they can resume their important work of vitalizing the mind and exploring the environment. Through the impact of dynamic psychotherapy, the psyche ceases to hold on to the narrow and arid outlooks to which it has been restricted. It expands, it becomes refreshed and works with greater speed and precision unless the individual allows it to fall prey to manic highs for extended periods of time. Buoyed by feelings, the mind surveys a wider territory, abstains from simplified, narrow versions of situations or evaluations of other human objects, and definitely relinquishes the compulsive preoccupation with minute details which leads to a loss of perspective. Instead, mental processes which are being nurtured by affects make significant connections and obtain a comprehensive, assured, generous view of the world. Drugs, alcohol taken in doses which are not so excessive as to paralyze the mind, and, apparently, hypnosis produce similarly expanding effects (Martin, 1952) but have the drawback that they increase dependency on effects which converge on the person from outside. By contrast, the lift, expansion, and elevation which the emotions lend to mental processes are entirely of the individual's own making since he or she is the agent who mobilizes the emotions.

The physical stirrings that take place when the affective life has been set free through psychotherapy are readily observed. Instead of merely contemplating an event in a detached and eventually depressing manner that exhausts energy, even very restrained persons show markedly more vigorous body movements, actually break into tears or unusually loud laughter, sigh deeply, and the like.

When the psyche grapples with events which promise to bring fulfillment, breathing becomes fuller and located in the chest, and the gait becomes wider and more bouncy. Alertness, a condition which anticipates the possibility of dangers and attacks, makes the senses work overtime to a point where, on the one hand, a slight pressure on the windows may be heard and possibly misinterpreted, but on the other hand, genuine dangers are more readily identified because awareness is heightened when body and mind cooperate. More often than not, the integration between physiological and mental processes which results from the free flow of emotions achieves more realistic assessments, more active, penetrating, and searching forms of thinking (Fried, 1970) which steer rather than sidetrack life and lead to more creative solutions. To be mentally healthy and productive, we need the cooperation of our emotions. The obsessing and paranoid preoccupation with insignificant detail is, as a rule, a collateral of emotional sterility and not of heightened alertness.

Emotions carry important messages to the mind—messages from what Freud called the "id"—which can be regarded as the primordial legacy of the instincts. Emotions thus enrich and refresh the

human being, who cannot live on cognition alone and is easily exhausted by long periods of intellectual pursuits. Sexuality, physical
motion, laughter, and humorous exchanges, all these activities
which draw on the body and the instinctual core, restore a balance
that is lost when the cognitive mind is in the lead for a long time. In
this way the emotions, as a bridge to the body, are invigorating and
refreshing experiences.

Besides acting as vitalizers, the emotions are the antennae of the
psyche and intercept signals that exist in abundance but are not
picked up by the cognitive faculties. They are indispensable guides
to the deeper motivations and feelings that underlie *our own reactions
to other human beings and their reactions to us*. Without full access to the
emotional antennae, it is difficult to assess in what ways one's own
self and that of others are genuine, or are false and therefore un-
trustworthy. Since human relations vacillate, as they inevitably do,
between higher and lower forms of cooperation and mutuality, individuals are guided by their feelings towards a clear awareness of
just what is going on. Feelings piloting individuals through the intricacies of their object relationships highlight what is difficult, but
also that which is rewarding in human life, for other people are of
extreme importance to us, and even the most skeptical minds know
that "without someone else none of us can understand himself"
(Sartre, 1953). Specifically, supreme joy is achieved through interaction and mutuality with others. We need others to correct our self-
representations, to shed old and primitive identification in exchange
for friendships (Guntrip, 1969), the need for which can be as intense
as the hunger for sex or food, and the more selective identifications
they facilitate (Jacobson, 1964).

Only when the emotions are present in full force can the individual feel the painful but necessary signal pangs of anxiety.
Obsessive-compulsive persons who keep emotions at bay often fail to
recognize or register anxiety, which is manifested, as a result, in the
form of somatic disturbances. Anxiety helps the person, of course, to
obtain timely warnings of various forms of dangers and thereupon to
take the proper psychological as well as practical precautions. We
master not our anxiety but the circumstances that cause our anxiety
to give a warning signal, although the warning signal, by definition,
brings pain and pangs of confusion. Another emotion, namely, gen-

uine optimism and hope as contrasted with manic and fleeting euphoria, lends us encouragement, supports tolerance of frustration, and frequently elicits superior psychological and technical performances. On the other hand, the feelings subsumed under the heading of caution help us discriminate between noxious situations and hostile intentions of other people and the good, well-intentioned plans of friends or newcomers.

Feelings, then, are not a luxury reserved for the young who are not yet burdened by life, or for the well-to-do or other special members of the human community. Rather than diverting energy from adult pursuits and responsibilities such as work, maintaining a healthy family life, and participating in public affairs, feelings, quite to the contrary, are an absolute necessity for self-renewal which, in turn, banishes fatigue and dangerous boredom. They provide a strong biological-psychological balance and offer crucial guidance in the pursuit of and discriminant participation in human relationships without which self-image, self-esteem, and the maintenance of cooperation go awry. Only when feelings are aligned with the various departments of the structured psyche, specifically ego and self, which sponsor cognition, judgment, adaptation to the environment, and the elaboration and coordination of human relationships, can the individual be assured that he or she is in full possession of a form of psychological equipment essential for survival and happiness. Persons who have "lost" their emotions have forfeited the mechanism that can steer a relatively safe course through life in the absence of full-fledged instincts such as many animal species have which sense the approach of a potential foe by intercepting atmospheric or olfactory alterations. Only when the emotions are or again become available, only if, as people are wont to say, they can "get in touch with their emotions," do human beings obtain important inklings as to what goes on in and around them.

With the emotions fulfilling the important functions of bracing the psyche and steering it, undoubtedly one of the prime responsibilities of all psychotherapy is to firm them up, help them come out of hiding, and safeguard them. This calls for a variety of therapeutic skills, most of them part and parcel of a kind of work that falls into the two categories of "emotional insight" and "recovery and articulation of emotions." Unless we rescue the emotions through emphasis on various forms of emotional insight and affective enrichment, self-understanding turns into a purely rational, arid, and altogether limited process.

The prerequisite for establishing emotional insight is the therapist's reliance on his or her own emotions as they come into focus more or less continuously, and particularly in counter-transference reactions. It is the therapist's own emotional response which helps one understand whether the patient is eager to allow the emergence of sadness and tears, whether the patient's stubbornness at a partcular time is penetrable or rigid, whether certain displayed emotions are genuine or false, and whether a perpetual warding off of feeling is caused by a desperate attempt to avoid dreaded rejection and hurt. Certainly, people undergoing treatment are, at least in the initial phases, often torn in two directions: They are fearful of sentiments while craving them thirstily like the wanderer in the desert who yearns for water. As a patient said who learned from earliest childhood to hide his fears, his soft sentiments and longing for caresses from a mother who used her arthritic condition to keep her son perpetually at a distance: "I feel at peace because I was able to cry. My body and my mind are getting full, round. I have three colleagues who tell me they never cried. They are tin soldiers who won't win any battle."

HOW INSIGHT HELPS TO DISCOVER OR RECOVER EMOTIONS

So far we have focused on the importance of recovering the psyche's full capacity. The emotions have been viewed as a precious possession that had been lost and must be found again.

It cannot be emphasized enough that many individuals are unable to recover emotional range because they never really possessed it. Emotions and the intuitive capacities from which they partially stem and with which they keep the individual in touch are absent from awareness and remain inaccessible, *either because they have been repressed or because they were never fully defined and formed* to begin with. They have to be put on the psychic map, so to speak.

When such emotions as love and hate are full-fledged or palpable, they meet severe censure and are repressed.* Human beings protect

---

*Ways in which to express aggression or love vary from one historical period to the next. In the sixties and seventies certain direct discharges of aggression and sexual love have been accepted in the U.S.A. Yet specifications as to how this is to be done clearly exist.

themselves against unrequited feelings of love because the ensuing rejections lead to intolerable depression and aggression directed against the self. They must also protect themselves against their own anger because the counterattacks and punishments that anger elicits from those at whom it is directed arouse devastating anxiety and fears of retaliation. In either event, the risky feelings are repressed and often eventually extinguished at the merest onset of affect, which usually registers in the form of physiological sensation. As a consequence, some of the most vital properties and functions of the psyche are forfeited.

In such cases, it is advisable to use the psychoanalytic method, which interprets to the patient the existence not of the feared emotion but of the defensive operations set up to disown and bury the supposedly dangerous affect (Sandler, Dare, and Holder, 1973). Such a procedure is apt to facilitate insight into the shunned feeling because it spares the patient anxiety, shame, and embarrassment by drawing attention, say in the case of love feelings, to such a stance as standoffishness rather than hot passion.

Other steps must follow. For instance, patients have to be encouraged to express even minute doses of affect in the transference, until the feeling attains full bloom. Since the most powerful emotions are invariably connected with physiological expression, such as changes in the voice, tears, floor pacing or waving of arms, a casual acceptance of such behavior is helpful in bringing submerged feelings to life, first through insight and then through expression. Strict censure of acting out encourages small repressive steps. While patients have hugged me, screamed at me, and stamped their feet or an umbrella on the floor, no one has struck me a blow. I think this means that the patient looks after the therapist enough to avoid true harm even at the peak of emotional arousal. Even when patients repeatedly lose control of their feelings following insight and expression, they are cheered by the influx of energy produced by the emerging and gradually stabilized emotions. They are relieved, too, when the mental clouds lift because the antennae (the steering facilities and the vision of self and world) obtain a crystal-like clarity with the freeing of affect.

In other situations and with other personalities, the point is not that important emotions have been lost through repression and extinction at an early stage, but rather that they have never existed to begin with *in articulated and defined form*. In these severe conditions of unemotionality which occur in certain borderline states but also in other supposedly less serious disorders, such as those of the obsessive-compulsive personality, individuals are bewildered, feel emotionally and physically clumsy, and are altogether convinced that they are not like other human beings. This is indeed true, as we shall see, and it helps little to reassure them, unless one simultaneously completes their emotional life which is stunted in a very special way. What is needed here is insight into the encompassing problem of an emotionally chaotic and thus confusing existence. The emotions have not been stripped away, as in the case of repression, but they have never been channeled into a network of separate and clearly delineated currents. Like the "fleeting images" discussed elsewhere (Chapter 6), they need to be recognized and articulated, either by the patient or the therapist or some other mediator, e.g. poetry or drama.

An example of such cases is the emotional confusion which results when the early environment has given mixed signals (Bateson, 1972) and created the so-called double bind to the point where one message elicited clashes with one or several other emotions. Instead of serving as clear affective structures to channel and guide life, emotions flow together and form a whirl. The whirl (rather than conflict) of emotions elicited by simultaneous, multidirectional, and partly-veiled messages arouses extreme irritability. Different nerves have received different kinds of impulses which have remained unintegrated; although the system is in a state of high arousal, there is no clear idea of how the excitation should be expressed. In this aroused but uncoordinated condition, people are highly uncontrolled and eventually force the environment they create as adults to shun them like whirling dervishes to whom one cannot relate because of their emotional chaos. The principal party, who has been the prime object of double binds, is confused both by his or her own inner formlessness and by seemingly inexplicable abandonments by partners or friends. The result is frequently a gradual withdrawal of a schizoid kind.

The talented, good-natured and handsome patient,

Friedrich, was the son and grandson of a double-bind mother and grandmother from whose confusing messages he protected himself through a withdrawal concealed behind amiable but meaningless chitchat. Having cut off communication very early with these two primary figures—the father had died a year after Friedrich's birth—this man's emotions remained unformed, raw, elusive and primordial, a condition he tried to repair by relying on pseudo-logic and intellectual hairsplitting. Unable to separate out what he felt or wanted, Friedrich was invariably confused, unable to carry to conclusion his work which demanded organization. Moreover, he, himself, transmitted bewildering messages of either a double-bind, primary process, or narcissistic nature. It was the custom rather than exception for Friedrich to ask a woman friend whether she wished to see a play and to suggest, as soon as an affirmative answer was obtained, that the couple could also have a quiet evening at home, thus denying the expressed wish of the companion and also acting as though two mutually exclusive possibilities were indeed reconcilable. Such confusion, contrariness, and contradiction created so much irritation and chaos in people, and especially in women who cared for this attractive and in many ways kindly man, that he was abandoned in the long run by friends who wished to preserve their own sanity. Only when the patient eventually entered therapy did he begin to get insight into the reasons why he was so regularly abandoned and to examine his own responsibility for this. This insight was continually augmented by a semantic education and gradual resignation from narcissistic omnipotence. The patient was helped to give shape to his needs and affects by articulating them one by one; in time, he was able to achieve a global integration of emotions and needs.

In his treatment, much emphasis was put on a linear, segmented approach to life which ordinary language favors because it proceeds sequentially in time, articulating first one and then the other part of a multifaceted constellation (Hall, 1977). The patient's needs and feelings were given shape through articulation and sorted out one by one. Integration came later and spontaneously.

Psychological and geographic isolation leads to arrestations of ego development which prevent the delineation and articulation of affects. In such cases feelings and their forerunners, namely somatic sensations, are not linked with clear, steady, and understandable signals. As Freud formulated it, unless auditory signals, namely words, are attached to such id content as feelings, the latter do not make contact with the conscious ego (Freud, 1961). This is seen in many borderline conditions but also in supposedly less disturbed personalities as, for example, obsessive-compulsives. They remain strangers to their own deep feelings even though they are verbal and capable of skillful articulation of their defenses, such as politeness on the one hand and rigidity and censure on the other.

A good example of persistent affective chaos and disorganization caused by isolation in the very first years of life is found in the story of Helen Keller as dramatized in the play, *The Miracle Worker*. Because she is deaf and dumb, the child, Helen, cannot communicate to herself or others what she feels and wants. Pressured by as yet unformed desires and feelings, she runs wild, shrieking and gesticulating and scurrying about aimlessly. Relief comes to the troubled child when her teacher-nurse synchronizes the desire for and interest in water with a signal, namely three taps on the palm of Helen's hand. This, at last, gives her a dawning awareness that there exist such things as signals by means of which to contain her feelings and let others know about them. In psychotherapy, we are able to help individuals who have remained isolated from an early age to grasp, through articulation, what they feel and want. The painful and psychologically costly isolations we observe are usually self-imposed, as when a child, sensing the psychic fragility of a parent, often the mother, holds back cries and vague feelings of desperation and demands that are in the making.

> From early childhood, Ivy had been compliant and undemanding, either hiding or burying her various talents and spoiling her good looks in the attempt not to appear more attractive, brighter, or more capable than her mother, who was a slave to the father. For thirty years such denial of a barely formed self had gone on until the patient could no longer bear the situation which she had set up. When she entered therapy, she complained that her emotions were tangled up and felt like a web that choked her. Her only refuge consisted of fantasies of a particularly repetitive, grandiose, and quite infantile nature. Feeling like a clumsy, overgrown child, she used these fantasies to see herself emerge many times each day as a glamorous creature, half nymph and half goddess.
>
> Gradually, we disentangled some of her feelings, especially

anger, and observed that she dug her long, scarlet fingernails into the palms of her hands as soon as she sensed any forebodings of anger. Eventually, she also joined a weekly group session; she wanted this because, never knowing what she felt or wanted, she welcomed the greater number of heads that could tell her what she really felt. To start Ivy on a course of tracing her emotions, I suggested that when she felt annoyance or anger she let the group and me know about it; when she complained that the stirrings were so faint that she inevitably lost them in the din of the group discussions, she was asked to wave her hand or jump up as soon as she felt something, in particular, resentment. After five weeks, Ivy, catching her anger clue of digging her nails into her hands, jumped up, started to talk, stopped, and then laughed with some embarassment at the opportunity offered her. The following week, she reported that the many reactions expressed during her anger episode, which she called "my gripes," had once again become entangled in poorly defined memories. Would everybody help her find her "puzzle pieces"? When a male group member remonstrated and accused Ivy of allowing her dependent needs to take over, there was disagreement on the part of the therapist and other members who were convinced of the validity of Ivy's desire to reassemble the as yet frail impressions.

The healthy person's self consists of emotions and needs that have been fused with verbal, visual, or tactile images and then been integrated into a structure. Insight into the nebulous fabric of a structure that lacks clear articulation is not enough to make up for semantic arrestations. Such patients have to be encouraged and enabled to say "what they want" and express "what they feel" (Spotnitz and Meadow, 1976). In many a way, *the word gives birth to the feeling by lending it form.*

This is not to say that the word is always paramount. Quite the contrary, as is so often the case in human affairs, two opposite approaches are needed in order to make a whole. While some persons occasionally must be provided with the right words so that they can get hold of their as yet vague feelings, words can at other times—and this is true not only of inarticulate inchoate individuals—overwhelm and destroy emotions and needs which are either fragile and incipient or else not released because the person wishes to keep them to himself.

Of course, concept formations, cause-and-effect connections, well-ordered priorities, and suitable articulations are needed when a weak ego cannot organize and master a profusion of stimuli. Yet, there are occasions when outside structuring, ordering, and articulation are counterindicated and silent attention is called for. The listening, then, becomes the cure. At such times and in such cases the issue in not fragility caused by the inchoate state of emotions, but a need for validation and dispensation from guilt over harboring feelings that others and the own self have censored or found irrational or unjustified. The acute and painful problem is that the words "Why should you feel that way, it makes no sense" have been heard too often. By contrast, persons with such difficulties need to experience in the attentive presence of the other person, for example the therapist, that they are not alone when they express what they feel and that they have a right to their feelings, such as they are. The most important experience for them is validation of their emotional existence. If the experienced and expressed feelings entail dangers and severe conflicts and the patient wishes to modify the affects, this will have to come later. To begin with, the therapist is primarily needed as the listener who remains unshocked and accepting (Fairbairn, 1952). The chief contribution to patients who possess full-fledged feelings but are afraid and ashamed of them is to share and not to interpret. Insight interpretations have to wait, such as separating defensive from core feelings, pointing out the true causes of feelings and showing how guilt is never reparative, while transformation of feelings and responsible action are remedial. These and other insight interpretations have to wait until patients have become able to own up to their feelings and realize they have a right to their feelings regardless of the subsequent changes that may be found necessary.

Schizophrenics and borderline personalities are particularly articulate about clashes between affects which they are trying to absorb and the verbal labels for them. Lorraine, an articulate borderline personality, asked me explicitly to say nothing at moments when she, usually devoid of body awareness or emotion, became sensitized to her body or genuine affect. What borderline people feel to be true holds to a lesser degree also for less disturbed persons, although they do not always have the same degree of awareness. If language is needed to proclaim kinship with the emotions and, indeed, to assist their birth, then it is the language of poetry or drama or of visual imagery and color in the arts. Real poetry is neither sentimental nor imprecise. It makes selections of special words and sounds, stringing them together not by logic but by other kinds of significant connections. What is accomplished in ordinary language through logic and adverbs such as although, yet and but, etc., namely an ordering and, thereby, a mastery of the world, is paralleled in poetry, drama and painting in a different way. The arts, for example, help us to master the world by making explicit fears that have been merely implied for too long; by evoking visions of what could exist in the future; by juxtaposing the unexpected with the anticipated, etc. In short, the arts sensitize us to what we can feel, if we give ourselves permission, and provide us with the means of expression.

CONCURRENT SEARCH FOR PROBLEMS AND SOLUTIONS

The chances for recovery increase with simultaneity. People who are trying to figure themselves out need synchronization. Concurrently with discovering what is wrong with their emotional life, their psychological organism, and their way of functioning, they need to obtain a fair idea of how to solve the dilemmas and shortcomings that are being unearthed. Insights into problems that exist and the related difficulties are more readily tolerated, less vigorously resisted, and indeed given a welcome if at the same time therapist and patient envision, discuss, and even try out ways to overcome the newly discovered obstacles.

When Suzy, a divorced woman of 33 who was eager to find a husband, discussed a recent visit to her orthopedist, she cried slowly, evidencing deep pain. She had been told that a curvature of the spine which she had since early childhood had become worse and that she probably would need an operation in case a course of planned exercises proved inadequate. She mentioned, her tears now flowing more heavily, that her specialist had been very kind. He had said to her that she was no longer the young unworried girl of seven years before when she had consulted him for diagnosis and help, but that she was very lovely and still young enough. "When a fellow puts his arms around you," so the kindly doctor said, "we want to give him a nice straight back to touch. You will see that if the exercises won't do the straightening out, the operation will do it and it won't be painful or keep you bedridden long." I asked Suzy whether she cried because the doctor had given her hope and some idea of her future prospects. By contrast, earlier in the session, I had only pointed out her fear of meeting men without suggesting how we could proceed to the greater social gregariousness she desired. Suzy agreed and cried even harder. An accessible and appealing patient, she whispered, "Please, let's figure out what I can do. I want a baby very much. I want to live with a man and do things together. I no longer want to be alone."

It is imperative to weigh problems and solutions conjointly since every person's psyche is a structure, a living system with coexisting currents. While we cannot survey everything that goes on inside and around the individual at once, we can master the *simultaneous* review of several connected problems. We need to consider what such related problems are and the possible directions for renewal and improvement. Everyone who desires a reconstruction of personality senses that one change will necessitate other changes. As a result of a concurrent search for problems and for solutions of those problems, people contemplate the road they are to travel more calmly. They feel less compelled to resist if they have a pretty good idea, and preferably an experience, of at least *a few answers,* since this gives some reassurance that a whirl of total chaos will not take over.

After separation from her husband, Bettina, who still loved him although he had initiated the breakup, avoided her friends, acquaintances, and relatives. Always in the habit of seeking refuge at home, she now buried herself in her little apartment, virtually restricting human contacts to her work situation. Bettina was enraged when her gravitation towards solitude was pointed out. "I don't want to know that," she screamed. "For goodness sakes, don't talk to me of my problems without giving me some little ways out. Why do I stay in my living room since I broke up with Claude? I am angry, is that it? I don't want people to stare at my rage, is that what it is?"

As I reviewed and tried to explain several episodes Bettina had reported, she listened, not patiently but pounding the table in front of her, with questions obviously swirling around in her head. Bettina had often been harsh, indeed cruel, towards her husband, as she had repeatedly remarked. I said that one of the relevant problems was her fear that, were she to go out, she might again be hurtful and, as she had called it, sadistic. And then the point was made that the patient's harshness, ridicule, and rage towards males, already evident in her early teens when she stuck pins into a younger cousin's leg, were probably what we had very soon to consider, understand, and change. Bettina, not exactly content, was nevertheless reassured. "I need those little maps," she retorted in a sarcastic tone characteristic of her. "A map makes me feel less stupid, do you understand?" I told the patient to hold it right then and there. "Now you are furious at me and probably feel sadistic. Don't push the rage away; stay with the cruel impulse but try to put a hold on it, as though you were singing a high C. Make it clear to the rage that you are its master." The patient understood what I meant, stopped hitting the table after she had given it a hard slap, and put her fist on it. Her breathing was heavy at first and then got lighter. "Golly, it worked," she exclaimed. "When I tried to tell those floats of rage and sadistic lashes that I am the master, they rolled off, they broke like waves on the sand."

This experience of mastery, very different from repression, gave Bettina a vision of what could be. Instead of going through the taunting feelings created by the back and forth between ego weakness and rage which led up to the sadistic thrill (Fenichel, 1955), she got a taste for a different and calmer kind of psychological-emotional management.

Having experienced an emotional alternative to repression by experiencing on-the-spot the deliberate prolongation of a usually quickly shunned emotion, she could embark on a reorientation. She discovered more tolerance for insight because she had caught a glimpse of how reconstruction proceeds.

It cannot be emphasized sufficiently that many an insight remains sterile because the psychic structure cannot mobilize the wherewithal to put the new understanding into practice. Let us stay with the issue of aggression. People gain nothing but more conscious guilt feelings if they are made more aware of their rage without at the same time being helped to learn how to convert anger into energy. Insight into unconscious, buried rage leads to improvement and healthy reorientation only if simultaneously the steps are discussed and practiced which allow the psyche to utilize the newly-discovered rage.

3

*From Repetitiveness
and Mechanization to
Variation and Innovation*

Repetitiveness is inevitably a sign of psychological disturbance. Often we see men and women exhausting themselves by running through the same old emotional and behavioral mazes again and again, getting nowhere. When this happens, we need to understand why the individual is resorting to stereotyped and thus maladaptive ways of perceiving, feeling, thinking, and acting.

Repetitiveness is a core feature in virtually all forms of pathology. For purposes of this discussion, however, we shall focus mainly on those situations that are primarily related to ego arrest and are remedied through promotion of ego growth. In such instances people often understand that they are about to make the same error, but they do not possess the psychological wherewithal to pursue truly different pathways and ventures.

It was Freud (1962) who first pointed out that the human need to practice repetition is so strong that one can speak of a *repetition compulsion*. But in using the concept of the repetition compulsion, we have to distinguish between different dynamics and different uses of repetition. There is a type of repetition which reflects and intensifies ego strength. And there is another type of repetition which cuddles

64

the ego, protecting both the repressive mechanisms which it uses and the gaps in development which exist. *Repetition compulsion* #1 can be found in healthy adults and is especially visible in determined children bound on learning important life skills. This is the strong and active form of repetition compulsion that induces us to try out feelings, thought, and actions over and over again, thus mastering difficult situations in which one initially failed—often because one was overwhelmed by the stimuli emanating from a new task or was insufficiently prepared to cope with its unaccustomed challenges.

In a second and quite divergent sense, the practice of repetition stems from entirely different dynamics. The goal of these repetitions, which are automatic and passive, is to protect either the defenses of the ego (Freud, 1959c) or certain damaging ego arrests and malformations. In these instances we need the concept of a repetition compulsion #2. Any failure to distinguish between the two types of repetition and to discern whether diagnostically we are dealing with repetition compulsion #1 or #2 misdirects treatment.

In the case of the second repetition compulsion, repetition is not used for the sake of establishing mastery over the environment or the self, thus expanding the psychic structures. On the contrary, the reruns of certain routines keep the ego confused and depleted.

A prime example in the second category is recurrences of choice due to the influence which repressed motivations have on our life. An example, to choose an oedipal illustration, although within the context of this book other motivations are viewed as equally or more important, is the repeated pursuit of a love object who resembles a parent. In such cases the individual has repressed the erotic and sexual desire for the parent who is to be resurrected. Yet the sexual taboos surrounding such a parent are still alive, though also repressed. Hence repeated pursuits are undertaken to conquer such a human object, but the urgings of conscience forbid the enjoyment of the ultimate conquest or tamper with it in many other ways. In any event, as long as the oedipal motivation remains repressed, the fatal chase goes on.

Other recurrences of fatal choices and decisions which occur due to the workings of repetition compulsion #2 have the function of protecting various defects of the psychological structures. What prompts the person in such cases to repeat previously doomed forays is the existence of ego arrests. Many human beings set up and select over and over again situations which failed them in the past. They allow, nay drive, themselves to get involved with friends, business partners, and lovers who resemble in basic ways primary people who proved disappointing in the past. If one looks closer, one discovers that these "new" people are basically chosen because they make up, in one or several ways, for ego defects from which the repeater suffers. The personalities thus wooed despite previous disappointments with similar candidates are expected to provide a form of psychological "foreign aid." It is hoped that their presence and the connections with them will make up for gaps and malformations that exist in the ego of the wooer. In actuality, the method never works, and the repetitiveness ceases to exert its eventually damaging impact when genuine ego and self-growth are accomplished by the person who heretofore fell victim to the repetitions.

ACTIVE REPETITIONS

We can observe the first kind of repetition compulsion—the kind that aims at overcoming defeat and trauma—in emotionally sturdy children. When restrained or scolded by authority, children often take refuge in sulking or withdrawal—responses which are obstacles to growth. But other more creative solutions are also possible. For instance, they can invent a game that turns the tables and gives them the upper hand. I recently overheard a little girl telling her mother: "I am the mother and you are the Elizabeth, and you go and 'have [behave] yourself." Elizabeth had found a way to escape her passive position and put herself in charge of her own conduct, while still meeting the legitimate demands that had originally been her mother's. (Yes, her mother's demands, by any normal standard, were legitimate, so that Elizabeth's "identification with the aggressor," while defensive in a sense, was also an adaptive internalization.)

Among adults, athletes achieve mastery through the use of repetition; after a failure, they are urged by their coaches to avoid passivity and return to active practice in order to avert defeatism.

Regarding defeatism, we should be aware of an error or fallacy which underlies this negative attitude: The defeatist does not distinguish adequately between external facts, which often cannot be changed, and inner capacities of his own which can be realigned and strengthened for the purpose of recouping his losses and going on to success. The defeatist outlook focuses on circumstances where the going was rough and dwells on the experience of failure. This attitude blinds a person to his or her inner resources and to the possibility of making a fresh approach, and forecloses opportunities for change and mastery. Whereas human beings are indeed often unable to alter external facts, they *can* change the way they tackle trying situations if they will put defeatism aside and take a fresh look at themselves.

As the intuitive "mastery games" of children show, the repetition compulsion, viewed as the motive to turn from passivity to active coping, is innate. But it can be undermined by prolonged emphasis on static facts and neglect of the flexible ego and self which are capable of creative problem-solving. By shifting the focus to inner resources, the compulsion to repeat becomes the source of human persistence and invincibility (Menninger, 1959), and reflects the organism's capacity for self-remedy. Unlike neurotic methods of self-protection, the repetition compulsion utilizes *conscious, straight,* and *creative* activeness, whereas passive repetition is based on primarily *unconscious* and *defensive* activeness. By making constructive use of the repetition compulsion, we demonstrate that immediate self-reactivation and practice enhance our skills and courage. Through the ensuing growth we come to master not only our previous failures but also the anxieties formerly connected with them.

The repetition compulsion, in this constructive sense of the term, engages the person in autoplastic activity: It leads to immediate enhancement of capacities, increased courage, and a revival of hope. In the process, the ego and the self are expanded rather than being restricted to existing levels of functioning.

Such recourse to the repetition compulsion helps people react assertively to abandonment or object loss—the most threatening of the basic traumata. In the face of desertion, the person can make it his business, after a period of mourning and self-search, to venture forth once more and gather new friends. This involves use of the contact function and of approach behavior, in contrast with the tendency to withdraw. The healthy appeal of making new approaches wins out over the self-defeating inclination to pull back into a corner. It may be added that approach responses draw much more on a person's inventiveness than do withdrawal maneuvers. A more neurotic choice would be to become hostile, disinterested and detached and thereby compound the effects of object loss in restricting the growth and use of the ego and self.

Constructive repetition marks a *voluntary return* to the scene of painful experiences. Strong, courageous, and determined people are likely to deal intuitively as well as rationally with psychologically challenging situations because they have not been alienated from their feelings and their inner life. Disturbed persons can discover through guidance and learning opportunities that the flood of stimulation that is invariably unleashed by traumatic experiences needs to be dispelled as quickly as practicable in the interest of psychological survival. They become aware that protest, challenge, and fight are necessary in order to avert regression to passivity, with its concomitant abandonment of previously achieved active positions.

In large measure, the organism achieves sturdiness of ego and solidity and coherence of self—despite inevitable disappointments and setbacks—precisely because of the repetition compulsion, which could just as well be termed *developmental tenaciousness*. Unless the psyche is chronically discouraged and its forward movement persistently thwarted, there exists in human beings a substantial measure of patience, hopefulness, courage, and willingness to learn in an active way from experience (Bion, 1962). Active learning occurs when one experiments with life and within life situations to bring new skills into the picture while trying once again to succeed where formerly one had failed. If we can make good the second or subsequent time around, then the repetition compulsion—the drive to gain the upper hand where once one had suffered defeat—has become our ally. Strong personalities, as a rule, not only make good use of the repetition compulsion, but also are future-oriented and hopeful. Indeed, successful repetition, future orientation, and hopefulness usually go together as an inseparable triad.

In psychotherapy, we join forces with the healthy repetition compulsion by encouraging patients not to give up and by helping them realize that unprocessed traumata and defeats foster anxiety and a return to the passive position.

PASSIVE REPETITIONS

In contrast to the active life- and strength-preserving tendency to approach traumatic situations over again in the hope of gaining mastery on subsequent tries, there exist passive repetitions that do not strengthen and enrich the mind. Passive repetitions lead to exhaustion of energy, an encompassing sense of defeat, and eventually to depression. Interestingly, many persons are unaware that their "downs" are actually the result of a lifetime of unaltered and unexamined repetitions. Indeed, the passive form of repetition compulsion is one of the core features of neurotic behavior. For this reason its correction has always been a prime target of treatment.

As stated earlier, we need the concept of a repetition compulsion #2 to explain the occurrence of repetitive behavior which contributes nothing to the strengthening of the ego structure and the self. Quite to the contrary, many repetitions that can only be explained by a second kind of compulsion stem from significant ego arrests and malformations which they cover up and perpetuate, for many disturbed men and women persist in recurrent behavior which proves to be destructive in the end because they suffer from developmental gaps. These are perpetuated rather than amended through the repetitions.

To illustrate, let us look at the phenomenon of procrastination. Procrastination causes not only friction with the environment but creates intense anxiety in many persons who feel that their habits of postponement are suggestive of some form of inner disintegration. Upon closer investigation we find that procrastination is determined by multiple and often interlocking causes, all of them the result of serious deficiencies of ego development.

Many a time one reason for procrastination is an unconscious wish to defy authority. The patient puts off tasks because the completion of duties is perceived and experienced as a way of yielding to seniority and coercion. Persons who have never completed their individuation and who feel that the primary way to protect the existence of a separate self is to flaunt rules and neglect duties such as clearing their desk of accumulated tasks procrastinate to emphasize their individual freedom. In procrastinating, they often fight no party in particular, but internalized voices that represent authority figures from childhood days. Being late, which can be considered a form of procrastination, is frequently experienced as a way of resisting the person with whom an appointment is scheduled and who is unwittingly placed in the role of an authority. Naturally, latecoming plays a role in dynamic psychotherapy, when patients keep the therapist, to whom they have assigned the role of a coercive authority figure, waiting.

In cases where procrastination represents a form of rebellion, albeit often against internalized rather than existing authority figures, the encouragement to practice direct and open opposition proves helpful. Fighting openly rather than by way of the circuitous route of procrastination, the person who never completed individuation gradually obtains a sense of independence and selfhood. A certain level of inner freedom is achieved. Procrastinations that stem from the need for non-compliance with imaginary or internalized authority figures fall by the wayside. The relief that greets the ability to give up the compulsion to procrastinate is unexpectedly great, since the negative freedom gained by procrastinating leads to various forms of bondage rather than to a sense of liberty.

The phenomenon of procrastination, determined as it is by multiple and varied causes, is many a time the result of another kind of deficiency in psychic structures—the fear of emptiness. While persons may be dismayed by long lists of neglected "musts," such as a jumble of unpaid bills and unanswered letters on their desk, they sense in a vague manner that if they were actually to work their way to the bottom of the lists and heaps, they and their world would feel unbearably empty.

Borderline and neurotic patients are apt to fear emptiness, as did one articulate but seriously disturbed woman:

> "I figure that as long as there are things to do, I can't get too lonely or disappear into thin air. In essence, I consist of these heaps of paper. If I finish them off, I might have nothing to do, no reason for existing. There would be no 'me' left, if everything got done."

She added, quite rightly, that she was sure she would stop procrastinating once her self, her identity, and her inner processes became filled out and she could feel she had achieved inner substance. What caused this and other patients' repeated and tiresome procrastination was, then, not some unconscious thought or wish that could be laid to rest through an uncovering type of therapy, but the more fundamental problem of a gap in the self that had to be filled before the "habit" of procrastination could outgrow its value as substitution for a true self and be dispensed with. The empty self is frequently found in persons with pronounced narcissistic inclinations who are used to role playing and pseudo-emotions and do not possess an authentic core.

When the ego and self are incomplete, patients often help themselves in ways that simply extend the chains of repetition. They seek out and find people and situations whom they expect to "help out" by serving as buttresses for their unfinished egos and selves. The tragedy of this approach, in which others are pressed into service to help one win life's battles without a full set of ego functions, is that the patient remains stuck despite all the effort and disruption. Another response of such patients to the paucity and imperfection of ego functions and the fragility of the self is to limit themselves to the relatively few situations and people they do know how to manage. Thus, existing personality flaws remain largely hidden and undiagnosed, and nothing is done to make needed repairs. The seeming activeness with which the person navigates through a limited range of situations is a defensive, not a fruitful kind of activeness (Fried, 1970).

It is amazing how few variations of feelings and behavior confirmed repeaters will permit themselves. They have to do with a few safe moves as long as their psychic structure remains archaic, poorly integrated, and generally inadequate, and their ego functions arrested. They resemble inexperienced chess players who arrive quickly at the end of their game. Because they lack versatility, they quickly forfeit many of their more valuable pieces. Through their automatized, passive repetitions, existing shortcomings are preserved rather than corrected.

Many persons manage to sustain the self-made unreality and monotony of intimate relations with others by treating the connection as merely temporary. Another relationship, to be formed eventually, will bring real human sustenance to their lives. They make *imagined variety* rather than *practiced and real variation* the invariant element which is repeated. To illustrate, a highly narcissistic man, who was so self-preoccupied that he did not notice needs and peculiarities of appearance in others, finally ventured into marriage at the age of forty-five. The union with a woman of identical age proved totally unsatisfying, but he succeeded in staying married by telling himself that soon he would find another very different partner. No obstacle appeared real to this male since he had developed the practice of dealing with this and any other difficulty by fantasizing situations, liaisons, and opportunities of a very different kind. In thought this man tried everything. In reality he did nothing of consequence.

WHY INSIGHT IS NOT ENOUGH

The person who settles for repetition usually does not know how to expand the ego and the self. Gaining insight into the situation, while certainly essential, does not suffice to overcome the psychological poverty and emptiness which cause the many standstills. In addition to grasping what is wrong, such individuals have to acquire psychological maps and visions. They have to be shown in what ways the psychic structure is inadequate, as well as shown ways by which the deficits can be made good, through learning, inventing, growing, and cultivating new psychological territory. These repeaters lag behind as a matter of psychological impoverishment and not by choice and must learn to fill their lacunae, as the following case demonstrates:

> Charm, a light touch of wit, politeness, and agreeableness were the surface qualities that made Sam a popular acquaintance, guest, and companion. He seemed always willing to give in to others and "adjust." There was no end to the round of parties to which he was invited. But the fact that all his relationships were marginal—that he could not permit himself to become personal or intimate—depressed Sam, even though he did not know the reasons for his predicament.
>
> He spoke and dreamt frequently of death. "The endless repetitions which I undertake because an unknown 'must' pushes me in that direction fatigue me to the point of either wanting to go to Asia or shoot myself," he would say. In treat-

ment, it gradually became clear that Sam had been held in check as a child by the stern admonishments of his two older sisters, a hostile brother, and a rigid mother who tolerated no rebellion. He had been expected, by silent conspiracy of his family, to perform household chores on the one hand and be a first-rate student on the other.

Sam never dared to oppose the manipulations he was subjected to, nor risk open refusal or confrontation; inwardly, however, he wanted to shake his sisters and mother into a state of trembling. His pleasant ways of going along with others were the predictable result of being unable to voice his private monologue of stubborn opposition and turn it into open dialogue. His ego deficit was his inability to go public as a dissenter—in short, to demand his independence. Always inwardly, he wished that he could run away to an island where he could live alone and be self-sufficient. His great desire was to turn a magic knob and switch the world off. As a result, he became a detached person who used charm and quick agreement to obscure a pervasive incapacity to relate to anybody.

This patient learned in his treatment what it felt like to go through the successive phases of making contact with another person—that is, with his therapist. The open expression of his desire for distance helped him the most. On one occasion, when a session had to be cancelled, he said: "I wonder when you will be going away. There are a lot of things I have to take care of, and when you leave I will have a chance. I am angry; I want you to be quiet; you don't deserve me. You make me a puppet that dangles. Don't touch me, go away, leave me alone. I don't have to care about you. I was right all along in thinking you were dispensable. It is all fake; you don't care."

With these and similar words and feelings—never previously expressed—this man made contact with his need for affection and at the same time established a sense of independence and a range of self-expression that strengthened him. Eventually, he no longer felt a need to run away to a remote island or to shoot himself. He came out of his depression, made more meaningful and solid personal contacts, especially with intelligent men, and finally gave up his impersonal hotel room and took an apartment. He stopped using the blabbering kind of speech he had loved before, and indeed quit going to a small "literary" salon where it apparently was the custom to talk and act like a child. He came to prefer serious discussions and arguments, especially when they pertained to the community at large, which he had previously ignored.

If a patient is arrested at an early level of development, the conse-
quent deficits in his ego capacities will preclude free movement and
exploratory behavior. The variety of life becomes whittled down.
Self-esteem will be low; therefore, only a limited variety of situations, namely those which promise a degree of guaranteed success,
will be sought out or tolerated. If the self-image (self-representation)
is shaken—as is apt to happen in new situations—it will be difficult
to stay alone. To be by oneself, one must be able to sustain a stable
and acceptable self-image without constant resort to the
reassurance, feedback, or even provocations of others. People,
crowds, and alliances are pursued, not out of free choice but from
dire psychological necessity. The end result is a sense of living with a
compulsion to socialize, which makes for hectic and indiscriminate
contacts rather than the easy alternation of solitude with the company of people one can truly enjoy.

In all such cases, the cure calls for a resumption of growth. For example, the hectic socializer can begin to tolerate solitude, which part
of him has always wanted, when he acquires, through therapeutic
ego-building, a clear self-image and a sense that he can be his own
person. Without continuous outside confirmation, his self-image can
become a clearly demarcated, active, and autonomous constellation
in the psychological firmament that has its place in relationship to
other such systems. No longer is he under pressure to pursue the
search for others who will supply the personal references, positive
and negative, that enable the patient to feel he really exists: "How
are you?"; "When will you pay me the money you owe me?";
"Can't you do better than that?"; "You're being silly." These are
among the hundreds of everyday questions, comments, accusations,
strokes, and other personal references that disturbed people need
constantly in order to be reminded of the reality of their existence.
These references, beyond an irreducible modicum, become unnecessary, once the awareness of one's reality as an individual rests
firmly and calmly inside the self.

The development and consolidation of the self-image are but one
facet of emotional recovery and independence gained through genuine personality growth.

A married woman who became anxious whenever her husband was out of town found herself unable to take care of her children and her work unless she could arrange to have company during the evening. As a rule, she got together with people, preferably men, who were as isolated as her mate. These companions served the function of giving her an island of safety, a base to touch down upon. Who the people were was not important; they merely had to be able to respond to her questions in a monosyllabic way. This patient remarked: "I notice that when my husband is around I try all the time to make him aware of me. I want him to respond to me continuously. If he doesn't, I am less there. That's why I must find other company immediately when he is gone."

This patient's inability to stay by herself and her compulsive need to replace one human contact with another were due to a dangerous diminution of self-awareness when she was alone (Fried, 1955). She was helped greatly through the gradual establishment of self-awareness, largely by acquiring a more deliberate and articulated use of her body. Whereas she had previously sort of pushed her body about when erect and then, when ready to sit, dumped it like a lump into a chair, she eventually learned to use her muscles, to enjoy taut movements, and to become a flexible person. Such were the beginnings of her personal and immediate, rather than second-hand, self-awareness. And with that eventually came freedom from repetition and substantial personality change.

It is not enough to simply identify or diagnose the existence of the second repetition compulsion and the recurrence of certain feelings, actions, and fears. To emphasize the consequences of certain psychological habits has some value because this highlights secondary gains that are achieved through repetition. But the chief purpose of any interpretations and explanations in this case is to make clear to individuals the specific nature of the inner limitations that force them into the straightjacket of automatic, passive repetitions. People become motivated to seek change when they understand life failures through repetition and the fact that they have left undeveloped large chunks of psychological substance that need to be structured and processed for psychological creativity to emerge.

As a second step to bring about change, *the individual needs to convert arrests into assets by discovering "turning around experiences."* This is often called the working-through process and encompasses that part of dynamic therapy which has met with the least success. It is equivalent to the building of new psychic structures; to the shaping of a different grasp on reality; to the acquisition of more developed ego functions and the making of a more authentic self. To work through, we not only remember and understand, we invent.

To illustrate, I shall report here the case of a young woman who became more creative and more content once she gave up a narcissistic need to rescue others. Outgrowing this need, which is used in the service of preserving a fantasy of being powerful and extraordinary, permitted this patient to finish a number of poems and stories that she had previously succeeded only in sketching out in a tentative and hurried fashion. Although her improvement was accompanied by greater calm, she did not settle down to a bland existence but instead devoted herself vigorously to creative pursuits.

The patient, Beatrice, was the daughter of a seductive and promiscuous father, whose charm and popularity she admired and emulated, and whose coldness towards his family she resented. At an early age, when her father was away from home for increasingly long periods of time, she took up mothering her own mother—a self-righteous woman, somewhat arrogant and highly intelligent, who drifted into alcoholism and died several years after Beatrice's marriage. Looking back over her life, Beatrice became aware that she had discouraged at least three capable, earnest, and marriageable men and had instead taken a husband who proved unsuitable. He flirted ostentatiously with other women and depended on Beatrice to the point where he could hardly speak to another person without first making eye contact with his wife as if to ask, "Is it okay for me to talk?" A hostile, passive man, he shared housekeeping and child care responsibilities only reluctantly; in general, he relied on Beatrice's strength and initiative much as her alcoholic mother had done.

Beatrice eventually separated from her husband. She had hardly done so when she met and became infatuated with a man even less responsible than the man she had left. The new love, Troy, enchanting her with his exceptional good looks, pouted like a boy unless she gave him undivided attention. He returned her attentions by popping in and out of her life as though he were an occasional visitor. Beatrice was certain she could eventually transform Troy. As a member of a therapy group with four men and three other women, she was also attracted to a male group member very similar to Troy.

However, a more mature, more realistic, and hard-working male group member, who was showing increasing responsibility towards his two sons, remained unappealing to Beatrice. She was aware of the more mature man's assets, yet felt attracted only by the "playboys" who needed her but gave little in return. It became clear that unless she could give up her appetite for the seductive young-prince kind of man who stirred her narcissistic rescue fantasies, she would continue her unhappy, repetitive choices.

The patient was strongly drawn towards inappropriate men as long as she remained stuck in a narcissistic condition. As long as she needed the excitement of erotic hide-and-seek games played by the men she found attractive, as long as she needed to indulge in rescue fantasies to obtain a narcissistic "high," as long as she craved feelings of omnipotence and elite status, she would predictably make nearly identical choices in men, however they might differ in age, appearance, and interests.

As it grew clear in therapy what a huge stake Beatrice had in rescuing people—not primarily out of a sense of caring, but for the sake of experiencing a sort of "St. Joan" type of exhilaration—she began to see how really dubious her jubilant rescue daydreams were. She "tuned in" to the fact that the people she attempted to support emotionally were really preoccupied with themselves and not with her. Eventually, she made up her mind to restrain herself from future emotional involvements unless she first found the other person worthwhile.

A social evening provided her with the opportunity to apply her new insight to an actual situation. Two available men had been invited to dinner, along with Beatrice and a number of other guests. Immediately, she felt drawn to a man whom I shall call Guest A—an attractive-looking person who confided that he was miserable over his recent divorce. The other man, Guest B, was average-looking and cheerful. Beatrice noticed herself becoming drawn to Guest A, but pulled herself up short when she heard him opine that if she, Beatrice, had four children from her first marriage, that should be enough to keep her happy. To her own surprise, the patient heard herself reply: "Hell, I'm not over the hill the way you think I am. I love the kids, but I need other kinds of companionship, too." Whereupon she turned her attention to Guest B, not for a rebound flirtation, but in an effort to trade in her old rescue dreams for the reality of simple and direct interest in other people.

Through psychotherapy, patients come to understand that although they believe that they are trying to change, they repeat themselves in ways of which they are not so much unconscious, in the sense of acting on repressed urges, as they are simply unaware. Certain patterns, like the creases in an old shoe, have become part of the sense of self with which the person lives.

It is important to define what psychological progress really is; however, since it resembles a multifaceted structure more than a limited, two-dimensional continuum, this is a complex undertaking. In the present context, we are concerned primarily with development of fuller and more solid psychic structures, with ego and self growth, and with concrete psychological developments that enrich the psyche so that it can engage in more varied and versatile interchanges with the environment. From this standpoint, the cessation of passive, automatic repetitions is a key requirement. It is preceded by the search for and activization of heretofore impaired psychological structures and abilities. Among such structures and abilities we develop, for example, ego boundaries with heightened flexibility. Patients can learn in psychotherapy how to tighten boundaries that are too permeable and, vice-versa, to loosen up boundaries that have, for reasons of early personal destiny, become too rigid. The gradual evolution of heightened psychological functioning facilitates, in turn, the pursuit of other treatment goals. For instance, persons who learn gradually how to relax the previously rigid ego boundaries invariably bring forth previously warded off emotions and begin to illuminate many heretofore disowned corners of their own psyche.

NARCISSISTIC INACCESSIBILITY AND REPETITION

Every form of pathology creates its own constellation of defenses, its own kind of suffering, and its own varieties of repetition. Specifically, narcissism is bound up with a certain approach to the world—with characteristic and habitual ways of perceiving and evaluating people and events. Because narcissism is a core factor in basic human neurosis, the narcissistic perspective enters into the functioning of everyone from time to time. In the narcissistic personality disorders, however, its influence is blatant to the point of coloring virtually all perceptions and judgments.

In narcissistic personalities, perception is regularly afflicted by a tendency to stay away from the world and favor existence in a relatively closed cocoon. Although such individuals are capable of distinguishing between themselves and their object world, their perceptions are one-sided, highly subjective, and not well checked out against facts that are readily visible to others. In short, narcissistic perception is not a product of mutual exchange of views and feelings.

Instead, the traffic of ideas and assessments moves along a one-way street, namely from the narcissistic individual to the world about him. As a result, his observations are apt to be highly subjective. This happens to such a degree that his perceptions and assessments fail to provide him with essential navigational information. In consequence, his journey through the world takes place without the normal safeguards of objective understanding, and repetitious errors result. In the process of consigning one's faculties of perception and evaluation to the more or less exclusive service of subjective needs, many wrong choices of human objects and situations become inevitable.

Narcissistic men and women see only what they wish to see or interpret what they do see in accordance with their desires. A narcissistic woman who had recently recovered from an unfortunate love affair said: "I told Harry (her equally narcissistic lover) that we both had an ecstatic infatuation with someone we didn't know." In such cases the psychic structures have to be developed until, for example, perception and judgment are freed from the pressure of personal needs and become psychologically autonomous. Until this is accomplished, the odds are great that narcissistic personalities will continue to allow themselves to be led astray by their desires. They will find themselves drawn again and again to essentially similar situations and people who offer more or less the same gratifications craved before. Outwardly though, the people and the satisfactions they offer are clad in different garb.

Such personalities are repeatedly disappointed, letting themselves in for promising beginnings which have unhappy endings. Discussing in this context how the structure and functions of the ego and how the self can be altered and enriched, it becomes clear that the therapist treating narcissistic patients faces a choice: The focus can be on the patient's underlying, primitive, omnivorous needs and the defenses against them. This is done with an eye, of course, to modifying both the defenses and the needs. Secondly, therapeutic endeavors can deal directly with the patient's perceptual and judgment functions, with the aim of making them more realistic, objective, and serviceable. Or, thirdly, therapy can combine the need-centered and the function-oriented approaches.

The function-directed approach—designed to directly foster the ability to perceive and judge with a minimum of contamination by needs—is effective, in my experience, when patients are in the middle phase of therapy and have begun to see that certain of their needs are ultimately responsible for their repetition of basic errors. The function-oriented approach is both practicable and challenging. It relies heavily on the operation of comparison. For example, when a patient makes an apparently need-colored assessment of some situation, the therapist can ask him to reassess his position from an opposite, or at least substantially different, vantage point and compare the results with his original perception.

An example of highly subjective and narcissistically tinged perception and object choice is charmingly dramatized in *A Midsummer Night's Dream*. In this play, Shakespeare has Titania act under the influence of a love potion that has inflamed her need to find some creature on whom she can bestow her amorous passions. When a donkey ambles into view, she beholds him as the dearest and most exquisite creature and puts her arms around him passionately. Needing desperately to love, she becomes infatuated with whatever creature happens to cross her path.

While all of us occasionally confer desirability on each other in such happenstance ways, disturbed persons misperceive and misjudge others much more regularly. The nature of unwarranted choices, doomed alliances, inappropriate work situations and the like differ from person to person. What is common to all, however, is the distortion and subjectivity of functions which ought to be reasonably autonomous (Hartmann, 1958). The subsequent reappearance of nearly identical errors is especially conspicuous in the selection of human objects and situations when they are chosen under the influence of narcissistically distorted perceptions. In such cases, the individual does not allow facts to make a dent in his thinking and is impervious to information that is right in front of him.

It is significant that while narcissistic personalities almost invariably misperceive and misjudge people and situations involving people, they can be exceedingly alert and objective about the world of *things*. Narcissistic personalities, who make misjudgment after misjudgment about other people, prove reliably selective in their choices of inanimate objects. They are discriminate when it comes to assessing the value of real estate, the virtues of a piece of art, the sturdiness of the foundations on which buildings rest. When it comes to *person perceptions,* their appraisals are contaminated by the pressure of urgent needs which do not apply, interestingly enough, to their *thing perceptions,* although these personalities value and accumulate possessions.

Another reason for the selective misperceptions of the human environment which explains the difference in accuracy between people perception and thing perception is the existence of a particular form of blindness. Early in their lives, upon the repeated infliction of narcissistic deprivations and wounds, the narcissistically impaired persons cut themselves off from interaction with their environment. This sets the withdrawal cycle going. They close their windows on the world, pull down the shutters, and undertake only sporadic two-way communications with the world outside. Thus they come to live in a fundamental state of focus on the self. Real connections are never firmly established, and what few connections are made are partial, distorted, and routinized to the point of mechanization.

These patients fail in two main ways: First, they remain inaccessible rather than open and do not undergo fully the gradual developmental transition from narcissism to interpersonal mutuality. They fail to open their boundaries. Second, they do not gather and pass along facts. In the terminology of general systems theory, they fail to exchange information—a task as well as a privilege of living systems (Bertalanffy, 1968).

Hence, there is very little progression towards dyadic relationships, and from dyadic relationships to multilateral contacts. The position vis-à-vis the world remains unchanged, and very few adaptive functions are solidly acquired. Transformation or metamorphosis does not take place (Schachtel, 1959) and sameness rather than renewal is the order of the day. Communications are sparse, active exploration of the human world with its life-giving energy is foreclosed, and the potentialities dwelling within the self remain locked in. The absence or scarcity of exchanges with the human environment, the rarity of new contacts, and the dormant nature of innate capacities—all these contribute to maintaining the status quo, to re-experiencing the past in the present, and to misperceiving freshly encountered human figures as revivals of old prototypes (Freud, 1959b).

Instead of becoming more and better acquainted with the world and enamored of it, the organism turns backward and settles for the limited arena of its own self. Such self-restriction—which of course leads to repetition—is reflected in what I call the "semantic impasse." We observe in highly narcissistic patients a tendency to repeat the same exclamations, phrases, key words, ideas and questions (Fried, 1960), thus choking off significant communication.

Narcissistically-based repetition changes when therapists, having explained to little or no avail how patients weave old expectations around new figures, undertake to force the rupture of familiar and constrictive patterns of repetition. One effective way of doing this is for the therapist to puncture the tranquillity of the patient's one-sided picture of their relationship by injecting an unpredicted personal element. This creates surprise and upsets the equilibrium the patient has found comfortable at the expense of growth and balance. When the therapist, at a well-chosen moment, makes it clear that he or she is not wholly predictable but is a living and, therefore, free and spontaneous entity—a distinctive human being with unique and divergent views—extraordinary transformation can occur. The challenge, the unexpected intrusion of a heretofore unknown or unnoticed possibility of behavior, becomes a catalyst. Suddenly the channels of communication open up, transference dies on the vine, and the patient's world undergoes a transformation.

Such transformations, while they can subsequently fade, can be revived through recollection and constructive repetition until they become part of the patient's way of life. The prerequisite for the patient's eventual acceptance of such a change in therapeutic behavior is a true absence of hostility on the therapist's part, combined with a willingness to stick to his or her guns and affirm that the startling change was undertaken on the patient's behalf and not as a whim on the part of the therapist.

Audrey, a professionally but not psychologically capable woman who had been in various forms of therapy for much too long, asserted monotonously that she was still living under the spell of her demanding mother, who had been dead for some fifteen years. She repeated on many occasions that she could not accept a compliment for fear that her mother would object—or that she could not let herself feel happy because, feeling her mother's presence, objections would be raised to her mood. Still intimidated by the now-imaginary mother, the patient felt compelled to treat her husband, her many friends and acquaintances, and of course the therapist as though they were merely new editions of her mother. Despite her years of therapy, during which her sex life and her relations with her husband and children had improved, Audrey still felt trapped in her mother-transference.

When, one day, she once again told me that she had missed the best half of her life because she still acted like an apologetic child towards her overbearing mother, I said: "And what do you plan on doing with the half of your life that is left?" Audrey's neck went red and she burst into tears. She asked angrily why I was so quick to confirm that she had wasted much of her life.

Answering herself, she said: "This is the first time I have heard anything, really. Whatever you have just done—and I know it did not come out of malice—has shaken me up. You penetrated, you injected yourself. I can't keep my ears closed, or for that matter my mind."

In this instance, as in many others, a surprise interaction upset an established pas de deux. With her mother, and afterwards with other people, Audrey had habitually put herself down in return for ritual reassurances which were so impersonal as to mean next to nothing, but constituted a token form of personal relating. The actual origin of this ritualistic pattern, that is, the masochistic self-abnegation she had learned, is not the crucial point here. What does matter is that it was the first break in the kind of routine sequence that characterizes narcissistic existence. When I broke into her routine, when an alien idea was injected into Audrey's habitual outlook, life seeped in and the prospect of real change emerged. I refer to this step as *the rupture of the narcissistic monologue;* its purpose is to clear the way for the initiation of dialogue. This procedure is related to what has been called the paradigmatic technique (Nelson, 1962; Spotnitz, 1962).

Different forms of pathology and of pathological repetition are caused by divergent forms of environmental interference with healthy development and growth. People who become victims of narcissistic disturbances have usually been subjected early in life to emotional inattention, absence of empathy, and unreadiness on the part of their parents to respond to the personal, idiosyncratic ways in which needs are expressed. While the child is satisfied physiologically, the parent's emotional responses are indiscriminate, shallow, and haphazard.

> An example of such inattention was the habit of a narcissistic patient's mother who, when she wanted to summon him, ran haphazardly through the names of her numerous children. Only after having called for Steven, Lena, Nicholas, and perhaps a few others would she finally hit on the patient's name. No wonder that, as a grown man, he rarely knew or remembered the names of colleagues and their wives—and no wonder that, like so many others, he fell victim to narcissism and retreated into a shell to avoid such slights. And finally, how predictable it was that this man failed to learn reciprocity in his relations with others, preferred monologues and daydreams to dialogues, and permitted himself only casual glances at the world of his fellow men and women.

The determination to avoid input by another person at the expense of losing all cross fertilization and remaining restricted to repetitive monologues with the self is illustrated in the following case.

> Saul, a homosexual patient who was seemingly docile in therapy and invariably polite, made it clear from time to time that he would never allow anthing I might say to him to make the slightest impression. "My sole purpose," he remarked, "is to defeat you, as I have always done with my mother, aunt, and sisters. Those bitches intruded in my life until I shut them and everything else out."
> When I observed one day that his primary problems were not sexual—as he had presumed—but his total isolation from

other people, he retorted angrily: "You talk as though I hadn't made any progress, so it is unnecessary for me to continue in treatment." I said, "You're right. You prefer to defeat me. You do not want to change." After a pause, Saul, his knuckles buried in his eyes, replied: "You win. This has just made an impression on me. I can't totally maintain the steel wall around my private circle any longer. Maybe I'll be better off for it."

A central problem in the above cases was to overcome the patients' "unilateralist" position in dealing with the world. They had allowed themselves to become imprisoned, and had lacked the will, perhaps the ability, to enter into true communication and reciprocity with others. They had not entered the arena of human exchange and had remained solitary beings; they propagated their one-sided expectations about others, and were satisfied to preserve their conclusions essentially in a vacuum without validation or correction from others. This *in vacuo* existence was reflected strongly in their life styles and, of course, in their transferences. To make change possible, a form of psychological puncturing had to occur. This is a delicate operation and must be carried out with care because it touches on, or passes near, some very raw nerves.

In a sense we can say that the entire phenomenon of transference is due to intransigence. Patients act as if it were superfluous to check out their ingrained assumptions. To them it is useless to find out how their impressions square with those of other people. It is when information is unexpectedly injected into the patient's field of experience, when the angle from which the world is perceived is abruptly changed, that a new outlook becomes possible. Dents have to be made in these persons. Above all, their habits of shutting out knowledge of the outer world has to be stopped. It helps these persons little to know who in their families were the original culprits whose behavior enforced their solitary existences. Although able to identify the original transference objects and their subsequent substitutes, the patients fail to dismantle the iron walls that keep them apart from others. Understanding the emotions they carry from old relationships into new ones and how they defend themselves against these emotions is "useful" but does not free them from one-sidedness and the ensuing repetitive transference compulsions (Fried, 1965).

What did finally succeed in producing the first harbingers of change was a strong startle, an important surprise. The self-perpetuating cycle of stagnation was broken when genuine disbelief, together with genuine new belief, was introduced. To help such personalities move, grow and change, they have to be startled. Their longstanding assumptions about themselves and their environment must be upset—not only rationally, but above all emotionally. In many cases, nearly every settled assumption, every habitual stimulus, has to be challenged (not all at once, of course, but over time) in order to make room for new growth and opportunities for living.

Certainly, such surprises and challenges are not the monopoly of therapists. It is also one of the missions of the novelist, the playwright, the filmmaker, and the artist, among others, to stir people up and upset the applecarts of hardened assumptions, notions, and life-styles which have gone undisturbed so long that consciousness is dulled.

BOREDOM AS A RESULT OF REPETITION

There are, of course, many ways in which to look at and define neurosis and other emotional disturbances. In the context of this chapter, certain connections between pathology and the self-restriction of ego and self-structure have been discussed. Originally, the ego and self are being restricted in order to avoid collisions with an environment that does not respect, does not promote, and indeed interferes with normal developmental thrusts. Unaware of their self-restrictions, and unfamiliar with measures which could expand their hemmed-in psyches, individuals further compound their handicaps by repeatedly seeking refuge in situations that conceal or compensate for existing deficiencies.

For example, many individuals who were hampered in the formation of a strong self because their environment was inattentive and uninterested later feel compelled to confine themselves to marginal relationships which allow the fragility of the self to remain undetected. They continue to sacrifice their potential for better things because, having rendered themselves partially crippled to begin with, they can navigate only in shallow waters but not in the open seas of the wider world.

The original self-limitations, as well as the consequences of subsequent avoidance of all but supposedly safe situations, typically serve to maintain a state of unawareness. For purposes of this discussion, the notions of *unaware* or *non-conscious* are as important as the concept of *unconscious*. The term non-conscious describes a primitive state that is characterized by the use of symbolism, by an absence of logic, predominance of fluidity and an absence of delineation. One thing, one process, one affect flows into another much like the stripes of an old-fashioned barber pole. In saying that a patient is unaware or non-conscious of a particular state, process, or structural deficiency is not to say that something once conscious has been repressed; rather it was never clearly delineated in the first place. It has not jelled, it lacks form, and, most important, it has not acquired a verbal designation. It is the joining together of process with words or other sensory signals that makes for conscious experience (Freud, 1961). Between the ages of three and four, often within the span of a few weeks, many children make a quantum leap into a more conscious existence. At that stage they begin to talk a great deal, cheerfully joining together real words with verbal inventions of their own. The reason they are overjoyed is that they have made the great discovery not only of language, but of the connection between the use of language and the creation of clarity. No wonder therapists are referred to often as talk doctors by children and the less sophisticated people. One of their missions, after all, is to help make people aware that without realizing it they are placing restrictions on their own selves. Many a time such self-restrictions are not unconscious in the sense that something is being repressed. Rather they resemble a kind of "house arrest." Men and women restrict themselves either because their psychic structures are so limited as to paralyze movements in a larger orbit, or because exchanges with the world are too risky. But regardless of the cause the "house arrest" is experienced as a deficiency. By articulating what is missing and highlighting what can be gained, the therapist sets up road signs to new destinations. If the patients want to use these for orientation they can lift the burden and boredom of repetition. To this end, people are given opportunities for formulating in their own words the nature of their ego and self arrest.

It is a consequence of self-limitation and the ensuing narrowing of his repertory of active and straight responses that the patient is robbed from childhood of experiences such as wonderment, discovery, and psychological experimentation and inventiveness. Much abused as the word "creative" has become, it is evident that self-restriction deprives people of that sense of exhilaration and joy that comes from shattering stereotypes, coining words of one's own, shaping love relations to suit one's own predilections and imagination, and carrying out even simple acts in varied and innovative ways. This is not selfishness. It is homage to the human spirit. To be deprived of it is to be consigned to boredom and eventual depression.

Dynamically speaking, boredom bears a resemblance to death. It is the individual's personal, subjective experience of the paucity of his or her mental and emotional processes. It is the result of a scarcity of stirrings on the part of the impulses and the ego (Fried, 1960). Basic processes are impoverished or enfeebled due to one or more deficiencies, among them those which lead to compulsively executed repetition. The more often an action is reiterated, the more it loses its distinctive outlines and its impact—not only on others, but also on the observing self. Its power is frittered away.

Boredom as a state of mind, especially in personalities with narcissistic or psychopathic inclinations, has been investigated far too little. It is not a neutral or innocuous by-product of repetition, but an important and painful pathological condition. Nor is it, as is often assumed, merely subjectively tiring and unpleasant. Quite to the contrary, boredom is a constituent element of every depression, which it in turn reinforces. It runs parallel to withdrawal processes, which it also aggravates, and is both a cause and a part of the loss of the all important contact function, which itself is a core feature of depression.

> Until his 28th year when he met a younger man who moved in with him, the homosexual patient Sean had never risked or felt capable of building a strong emotional relationship with anybody. His companion soon began to treat him in a humiliating and domineering fashion. Unhappy at his housekeeping duties, the younger man would send Sean out to shop for hard-to-find items such as rare imported spices and give him a tongue-lashing whenever he returned empty-handed. He threatened repeatedly to leave and to take some of

Sean's property with him. Sean, who had until now lived in a narcissistic fog, was exhilarated by this new sado-masochistic relationship and especially by the anal sexual activities involved.

He accepted the pain, the anxiety he felt over his friend's threats to leave him, and the sullen anger that permeated their relationship because these were "real" experiences as opposed to the previous repetitive monotony of keeping himself aloof from everybody and everything. After his lover had finally deserted him, Sean exclaimed many times in his narcissistic and repetitive fashion, but with greater ambivalence than previously: "I think the sharp pain I feel because I opened myself up to him and then he abandoned me is a better feeling. At least it is something new and alive, even if it hurts. It is new and frightening and better, but I don't know how to hold on to it. I don't want to live any more on the Island of Loneliness—the I.O.L., I call it. Am I forever to repeat something that is only grey, or do I want to take another risk? No, better to be alone. No, I *want* to take a risk, or I will fade and die."

To find relief from boredom and the monotony of invariant behavior, some people attempt to alter their external situations. As they change the world outside, their spirits perk up, but unless an inner burgeoning gets under way at the same time, their efforts remain abortive. Bored self-repeaters become habitual world travelers, consumers of ever more varied goods, seekers after ever more exciting entertainment. They move from place to place in quest for the experience of psychic variation, which in actuality is obtainable only through far-reaching self-change. When self-enrichment and self-expansion do not take place, boredom and its concomitant depression may lead to such despair that suicide becomes a preoccupation, and sometimes an actuality.

When we recognize boredom as a serious expression of pathology and set expansion of the ego and the self as a therapeutic goal, the results, though slow in coming, rescue the patient from self-destructiveness. Emotional and psychological variation are not luxuries, but urgent necessities.

4

Connections Between Past and Present

WHAT CAN WE GAIN FROM EXAMINING THE PAST?

The more effective psychotherapy becomes, the more fruitfully and meaningfully do patients explore the past with which they want to part. They learn that they cannot truly put the past behind them by ignoring it; they need to acknowledge, ultimately without fear or shame, what has happened in their lives. On the other hand, they also come to see that neither dry recitations of their personal chronologies nor obsessive stewing over particularly painful events will set them free. Instead, they are helped to review and reassess their past in a spirit of clearing the air and, thus refreshed, to discover present-day opportunities to alter the persisting noxious effects of prior experiences. As we well know, people with severe problems share the burden of having gone through a past that fettered rather than facilitated their development.

THE IDEAL BALANCE BETWEEN PRESENT AND PAST

The past must be acknowledged in a frame of mind that aims at making new connections between past and present. We have to take many things into account; all people who are disturbed need to acquire *new* assumptions, capabilities, functions, and ways of organizing their psyches in order to call a halt to the ill effects of the past. For this to happen, it is invariably necessary to enter into novel corrective and growth-promoting experiences.

Whether the psyche becomes more complete through immediate interpersonal experiences that are called into being in the therapeutic situation or whether this is achieved through the more indirect, cautious, and traditional method of verbal explanations and interpretations is not the main consideration in this context. Either way, it is *how* a patient comes to deal with his past that determines whether or not growth ensues.

The past bears upon the psychotherapeutic process in four basic areas:

1. The fact that a mature male patient was born in March of a certain year is, by itself, of little or no significance. What matters is whether or not March and early spring was a time of year when the mother welcomed childbirth; whether it was a time when the father could be near home rather than away on a business trip; whether the child's birthday fell close to one of his relatives' birthdays, and, if so, how significant the relative was. Patients without therapeutic experience tend to narrate bare facts and their reports often resemble the skeletal letters which youngsters dutifully send home from summer camp. In contrast, the person who has got hold of what matters in psychotherapy gravitates to the *emotions,* the *thoughts,* the *connections* that surround the landmark events and recurrent themes of his or her past life.

2. As they get the gist of what psychotherapy is about—namely, a process of liberation, rebalancing and growth—patients "stretch," trying to apply the therapeutic insights gradually and organically to their methods of living and to the ways in which their interpersonal relations are conducted in the present. They utilize their discoveries so that the "remembrance of things past" serves not only to connect them with their beginnings and to give them a sense of personal history, but also to liberate, enrich and otherwise alter the present and future.

3. In every therapeutic relationship—whether treatment is conducted on a couch, in a corridor, or on a garden bench (the practical limitations of time and space in crowded centers are many)—it is possible to glean the patient's past from the transference relationship with the therapist. In the case of groups, this information becomes apparent from his or her relations with group members. In this sense, the past is indeed the present. What the review of the past does is variously important: The person comes to feel and to relish the fact that, rather than springing into adult life suddenly as did Minerva when she issued from Zeus, he or she has a "genealogy," even if it might not be a royal one.

To view one's personal history without blinders and idealization gives perspective and meaning to the present. The historical vista not only shows us how we entered upon the path of our basic problems, but also emphasizes that it was to a considerable extent a matter of accident and circumstance that we adopted particular ways of dealing with these problems. We did not always choose our solutions; often we simply hit upon them fortuitously. Concomitantly, it becomes ever more obvious that quite *different* solutions and methods are available for the looking and the asking.

4. A continuously successful course of therapy means that the past retains an ever-diminishing grasp on the present, so that the autonomy of the here-and-now increases up to an optimal point. As a rule, a *gradual* growth of autonomy is more beneficial and ego-syntonic than a sudden emancipation, which tends to throw the ego into anxiety, reinforce old defenses, and make for a feeling of alienation. A more measured rate of growth allows for the pleasant experience that what is new becomes at the same time increasingly familiar.

The present also has an influence that extends beyond its own existence, not only towards the future which is being prepared, but towards the past which is now seen in a truer light. The past becomes less idealized, and yet, curiously, more acceptable; indeed, it becomes interesting and *new* because angles and corners that formerly lay in darkness are now bathed in new light. Actually, the very telling of one's personal biography becomes an accomplishment. As the past is gradually brought into the present by re-telling, it comes to conjure up a new vision of old realities, based as it is on new ways of comprehending what happened in one's life (Schafer, 1977a). Such altered modes of comprehension lead to new ways of dealing with the world. In this way, looking back on what was, can, if properly undertaken, carry with it the seeds of metamorphosis.

If therapist and patient together work out a good rhythm and fine integration, then the balance between reviews of the past and overviews of the present combined with new experimentations tends to limit any tendency for the work to become a mere historical review. We have to beware lest the telling of past history have counter-therapeutic effects. Instead of patients being liberated from whatever noxious effects the past has had, they can become fixated on the past and get bogged down in certain false notions. Individuals come to believe that to extend the past is their fate; or they may believe that the completed recollection of the past, and not their actual present, with its manifold potentialities and open-endedness, is the key to overcoming lingering misfortune.

Carrying such beliefs, many persons are unable to grasp the alternatives that are either available now or can become available if they make certain changes in their psychic organization and emotional/cognitive powers. As a result of overemphasizing one's personal history, self-pity can take over, misguided nostalgia capture the imagination, and primitive idealizations and blanket condemnations continue to flourish. Passive recounting and reminiscing without discernment encourage the "genetic fallacy," namely the notion that just knowing how a disturbance came to pass or what were the causes of a pathological line of development will put a stop to the process. Experience has shown that, in general, this over-simplified and overly intellectual view of the curative process is simply not accurate.

OLD GOALS AND NEW GOALS

As we, joining forces with many diverse branches of study that deal with the understanding of man, continue to discover more constellations that influence human growth and development, and as we come upon new ways of defining which events liberate and strengthen the psyche and which cause distortion and pathology, all monolithic explanations break down. There is no one category of events, no one type of cause-and-effect relationship, no single formula that explains everything.

It was believed that neurotic psychological suffering was due to the pressure exercised by unconscious forces, and that the all-encompassing cure consisted of making the unconscious conscious. Today, this elegant and simple tenet cannot be supported in the light of new data and observations. Psychological problems, which vary from person to person, are now seen to have multiple roots and to be the outcome of many processes. In order to restore a battered individual to health, many connections between past and present have to be seen and, above all, undone. This task usually cannot be accomplished through contemplation and understanding alone.

Classical psychoanalysis was concerned with hysteria, obsessive-compulsive disorders, and other symptom neuroses. Although severe character problems were also found in these disorders, attention was focused on the dramatic symptoms that called for treatment. Symptoms included a gradual paralysis of the ability to walk; obsessive and unwanted compulsions that forced cumbersome washing, counting, and other rituals on a seemingly unwilling person; and bizarre fears of normally innocuous events such as a mouse running across a room or a sudden inability to cross a bridge. Eye-catching eccentricities such as these were, in the early days of psychoanalysis, the focus of attention and cure.

The curative process seemed as simple as it was miraculous: study the unconscious in order to uncover repressions and make the unconscious conscious. The hidden wish that is responsible for the debilitating symptoms will, when laid bare and then sublimated, cease to exercise its pathological hold, and the person will go forth from the consulting room unencumbered. For example, the woman who could recognize that, at heart, it was her illegitimate wish to have intercourse with her brother-in-law which inhibited her walking (so as to avoid approaching the forbidden and hence dangerous love destination) could get around again once she was able to apply reason and will to the now thoroughly understood situation.

Even when the relationship between the prime departments of the psyche (the threefold structure embracing id, ego, and superego) was overlaid upon the earlier topographical model of unconscious, preconscious, and conscious, and even when it was clear that repression was not the only basic defense and that the ego in and of itself is an agency that can be set back by many kinds of damage and adversity, the traditional uncovering techniques were still for many therapists the main course that treatment had to follow.

There was considerable change, however, when characterological problems came to be understood in a new way—namely as products of interferences with normal personal development and ego building. The work of Wilhelm Reich, Erik Erikson, and the ego psychologists who studied pre-Oedipal childhood development (such as René Spitz and Margaret Mahler) brought much new understanding to the shortcomings—as distinct from the conflicts—of the personality. Their work helped to show us not only how the problems of character arise, but how they can be treated and prevented. Understanding of the psyche grew by leaps and bounds and expanded therapeutic vision. The fact that social conventions and strictly upheld codes of manners, which had once served to obscure personal flaws, broke down as we moved deeper into the twentieth century served greatly to expose human frailties to the bright light of psychoanalytic inquiry. As long as interest in symptoms predominated, the old, topographically-conceived formula that we cure and get cured by making the unconscious conscious held up very well. Indeed, with important modifications it still encompasses one of the goals of analytic psychotherapy — but only as long as we remember that therapy has to achieve *much more* than just helping the ego tolerate instincts and their many derivatives.

STRENGTHENING AND COMPLETING THE EGO AND SELF

The ego psychologist who is psychoanalytically oriented assumes that a large proportion of present-day problems are the result of interferences by the prime caretakers of the past, especially the mother, with the progressive development of the ego and self. For instance, many damaged people did not get enough opportunities to develop the kind of intimate relationship with their mothers which their bodies and inborn maturational potential demanded from the moment of conception. The course of the developmental seasons was not observed, not encouraged, and not facilitated. Instead, gaps, deficits, and errata became woven into the fabric of personality. The narcissistic bubble was not broken and the child was forced to stay in his or her cocoon; symbiosis was denied when it was sorely needed, or else encouraged well beyond necessary bounds; selfhood, independence, and individuation were steadily opposed and tabooed. Object constancy was not aided.

To cope with these incapacities, the psyche had to use tricks, make-believe, and clumsy, primitive modes of contact and interpersonal relating. In the course of this makeshift way of getting along, storms of anger became a frequent occurrence. Gaps, arrests of function, and malformations occurred which became part and parcel of the defective functioning which today's patient is bringing into his encounter with the present.

The pathological liaison with the past, then, consists primarily of severe cripplings and attachment to obsolete ways of perceiving, thinking, feeling, and acting. The tasks of therapy, whatever they might be in detail, aim at bringing development up to date. To do this, therapy must be reconstructive, corrective, and preoccupied with inventing ways of raising the level of psychic functioning from a primitive level to skillful, flexible performance.

All disturbed people, and not just borderline patients and schizophrenics, labor under specific structural deficiencies which must be repaired through belated growth experiences, for all problem persons, even those who have in some way matured, persist in carrying out mental functions and responses that are derived from states of mind that are primitive, deeply narcissistic, ravaged by fury, and non-integrated (Bion, 1965). These primitive and distorted functions are put right by means of new, reparative growth experiences, which come about as a result of several combined discoveries. First, the person comes to see which more or less continuing deprivations—rather than one-time, catastrophic traumata—led to the standstills from which he or she suffers. From this, the patient comes to the conclusion that repairs must be made. The therapist, in response, chooses or often devises simple, basic experiences that encourage and make possible the forward thrusts that are needed.

In child therapy, it is considered desirable to prepare the way for forward movement through reparatory experiences (Ritvo, 1971). Similar procedures, curiously, are too often considered overprotective, arbitrary or authoritarian in the treatment of adults. This fear is justified in the case of persons who have lived under the protective umbrella of an extended symbiosis, have not learned to cope with frustrations, and rely excessively on a continuation of dependency demands. But in the adult cases where symbiosis was terminated prematurely or where the seeming symbiosis was an overlay for the mother's own dependency on the child, warmth and encouragement are essential among the core reparatory experiences, though by no means do they comprise the full measure of corrective steps.

The therapist who deems interpretations alone to be insufficient and who offers experiential help knows the difference between autocratic intrusion and selected therapeutic interactions that are based on an understanding of dynamics. (Ritvo, 1971; Alport and Bernstein, 1959). The therapist acts to help the patient affirm his or her independence and selfhood, and then often interprets what happened. In so doing, he or she does not intrude, but rather facilitates adult, independent behavior. This, in turn, paves the way for explaining to the patients how they used to act as though they had to smuggle opposition into their behavior in subversive, hostile ways—but pointing out that today they can assert themselves openly, now that former obstructions to independence have ceased to exist in their minds as well as in reality. Having had a taste of independent self-affirmation, patients can now give up their nonsensical angers at an opposition that in most instances no longer exists.

A therapist who offers reparatory experiences is not to be equated with an overindulgent mother—one on whom the patient remains dependent because her presence has made it unnecessary to acquire autonomous structures within the self and ego that work independently even when the mother is not there. As a really good mother makes herself eventually dispensable and permits her offspring to take off freely, so the interactive therapist is aware that the aim of growth is to acquire internalized good feelings about oneself which make dependency an anachronism.

Reparatory experiences are comprehensive and numerous and by no means limited to blind support and praise such as is implied in the idea of "chicken-soup mothering." Corrective experiences come about when, in addition to the analysis of defenses, the therapist facilitates positive steps:

—The shedding of omnipotence and idealization can be accelerated by tactfully and humorously piercing grandiose fantasies.
—By behaving humanly and simply, we can help the person to express, for instance, disappointment or liking in human, simple ways.
—A display of focused attention, such as remembering small details of name and place from the patient's discussions, will be convincing and help do away with a hectic search for admiration and mirroring.
—In addition to dealing with the false self and "as-if" ideas, we can encourage through our own behavior a gradual show of genuine emotion.
—By pointing out their true assets and talents, we liberate patients from their fight against, or submission to, the internalized, old-time parental negative and oppositional atmosphere (Kohut, 1977).

There are, as will be shown, very many other positive experiences on which to build good functioning. The therapist can mediate these in order to lead the way out of the ways of the past into new pastures in the present and future. The dogmas of the past are inadequate to deal with the storms of the present and studying and understanding the old ways which have to be replaced is merely a beginning, not an end-all, of proper preparation for ego and self.

A CASE HISTORY: SANDRA

The patient Sandra came to therapy because she felt on the brink of breaking up her second marriage. She was previously married to a psychopathic man who took money from whomever he could get it, was absent when Sandra gave birth to their son, and had numerous promiscuous affairs. Her present husband was a devoted, serious and philosophical man whose presence was enjoyed by everyone. Sandra emphasized, as do many previously-married mates, that the big problem in the second marriage was the children: her own son and her new husband's youngest daughter, who spent long weekends with the couple. But it turned out after some preliminaries that the problems Sandra had with her 10-year-old stepdaughter reflected deep problems she had with herself, her husband, and the world.

Sandra was infuriated by Oona, her stepdaughter, and by the relationship between stepdaughter and father. In Sandra's eyes, the young girl had many situational advantages and personal assets which she, the stepmother, lacked. It was really a Snow White situation, in which the mirror of self-reflection told the older woman, Sandra, that she was not the fairest of them all. The result for Sandra was sadistic rage against Oona, whom she alternately suspected of sneaky flattery or else considered superior to herself. She wanted to beat Oona, push the child's head against a wall, and forbid her to enter the house.

The patient wavered about the reasons for her jealousy and rage, thinking at times that the child related incestuously to her father, who in turn saw nothing wrong with the stroking, the lapsitting, and the hugging that his daughter gave him. On other occasions, Sandra was convinced that her behavior towards her stepdaughter reflected her own deep disturbances, and that indeed it did not matter whether the intimacies between the father and daughter were excessive.

A review of Sandra's past showed that she always had difficulties with other women, starting with her own mother. The mother, a narcissistic person who invariably turned to her own petty concerns when Sandra needed her attention and help, emphasized the value of money and comfort and squandered a small fortune to look exquisite. By way of protest Sandra gravitated to flaunting a Bohemian life, an endeavor which prompted her among other things to marry her first husband. His exploitative, outrageous actions and sexual flings appealed to Sandra because he dared to flaunt contempt in a manner and to an extent which she desired for herself but did not have the boldness to risk.

The patient, eager to save her second marriage, was only too willing to discover and draw parallels between her hatred for her mother and the sadistic rage towards her stepdaughter. She recalled how frightened she was to realize that she wished to stab her mother with a kitchen knife, an urge she first discovered when she wrote a short story using that theme and locked the story away in her diary. She searched for memories of competition with other women, and recalled her continuous attempts to gain some power which she could exercise over females, thus proving her own superior position. But the parallels, some hastily drawn in the hope of resisting true understanding, did not prove remedial. Only when Sandra began to understand the intertwining between her mother's narcissism and her own callousness and desire for magical control did the first steps of recovery and reconstruction get under way. Sandra began to see how much she identified with her narcissistic mother and also how lonely, stranded, and closed she had remained because of her mother's inability and unwillingness to care for her family. She still found herself searching in vain for a smile of recognition and affection in the impassive maternal face. She feared the imminent disintegration of her marriage because her husband, she thought, had to find his daughter immensely more gratifying than her, his second wife. After all, Oona made him happy. She listened with rapt attention to his words, whereas Sandra barely managed to show interest in what he had to say. Oona was open and approached people with a smile and a question, whereas the patient, always on guard, retreated at slight signs of neglect. Oona was there first, she was the rightful aspirant to the father-husband's interest and protection, while Sandra was an interloper; the daughter, like the father, was an accomplished student, while Sandra was interested in clothes and pleasures but not in ideas.

Therapy dealt successfully with *both the past and present events* in the patient's life and with the ways in which the two periods in her personal history were interwoven. *When the past was examined,* it became ever clearer that Sandra never had the guidance, interest, and help of either a mother or a father and that her considerably older and very tolerant second husband fulfilled the role of both parents. How, then, was she to act in the present like a wife rather than a child? This was the question that emerged.

Being stuck in the present with many childlike feelings and longings that had not been fulfilled in the past, she disliked the childlike part of herself and thus hated the child Oona and envied her for the paternal love she received. Moreover, she resented the child for possessing emotional skill and presence in social situations, which the adult Sandra lacked. Having been deprived as a child of fondling by her mother, who stroked herself rather than her little daughter,

Sandra longed for physical tenderness, yet nevertheless balked at the caresses her stepdaughter bestowed on her. She feared Oona's advances and experienced them as lesbian approaches and pacifications, which indeed they were. Discovering these and many other connections between past and present, Sandra and the therapist recognized with increasing clarity the many layers and complexities of the problems that she faced as a wife and stepmother.

When the present is examined, it becomes possible to devise technical ways and means by which to create alterations within the ego (Kris, 1956). These alterations became the basis for major personality changes in Sandra and great eventual improvements in the marriage and in the stepmother-child relationship. Sandra was helped to discover methods of caretaking that benefitted herself as well so that she no longer needed to seek symbiotic-like satisfaction through her husband. The fact that the couple's sex life was good greatly enhanced her opportunities to shift from care-through-husband to love of self. More and more, childlike desires which had once been unacceptable came to the surface. For instance, the patient's carefully guarded wishes to talk baby talk eventually became an open secret that was occasionally indulged with a smile. She became both sly and charming as she amused herself in this way.

To be specific about the kind of ego alterations that were undertaken to bring Sandra up to date in her development of a mature self, I shall describe how she came to summon capacities such as persistence, patience, and dauntlessness, qualities she had always admired but possessed to a very small degree. The patient had been an addict, as it were, of the quick and magical personality change. When she felt impatient and shaky, not up to the demands made on her, she had practiced from childhood a manner of "upgrading" herself that cannot even be called identification. She would in such circumstances seek out a close association with some competent female, often her cousin who was two years older and a solid personality. To come into possession of personal strength and endurance, she used a method of "coupling up." She would call up the cousin during periods of anxiety and ask to spend part of the day with her. She ordered identical meals when the two women went to a restaurant. She shared the cousin's good moods. Sometimes this "coupling up" could be seen in the transference, when Sandra felt that the therapist happened to act or look a certain way which she on that occasion craved for herself. More often, a supervisor at work was the ideal figure she identified with. This route to "instant growth" was blindly imitative and lacked selectiveness.

From the fourth month of treatment, I regularly inquired what Sandra wanted when she asked (as was her custom) for extra sessions: Did she wish to absorb some strength from the therapist through proximity, or did she have other reasons, such as working on a particular problem? As time went on, her answers became more serious. As a result, when Sandra wanted to absorb some strength and skills that she had seen displayed through increased contact, I recommended that we *not* schedule the additional meetings and instead encouraged her to stick out some anxious day or weekend without resorting to magical unions. She would do better, I explained, to move along on her own strength. The method worked, and gradually Sandra's ego grew and expanded by calling on its own roots for sustenance.

When Sandra, who increasingly understood how fragile and narrow her relationships were—for instance with her own son, and certainly with her stepdaughter Oona—asked me how she could begin to feel more love so that she could show more love to these young people, I encouraged her to try, as a beginning, to be helpful. I explained that there was nothing wrong with making an effort to be of concrete assistance, even if the feelings were not yet present. It was quite possible, I said, to read and discuss a history book with her son and a simple art book with Oona without feigning positive feelings. Often genuine fondness follows on the heels of a shared activity. Indeed, the patient's many attempts to be a participant in the lives of the two children, while expressing in therapy her indignation and anger over the time and patience that were required, led to her becoming gradually and genuinely more involved. There was nothing wrong with deliberate interest, and there was much to recommend it. At any rate, it worked.

MAKING THE PRESENT AND THE FUTURE DIFFERENT FROM THE PAST

It is implicit in the notion of development that the familiar present and the future (dimly perceived by the disturbed, and more clearly envisioned by people of vigor), can never be a mere replica of the past. There must be "leeway for self-initiated change" (Smith, 1978). Adult human destiny is strongly influenced by what once was. It becomes the more satisfying the more it permits the individual to utilize the past as a springboard for behavior that goes well beyond what went before. Healthy personal development equals a harmonious evolution from early influences, rather than an abrupt rejection of them. From an understanding of the past, we gain a widening of vision and goals and attain higher psychological skills. But we benefit only if our minds are focused in two directions at the same time: on the forces and circumstances that molded us when we were little, and on how we can now acquire new capacities and outlooks that bring us closer to the envisioned future. Probably "what is influential in human behavior is more an envisioned future than a remembered past" (Smith, 1978). The human being needs goals, expansions, and new objects. While we want to be able to conjure up remembrances of things past, it is equally essential that we generate new anticipations (Ricoeur, 1966).

Whenever a person hangs on closely and literally to old psychological habits, difficulties abound. Freud's famous statement that the present is the past (meaning that the traces of early life remain vividly alive in the particular problems and transferences that carry into the present) serves as a reverse measure of psychological well-being. Mental and emotional prosperity and productivity are directly proportionate to the extent to which up-to-date behavior embodies fresh development, modifications, and variations as compared to the earlier stages of life. The ultimate purpose of all investigations into the past is *not* to understand how something came to be. We are not going after genetic facts *per se*, interesting though they are. Rather, we aim always to eliminate the faithful reproduction and re-use of former processes, because they will not do in the setting of adult life. While we remain receptive to the enthusiasm and freshness of the child-like mind and spirit, we become acquainted with our childish behaviors mainly for purposes of replacing them with adult ways.

When journeys are undertaken by therapist and patient into the past, the questions asked are often prefaced by seemingly innocuous but actually misleading "whys." The therapist may query: "Why do you treat your teacher today the way you behaved towards your father? . . . Why did you always fear that you were inferior?" And so on. These "whys" are used so often because they have become a handy overall umbrella and because they save us the mental effort needed to formulate *other* queries—those designed to establish connections apart from the simple causality with which the "whys" are concerned. Instead the "why" needs to establish a whole variety of psychological laws and meanings: "Are you aware that two sides of your behavior are contradictory? . . . Look at the implications your mother's feelings towards you had, and still have! . . .Do you agree that I should help you make up for a lag in development?"

Basic reasons for looking backward with clarity and courage are: inviting the help of those illuminating lights which we call free associations, getting ready for sudden recollections, and dwelling more leisurely than usual on small incidents to elucidate the *real* connections. The man who is today drawn painfully to genuinely independent women known to be courted by others and who has the awareness that something about them reminds him of his mother, gains nothing by stopping at mere recognition of the similarity. On the contrary, it can make his fixation even more intense. But if he should behold a certain important connection, then he is many jumps ahead of himself and can start anew. For instance, what if he either recalls, or sees, that his mother was the chief intermediator between himself and an emotionally cold and disinterested father? Is he still stuck at a point where he assumes unquestioningly that only a strong woman can mediate a pseudo-intimacy and third-rate peership with a man, without whom he would be left as a mere boy? If such a connection is made, then a key link has been discovered which must then gradually be severed. Only if the man who seeks the woman's help turns to other approaches, preferably to his own potential strength, will a true beginning be made. What matters in terms of change is not the similarity between the mother of the boy and the independent women whom the grown man desires. What matters is that, in making his way towards a retarded manhood, he has made his love life subservient to his growth. The connection involved. And the resulting mix-up, have to be changed. Only then will the present differ from the past as it should.

When health, strength, spontaneity, and creativity are encouraged by a facilitating environment and reign during the earlier years of personal development, the relationship between a person's childhood existence and his adult way of life is characterized by change within a certain order and by continuities at different psychological levels rather than abrupt change.

In unhealthy and confining conditions, on the other hand, the dissimilarities of functioning, though seemingly drastic, are of a surface nature. There is an abundance of artifacts and of sudden ruptures, rather than of significant transitions. Relationships and situations that once were very positive can become negative in the extreme—as when a son or daughter, formerly tied to a parent, proclaims loudly that the company of the parent has been foresworn for good. An individual who once clung physically to aggressors may begin to use verbal flattery to assuage those of whose friendship he or she is uncertain. When development is unfavorable, relations between the individual and those who are close to him become more involuted, or else they are severed abruptly and violently. Either way, in essence the underlying difficulty is still the same: a simple, durable trust in others has never come about.

In contrast to the troubled individual, the healthier person neither lives by hand-me-down precepts nor does he or she defensively go into reverse gear. The sound man and woman, while connected with the past, functions differently as development proceeds. It becomes possible to challenge others; hollow threats are distinguished from real and clearly defined dangers; admirable figures are liked and observed, and one or another of their assets or skills is adopted or adapted on a selective basis, without the clumsiness of global, all-consuming imitations and identifications. All progressions, though gradual, produce some things truly new and do not involve total reversals or sudden ruptures.

We are used to regarding psychological problems as the legacy of past conflicts and arrests of healthy development which have left ego and self incomplete. Another legacy with which the psycho-analytically-oriented therapist upon occasion deals is the individual's body of false expectations, blind preoccupations, and unfounded assumptions. These are carried about by the psychological straggler who had not completed his development in a comprehensive way. We all approach life, and especially its more critical situations, with our very own cognitive equipment that is the result of psychosexual history, ego and self development, environmental influences, as well as the many accidental happenings to which we have been exposed. The early phases of life, adolescence with its exposure to various peer groups and teachers who function outside the family, clear or hazy perceptions of science, philosophy, art and religion—all these converge and come together in the set of expectations and beliefs which play a central role in our lives.

For instance, during the first two or three years of infantile dependence, not only are biological needs closely tied in with nurture and symbiosis, not only are relationships guided by the turning towards other and stronger persons who are instinctively expected to be the caretakers, but in addition there is a set of notions about life that come from outside the arena of psychophysiological needs, even though they find their place in the matrix of the developmentally primary mode of existence. During the period of nurture, dependence and symbiosis, the expectations and beliefs in other areas of experience structurally resemble needs for nurture and its satisfaction. To illustrate concretely, from the period of nurture and symbiosis there stems the individual's expectation that his or her survival and well being are best served through pleas for help from others. The other person's ministrations are the instruments through which self preservation is expected to be guaranteed. In any case of true or imagined danger, cries are uttered and the notion rules that the harder one screams the quicker the relief; that gadgets, machines, and systems will work if the right switches are pulled or buttons pressed by someone; and that technical intricacies cannot or need not be understood. From there to resignation about the complex ways to which bureaucracy subjects us is only a small conceptual step. Because time has not yet become a matter of experience and contemplation and has not been subjected to organization by the self it does not exist. Many such expectations, focal experiences, and beliefs are closely related to and fitted in with ego and sexual development (Schafer, 1977a). They are primitive, intimately connected with body feelings, highly idiosyncratic, contradictory of each other, and out of step with what we call rational and commonly shared ideas. The expectations and beliefs I am referring to, although co-existing with many validated and updated outlooks on life, are part and parcel of mental disturbance. They are partly derived from the philosophy of the nursery; some are found in simpletons or in *Alice in Wonderland* figures; sometimes they resemble in certain ways the superstitions and rituals of primitive tribes and are at times called cockeyed or outlandish. Their believers defend them ardently and often tenaciously, and they defy therapeutic interpretations aimed at showing how these focal concerns cause short circuits, lead into blind alleys, or encourage barking up wrong trees.

The convictions and concerns have gradually built up over a lifetime without any clear awareness on the part of the believers—as though they represented a kind of doctrine never spelled out, discussed, or challenged—yet they are not strictly speaking part of the domain of unconscious ideas, because they were never conscious in the sense of being in awareness in an explicit form.

Many essential pursuits throughout life have been undertaken on the basis of the concerns and beliefs which the therapist now exposes as dubiously founded, and which he now calls into question. The revisions in world- and self-views, and the changes in their future conduct implied by the therapist's challenges are so fundamental that patients initially prefer to stand pat. They balk at the enormous reorientation they sense to be ahead, should old concepts be exchanged for new ones.

To illustrate, I shall set forth some central expectations, basic assumptions, and ideas about life that surfaced in a group therapy session composed of seven patients. The participants, though behaving and proceeding on the basis of these beliefs, were not explicitly aware that they had extracted them from their life experiences over the years. It was one of my prime goals to help them realize by what mottoes they lived and to examine and question these tenets and slogans. In encouraging them to do this, I found myself saying repeatedly: "Now take this further"—thus helping and indeed directing patients not to take for granted certain dogmas about life that they held.

> *Laurence:* I am primarily concerned with my and other people's relations to authority. My basic question is invariably whether authority will dominate me, or vice versa. [His preoc-

cupation was determined by the coercion which his father practiced from the beginning, and which his mother also applied as soon as her son showed signs of individuation.]

Kay: Will I be ridiculed? Ridicule is the greatest threat. I can avoid it by acting inconspicuous. [Related to her mother's use of derision as her preferred mode of competition during the Oedipal period, and then again from puberty on.]

Beverly: I shall be ignored. I must make all plans by myself. [Related to her father's sudden death, and to her mother's quasi-Lesbian involvement with her best friends, with whom Beverly was often discussed.]

Jonathan: I must make an impression on the people here. It has to be something spectacular. [Jonathan, a painter of very short build, was narcissistically injured by both parents and tried to remedy this through certain forms of moderated exhibitionism.]

Lisa: I am not in the same league as the others. I am above or below them. [She is the daughter of an inept father, and she overrated and hated her brother and mother.]

Morris: I want total silence and no contact with others. [Longstanding defense against an intrusive mother who, among other things, examined his stools until he was seven years old.]

Ada: This will flatter L. I hate everyone here. I must imitate L and K—no, better P. Nothing here applies to me; I'll buy that "how-to-live" book tonight. [Schizophrenic patient who wavers between contradictory beliefs assimilated from constantly shifting parents.]

While it is valid and useful to deal with connections between focal concerns, expectations, and beliefs on the one hand and marks left by early conflicts and developmental gaps on the other, the *first* therapeutic objective is to demonstrate to the patient the *existence* and *content* of these lifelong orientations. Their guiding ideas, accumulated through the conflux of all life experiences—conscious, unconscious, and shapeless—are the result of abstraction and distillations made over the years. Helping patients recognize the occasions when their mottoes (implicitly and, rarely, explicitly) guide their feelings and behavior furthers their liberation from the past. The mottoes infiltrate the mind by way of cognition and are discovered through cognitive pathways, but they exercise great emotional influence and shape behavior as if, in Adam Smith's phrase, by an "unseen hand."

The questions we ask when we uncover the patient's early experiences are not primarily concerned with the "whys" of the past. This point is among the important contributions of the Gestalt school of psychotherapy (Perls, 1973), which has stressed techniques of recognizing and correcting present-day deficiencies of ego and self. When we automatically slip into "why" questions, the intention is frequently not to find out how an event occurred. Often we attempt to discover whether the patient's reactions to it provided temporary safety, whether the reactions left scars, etc. How, for example, did abrupt terminations of love relationships come to be adopted with regularity? What form of self-help did these many abrupt breakups serve? If a patient discovers that his or her fear of abandonment was so great that ties were severed prematurely so as to preempt the possibility of their being severed by the partner, then by knowing the function of the unnecessary breakups we have a better chance to be of help. We then know and can point out how important it is to put an end to years of abandonment—real, imagined, provoked, or arbitrarily anticipated—so that the superficially perverse practice of discarding viable relationships can be dispensed with. In such cases it is not the "why?" in the sense of prior cause, but the teleological "why," that is, "what for?" or "to what end?," that is the real aim of our questions concerning the past, the present, and the nexus of connections between them.

At other times, a "why?" question referring to the past is designed, not to establish any simple causality or purpose, but to encourage a patient to search for various experiences that have contributed to a chronic state of confusion. Thus, I might ask Linus, the gifted and capable son of an overpowering father who usually treated Linus with disdain but sometimes expressed admiration and envy for him, *why* he has such a poor sense of self-worth. But what I mean, and ought to convey through the tone and wording of my question is, tell me all you can conjure up about the ways in which your father's behavior confused you; let us find out what, in retrospect, makes you convinced that you are doomed to go under as your father predicted.

Questions, particularly ones that are phrased in such a way as to allow leeway in answering and do not steer the patient into a cul-de-sac or tempt him to explain a present-day occurrence in terms of some past difficulty, are among our most valuable tools. They are especially well-suited to unsettle firmly entrenched assumptions, expectations, and motivations that have made a tyranny of life and pitifully limited its scope. What were some of the absurdities to which the patient consented as though they had the force of law? How do different psychological facts, perceived by the patient as belonging together, fit in with each other? For instance, what do you expect your cries to accomplish? Do you just want to express dead feelings or do you want to alarm somebody? Whom do you want to come to your aid?

Although "why" questions have to be chosen judiciously lest the patient be lured into a search for simple connections between one effect and one cause, the opposite form of the question, namely the "why not?" variety, often proves very stimulating and helpful. The query "why not?," because of its provocative form but also on account of the mental orientation behind it, conjures up ideas about the abundance of possibilities that lie open to action. After all, it is one of the primary goals of therapy to help the patient envision *a world with possibilities*. Then, we can turn to developing the functions that truly enable the psyche to have access to more than one alternative; finally, we can impress upon the person the fact that he or she has the capacity as well as the opportunity to *choose*. As long as patients suffer either from conflictual problems where heavy defensive bulwarks are erected against a desire or from developmental arrests, they cannot make choices because they are too lame to go after them and because they cannot envision a world with opportunities.

A two-pronged approach is available and indicated. First, the patient is mobilized to work in therapy because the idea of a world that is open to many approaches comes across and serves as an incentive. Second, the steps in development are accompanied by the illumination of a range of available choices. Questions of the "why not?" sort open up avenues of new experience by expressing wonderment at past choices made by patients. Such questions make it clear that long-held beliefs and habits are by no means as obviously preferable or inevitable as patients have thought, and that the modes of functioning they have settled for do not measure up. Questions, among the royal instruments of psychotherapy, are reserved neither for unconscious motivation nor for identifying the time or circumstances of origin of certain behaviors. They can reveal, additionally and usually more to the point, that a preference for or rigid attachment to a certain behavior, past as well as present, does not make the undeniable sense that the patient attributes to it.

The origins of problems usually lie in early childhood, but the reasons why these problems remain acute *today* do not lie in the past. They come from processes that are active in the personality here and now. As it has been put, "the child is a collection of reactions to [painful] impingements" (Winnicott, 1965). To bear the pain and to protect against future impingements, defensive postures were developed in the past that appear as artifacts and obstacles in the up-to-date world of the adult. But the patient is unaware of this, not only because his or her defensive character-postures and beliefs have become unconscious, but because many never were conscious in the first place. Having become habitual, they are regarded as natural, matter-of-course appendages of his or her mental life. Psychotherapy takes on the assignment of making clear just how nonsensical these positions are in the light of adult reality. The difficulties which the past imposes on the present are in the eye of the beholder, for he or she cannot distinguish, unless helped, which of the restrictions or laws he imagines to apply in the present are the mere pangs of a chronic hangover. To behold the world in true as opposed to simulated light, one has to discern that there exist many vantage points and that only by looking around from some that are newly-found can one get a view wide enough to encompass the things that really matter. We need to understand both what is and envision what can be if the past is not to choke off the progress of life.

THE INNOVATIVE USE OF RECOLLECTIONS

The practice of living on a diet of warmed-over remnants of the past stems from old cut-offs and, as pointed out, the early paralysis and limitation of the self. Random and unprocessed recollections can, instead of leading to innovation, take the person into dead-end streets and keep him stuck there for good.

Yet, there is another angle—and it is a very important one—from which the individual can approach recollections fruitfully. There exists innovative approaches to one's past that promote growth, rather than keeping impressions and actions of the formative years relegated to hermetically closed intrapsychic departments. We do not need to inspect recollections passively, without passion or purpose, nor to imprison them again, thus risking that they, as if pent up in a cauldron, might seethe and explode. We can make recollections our helpful friends who steer us toward *new directions which have a kinship with the past.* We can walk arm in arm with these helpful recollections, allowing them to tell us what powers are slumbering inside and can be developed along lines of vitality and health. Our recollections can indicate to us, if only we listen to them, what stuff and origins we are made of, so that we might process the givens for a better life. As we shall see, we also have to listen to our memories in order to discover and own up to certain inevitable limitations on growth and potentiality.

Recaptured memories, then, are not in and by themselves necessarily liberating but they are highly useful in another sense: they clear access to existing psychic energies that were dormant; *they help to shape those building blocks for new psychic structures which are indigenous to the individual;* they give the person the courage to acknowledge limitations that are insuperable. To design and craft the building blocks for new psychic structures is one of the chief aims of dynamic psychotherapy. Awareness of the injuries and structural defects, as well as of achievements which the past produced, indicates the directions which, as the most indigenous, should be pursued. And early memories, if carefully handled, instill the realistic and courageous acceptance of limitations which are also indigenous. *No person can be everything, or achieve everything.* Through individual recollections the psyche which, as result of dynamic psychotherapy or of other formative life experiences, is once more in an incipient state, finds out how and in what directions to stretch and to progress. In order to become or to remain healthy and authentic we must respect the residues of our past. We cannot disclaim them without threatening and uprooting the authenticity of the self. But the aim is not repetition of the past; the aim is, on the contrary, innovation, imaginative expansion, variation, and, since sublimation can take several forms, the selection of the types of sublimation most appropriate for the specific situation. A case will illustrate the points made.

Minerva, a woman of 32, went into treatment because she realized that she had repeatedly destroyed relationships with men and had thus herself thwarted her desire to share her life with a mate and have children with him. During the first year of treatment she became increasingly aware of the pervasive character of her feelings of dissatisfaction and restlessness but she was unable to unearth her true proclivities, for she had buried them and thereby her true self and real identity under a thick layer, namely, her desire to live up to external expectations. Born and raised in a small town, Minerva hid her timidity by subordinating herself to the clichés and value judgments of her environment. There was above all her wish to continue depending on and thus to please her father whom she loved affectionately and sensually.

A beautiful woman, the patient worked for a metropolitan fashion house where she had moved with fair although not dramatic speed to a rather high level of corporate responsibility and success. The father, hinting in a very indirect manner at the accomplishments he expected from Minerva, his first child, wished her to be very slender, regardless of the fact that her rather strong bone structure and broad build did not allow the kind of appearance he fancied for her. He wanted his daughter to be not only well-mannered, which indeed she was, but to exhibit the gloss associated with high fashion magazines. He persisted to allude to these expectations although the patient still revealed remnants of an outspoken, counter-conventional personality. The father also made clear, through frequent oblique inquiries about her corporate status, that he expected her to identify herself completely with a milieu that clashed with the one to which she had exposed herself in her early twenties.

At that time she had, in a period of emancipation, obtained a three-year fellowship to study old dances and other art forms in Asia. But when after two years her father called her back in order to start a "real career" she obeyed.

Eventually, she suffered perturbing moments of depersonalization, and felt increasingly "awkward" in many human, social and occupational situations. All this was, as became clear, caused by the way she had incorporated her father's wishes. Now she gradually grew out of the harness into which she had forced herself.

When, after a summer vacation, I saw her again, she reported that she had reached the conviction that she had to liberate herself from actually self-imposed fetters and, as she put it, to run and roam through open psychological territory. She decided to give up her corporate position with its good pay and to acquire the strength to adopt a different life-style and pursue different interests, closer to her past. This, in turn, enabled her to add still another building block for her future, namely, to choose between two men, both of whom she had previously antagonized by playing one against the other. "I have decided to make myself a new dwelling out of the building blocks of the past," she said. "I must have physical and psychological space. I have to regain the opportunities to dance, psychologically speaking, as was my habit when I grew up. I must have a husband who allows me a free inner reign. Rodrick is older and better able to grant this to me without suffering in turn, than is Halbut who needs to cling because he feels helpless. He'll always do some clinging and I'll always be impatient with it. The life I led in Asia really suited my nature and whatever work I'll gradually get ready for, I must find in it some echo of that wonderful time. Probably it goes back further; I don't remember how far back. But I know I need to work with gentler people, though this will bring new challenges. The past gives me my stepping stones. It is not a prison that holds me back but offers a harvest that must be reaped. I've become reconnected with my experiences in Asia, and this gave me the strength to make the decision, although I know that my father will always have some grip on me."

Nearly everyone has more options and more room for development than is usually perceived; but the directions in which a person can move are not unlimited. Natural endowment, health, and talent, as well as the deposits of the past, determine in some measure the scope and nature of expectable growth. Thus, we can say that remembrances expand the individual's vista, even while it must be acknowledged that the past also determines specific limitations of growth.

On the whole, psychotherapy has often assessed given factors too pessimistically, and considered them *a priori* as unalterable factors that limit growth and necessitate various forms of standstill which the disturbed person must accept. Even the chances for so-called borderline cases to gain considerable self-liberation and expansion have been underrated. In general, the mental health profession has, starting already with diagnosis, erred more frequently on the side of pessimism than on the side of optimism. At the same time, unlimited optimism is also unwarranted. What is required is greater specificity as far as the two poles of optimism and pessimism are concerned: 1) It is possible in very many cases to outdistance the limitations imposed by the past. 2) Yet, the past also puts limits on the directions in which individual growth can proceed. It is not likely, for example, that the heavily traumatized person will totally change and become an unworried creature. *"Semper aliquid haeret"*—something always sticks.

What is true is that an individual who was deeply and frequently traumatized as a young organism can later on still acquire helpful psychological know-how. He can acquire the ability to "speak to himself" in a crisis and "remind himself" that he has become a much broader person. He has developed through dynamic psychotherapy or positive life experiences a number of important new psychological processes. Hence, when threatened by panic, he need no longer react with counterphobic posturing, because he has convinced himself and others that he need no longer be overwhelmed by fears. A form of bluffing which he previously would quickly seize can be dropped.

Such an individual can, on the basis of the insight he has gained into the old habit, make use of some psychological innovation which is now at his disposal. Also, when facing odds that to him appear overwhelming, he will be able to call for assistance, regardless of whether those odds may be deemed by others to be trifling or realistically huge. Instead of withdrawing and pulling inward, or pretending that he is unafraid, he has become able to reach for rescue through contact making. Yet, although he will now be less prone to panic, he will remain easily alarmed—an emotional and cognitive inheritance from his past. The fears gradually lessen but might never completely disappear, representing a limitation caused by the traumata of early years. Modification, and not total renovation, is often the only realistic, but still highly worthwhile, goal.

5

The Future: The
Forces of Progression
and Construction

Striving to be open to revisions in theory and to innovations in treatment techniques, dynamic psychotherapy can be thought of as a pioneer and not some illegitimate offshoot of psychoanalysis. A considerable enrichment, for example, is being achieved by some practitioners who are undertaking to integrate the theory of living systems with psychoanalytic findings. Important advances have been made through the study of human communications (Bateson, 1978; Watzlawick et al., 1967). Gestalt therapy, with its emphasis on the here-and-now, has made an important contribution, as have other systems. Thus, psychotherapy is enriching the field of treatment as a direct result of its eclecticism.

The various techniques that are being subjected to experimentation, discussion, and prudent selection allow for flexibility, so urgently needed because psychological life is not regulated by one but by a variety of principles. Human beings not only have psychobiological hungers such as sexuality, but also feel social hunger, for people (Guntrip, 1956). The chief goal of human beings is not a state of equilibrium or homeostasis; they need active movement and change, seemingly in the direction of ever new balances between self

116

and environment. My own belief is that human organisms need those kinds of inner changes and interchanges that will make the organism increasingly independent of the environment while simultaneously stimulating a lively interest in the happenings that take place in the world around us. We become less dependent on parents and other nurturing figures as we grow up, even while we have an increasing stake in what happens in the world around us. Narcissistic inaccessibility wanes, ego trips, as the public calls them, become rarer as the organism matures, but mutuality and love for the world continue to grow.

Not only does the human psyche pursue a variety of principles, but it also has various branches and organs in the form of different capacities which follow somewhat divergent laws of growth. Among these are the passions, the emotions, human perceptions, the processes of thought, different forms of self-control, and the contact skills. In view of all this complexity, it is more appropriate to talk of specific psychological cures rather than of one overall strategy that can accomplish all the healing that needs to be done. To understand how these various organs function and how the psyche as a whole maintains its life, elasticity, and effectiveness, we rely heavily on the body of knowledge established by psychoanalysis which has altered mankind's understanding of human nature. In order to heal specific functions as well as the entire psychological system, psychotherapy borrows some technical knowledge from psychoanalysis and adds other valuable techniques, some to be synthesized, some more fundamental than others, but all allowing for a high degree of flexibility (Rangell, 1954).

One technique that I find very useful when fitted into a broad understanding of developmental psychology is that of specific ego building. To survive, the grown-up adult has to be so infinitely more highly structured, integrated, and complex than he is at birth—a structuring which is so dependent on understanding of and facilitation by the environment that in many cases of disturbance one of the prime tasks is to complete several ego capacities which have remained backward· and stunted. Of course, such strengthening and completion of distinctive functioning have to take place within a broader framework of personal growth. But the overall treatment goals are related: to enable the whole person and the afflicted function to serve the principle of independence; to enhance chances for participation in the social, material and artistic world; and to experience changes, transformations, and movement as the essence of rather than an obstacle to the life force. Change is man's heritage and destiny (Levenson, 1978).

Ego-building is necessary even in cases where the ego is sufficiently intact to qualify the patient as a neurotic person rather than a borderline case. Patients who function perfectly well, often splendidly, in several areas (such as work), who have no doubt about clear distinctions between self and object representations, and who are not given to wild excesses of rage, frequently have ego arrestations and deficits. They may also lack integration and authenticity in their self-feeling to the extent that extensive correction and building of the ego and self are needed. The self-representation is often marred by excessive, yet fleeting, identifications with others. It thins out and becomes vague when the patient is alone and lacks geographic-physical-direct human reference points to affirm who he is and to render the self a conviction of reality.

Such patients may be perfectly able to develop explicit transferences to the therapist, projecting on him or her feelings that belong to objects in the past without getting confused about the lines of separation. Yet they exhibit relationships to other human objects that are so bad that interpretations alone are not sufficient to extricate them from their crises with people. They may have extraordinary symbiotic needs which drive away close friends, mates, and children. Or they have so great a need to catch up with unfinished individuation that they take extreme stands of independence on the most insignificant occasions, thus making it impossible for other persons to live with them permanently.

These cases make up the bulk of many a practice in psychotherapy. Mere support keeps crucial feelings under the cloak of repression and is not enough. Nor does interpretation suffice. These patients need skillful egos and self-building like that outlined throughout this book. Such ego-building and self-consolidation are not undertaken in lieu of uncovering, but rather along with and in addition to it.

Most importantly, these processes rely heavily on reparatory experiences in the relationship with the therapist. The patients (who are not borderline cases) need the treatment situation in order to make up for gaps in development. In these efforts to sprout fresh growth which, in turn, influences the growth of the psyche as a whole, the relationship to the therapist plays a central role. A therapist, by most recent definitions, is both recipient and reciprocal. Dynamic psychotherapy has parted with the role of the therapist as a silent observer, a neutral bystander, a person primarily engaged in scientific objectivity. Nor is the therapist a person who dispenses mother love in unspecified quantities, as critics of the reparatory experience often charge. Rather he or she is a participant in the growth process (Sullivan, 1952) who allows the patient to open up, to soak up contact experiences, and to gain new information so as to learn belatedly how to invoke and use growth experiences.

DISSOLVING OUTDATED BEHAVIOR

The basic psychoanalytic notion that archaic, primitive structures on which even a relatively intact ego and self rely must be razed is modified in a significant way. The razing of the old structures must be combined with the production of new building blocks and the construction of a new psychological "home" for ego and self. However, the dismantling of the old structures does not require full-scale regression. Even though it is essential to get away from intellectualization, for relaxation and capture of emotions are far more likely to bring results than compulsive and logical thought, yet ego- and self-building require learning and practice. As such, they overlap with learning theory.

The proposition that "regression must precede the new and better resolution of conflict" (Zetzel, 1970) has been abandoned, at least in large measure, because of convincing positive experiences in the treatment of developmental arrest. Once new capacities of ego and new qualities of self are envisaged, captured, and tried out, the old, indeed archaic, predecessors fall by the wayside.

Gordon was a 50-year-old patient who originally wished to be treated because of nearly persistent anxiety with which he tried to deal not only by staying within his small apartment but also by remaining in bed till mid-afternoon. He had overcome this condition, but continued treatment in order to muster the strength to find work in the entertainment field, in which he had abandoned a job which he had loved. He had the dim and always quickly denied hope that he might yet become an effective person, even though he had always looked upon himself as a failure. He traced his conviction of being a nothing back to the relationship with his mother who never allowed him to give her anything, even a book or a bouquet of flowers. "I feel that what I do never matters," the patient would repeatedly say. "Once when I told an actress to have her teeth capped and I later saw a photograph of her and noticed she had acted on the suggestion, I jumped to the conclusion that someone else had given her the same idea. She denied this when I had a talk with her. I have convinced disturbed playwrights to go into therapy, but I never believed it was for me."

Fully aware of this patient's masochism, which went back practically to the first year of life, but wishing to give no more interpretations to Gordon, who had been in therapy and read nearly every book on the subject of psychotherapy, I asked: "Since it is not you who has an effect, who exactly is it?" The remark, which cut short further evasions and denials of power (in part because the patient shunned display of his substantial aggression), was repeated at intervals and helped, together with other interventions, to lead to articulate ego- and self-awareness.

Alterations within the ego are accomplished through ego-building techniques which have in common the concern with what it is that the patient desires to accomplish, either despite or through various defensive deviations that are pursued. This goal of achieving ego alterations will often parallel though not supersede attempts at uncovering the repressed (Kris, 1956). We no longer wish to overemphasize the genetic inquiry into heritage, the inflictions of early trauma and parental teachings. For the reasons discussed, we place equal emphasis on the developmental capacities—and even greater emphasis from the middle of treatment on. The prime concerns are to draw patients' attention to the possibilities for catching up with missed development and to convince them that innovations in the realm of emotional-cognitive life are within their reach. Future development is as important as past genesis; attempts are made to help individuals run into the thick of the fray (Abrams, 1978; Piaget, 1963).

To illustrate techniques of building ego competence and with it heightened moods and optimism, I shall present a vignette from a well-run ward which treated a primarily borderline population of abusers of drugs and alcohol. The staff members were well trained in following diagnoses and knew how to combine acceptance and firmness, ego-building techniques and, on proper occasions, techniques of uncovering.

The patients, who were on the young side, suffered from anxiety attacks, depressions, and all-encompassing convictions of worthlessness often covered up by bravado. They had reached for drugs and alcohol for support. A general listlessness prevailed much of the time, as is customary on many psychiatric wards. Most patients were convinced that they had no chance for a fresh start and some had made several suicide attempts. All had suffered serious psychological arrests in their early development. Still depending on their parents as if they were children, most of the patients alternated between defiance as a show of independence and attempts at reconciliation which were, as a rule, cruelly rejected. Most bemoaned the rupture of relations with "the old man" or "the old lady" (referring to marriage partners or common-law mates) and were only too willing to assume a sad and resigned responsibility for the break-up.

Towards this alternately depressed or raging crew of patients the staff assumed an outlook that emphasized a moderate optimism. Group treatment was stressed and combined with individual sessions. The group treatment allowed patients to air problems, gripes, and planned aggressive acts towards other patients. Opportunities for friendships and for the making of a peer community were stressed (Riess, 1976).

In this context, an extremely important factor in dissolving outdated behavior is *the creation of a new family, often one that gradually becomes quite extended.* The clinging, anxious waiting for forgiveness from disappointed and rejected members of the original family, the abject self-remorse and defiance vis-à-vis the original family, the desperate sense of isolation, all gradually abate as the new circle is built. Parents, grandparents, and siblings are found through "adoption" amongst individuals met when the patient has begun the road towards recovery (Howard, 1978).

As to ego-building, each patient and his or her peers were helped to become aware of *specific* steps that could be practiced to make for greater ego competence and, thus, a rise of self-esteem. The emphasis was on the need *to talk and to do something constructive* by making life better in the present for oneself and other persons. The patients were encouraged to make *tangible* products to improve and embellish the quality of life, to express their feelings in a drawing, a poem, or through a craft.

Fred, a 42-year-old black patient who had been depressed, very withdrawn, and unkempt when he was admitted, can be cited as an example of how progressive forces gain the upper hand over regressive ones if the therapist and the milieu cultivate the developmental direction with the awareness that it determines life at least equally as much as the genetic pull of the past. Fred often spoke in group meetings of the poverty, sleaziness, and periodic outbreaks of violence in his parental home and justified his dirty, neglected appearance with claims that he did not know any better. Joined by a small subgroup of other patients, the therapist asked Fred whether he wanted to do something about his looks. When Fred began to complain once more about how hopeless the situation was, someone who interrupted was encouraged by the therapist to go on. At the end of that meeting, Fred remarked that he used to be somebody when he bought hats and caps for himself. Several patients and the therapist said that he probably could look nice again. After all, there were lots of nice things that people were in the habit of throwing away.

Fred proceeded to set up a project. He went through the nicer looking garbage cans on the best avenue in the neighborhood and gradually collected 37 hats and caps. He had them washed, picked out 17 he liked best, mended them, and trimmed them with feathers and ribbons. Fred was quietly pleased whenever he wore his favorite, a small red hat with the brim turned up in the back.

In Fred's case, as in many others (see Chapter 2), change came before insight. After gathering the hat and cap collection, he often deplored the years he had wasted on self-pity. Fred began giving encouragement, as an assistant therapist, to other patients, thus gaining recognition and affection, and enhancing his self-esteem. Eventually, he ventilated his rage at his parents, at society, and at the counselors who had just "blabbered." His became a story with a happy ending, for eventually this man retrained as a baker, found a job, set up a little home, and got himself a new "old lady." He had been able to work from the outside in, from putting together with perseverance his hat and cap collection to a fairly good level of frustration tolerance.

The goal of any treatment is to free a person as much as possible from fears and restrictions. A psychoanalytic conception of what creates disorders is the assumption that most problems are caused by faulty psychic structures that were acquired early, for instance structural imbalances between the id, the ego, and superego. The appetites of the id must be harmonized with the capacities of the ego. This is accomplished by producing changes in the ego and superego. The classic psychoanalytic assumption is that by allowing appetites and needs for sexuality, aggression, and social contact that are repressed, denied (or otherwise hidden from awareness) to peep out from behind the defenses, the ego, which has meanwhile been strengthened mainly through interpretations, will gain a surer grip on the conduct of life (Guntrip, 1956). Affected by treatment, the ego is expected to be in better shape to settle conflicts, seen as the prime emotional-cognitive scourge, to deal more firmly with frustrations, and to acquire broader access to defenses which can then be used as desired. Also, the ego will have better judgment to decide when to use a defense and when to let matters run along.

Common to these ideas is the assumption that the psyche of the disturbed person is endowed with spontaneous recuperative power, provided the defense picture is in order. Once the individual is liberated from the pressure of unconscious processes and the clutter of defenses, previously scattered or repressed energies will now come to the fore and be harnessed by the person. Health will emerge without further construction and repair.

Implicit in this model are these basic assumptions: First, if the person can remember a previously repressed event, he or she will not be forced to pursue repetitively some powerful unconscious motivation. Second, damaging past events and repressed motivations, once they have risen above the horizon of awareness, lose the power to steer the patient back towards archaic behavior of which the up-to-date part of the mind, the other side of the conflict, does not approve. Third, once the ego is relieved of the nuisance job of using much of its energy for repressions, it will spontaneously take on new shapes and produce superior functions.

More recently, psychotherapy has been preoccupied with filling in ego deficits caused by environmental interference with orderly, step-by-step growth. This new emphasis has grown out of the realization of how profound the influence of the pre-Oedipal environment is on the formation of ego and self. Until deficits are replaced by assets, the ego cannot concentrate on the constructive tasks necessary to navigate through life. For example, it will not be able to produce such highly important structures as a healthy self-representation, a viable sense of identity, or solid self-esteem. Since it is not only the borderline personality and the psychotic who suffer injury from the environment, other persons too need belated ego and self revisions.

When it comes to helping an arrested ego develop stunted or misshapen capacities and to straighten out functions that have been twisted, interpretations are aimed at a new target. In cases of repression, the therapist usually tries to assist patients to discover that they are using defensive methods to repress something they do not want to face. However, when it comes to problems of ego deficits, the therapist aims at clarifying just what it is the ego in its restless search, despair, and repetitive hyperactivity tries to accomplish (Lachman and Stolorow, in press). The process might consist of three steps: 1) Patients who suffer from ego arrests are advised what capacities, functions, and structures they are missing or trying to alter. 2) They discover to their relief that many seemingly compulsive and odd forms of behavior are really psychological self-cures, though inadequate ones, meant to patch up existing gaps and malformations and to make up for deficits. 3) Therapy acquaints patients in various ways with healthy modes of feeling, thinking, and behaving. Sometimes it suffices, as the classic approach shows, to clear away outdated behavior. On many other occasions, however, it becomes necessary to introduce fortuitous experiences that awaken, kindle, and shape new ego assets and integrations, largely, as we shall see, through reparatory interactions with the therapist. For many, changes occur because old transference patterns break away like deadwood when the therapist makes independent and unexpected moves that gradually force the patient into new and healthy responses.

It is still true that anxiety, that worst of torturers, is often the result of clashes between an urge or unadmitted need and the ego and superego. It is still true that identifications are the forerunners of object relationships, that love binds while aggression assists separation, that an optimal degree of postponement and disappointment produces frustration tolerance. But the growing understanding of developmentally appropriate sequences and of developmental arrests has led to important changes in therapeutic process. Without healthy interactions with therapeutic figures and subsequent alterations of the internalizations, without a clear-cut range of reparatory experiences and without ego-building through guided growth, the ego cannot gain normal form. The purpose of therapy is not to help reconstruct but to construct, not to regain but to gain, not to rebuild but to build. Simply undoing regressive and past-oriented trends is not enough. The experience of existing has to be evoked (Lichtenstein, 1977) and "teased out" through interaction, and then it must become a basic internal fixture. Other functions likewise depend on guided growth, which in the case of treatment is largely the responsibility of the therapist.

BUILDING, ENRICHING, AND INTEGRATING EGO AND SELF

Low-level functioning is characterized by extreme dependence on the environment, which makes the vitally important exchanges with it one-sided. The environment not only neglects participation in the formation of the individual self, it not only negates or else stays indifferent to the individual's needs, but it continues to exercise more weight on the fate of the person than the person's own unformed self can possibly bring to bear. As a result, the individual stops being and becoming an evolving creature (Levenson, 1978), but stands still in his tracks, detached, withdrawn and isolated rather than autonomous. His boundaries are closed to commerce with the world.

In the therapeutic setting, the anger at the disinterested and deserting world is gradually expressed. Confidence, previously stunted, begins to bloom because the patient is given to understand that needs are perceived and heeded, though there remains the expectation that the patient assume responsibility, too, for growth. Enjoyment derives from *becoming* rather than *having,* thus sharply contrasting with the perpetual desire to assemble goods and treasures as shown by those deprived of opportunities for interchange. The therapeutic setting is sheltered in the sense that it is accepting of all emotions that burst forth. It is always understood that the patient will both investigate and gradually update his or her responses. Experimentation with different forms of relationship is encouraged. There is no retaliation for human errors since there is no need to gratify an adult who lets his or her own need prevail over the developmental requirements of the patients. Hence, it becomes possible to go from an apprenticeship in relating to other human beings to the final expertise of mutuality and genuine affection.

Persons bent on growth create new perceptions, recover, and then update archaic feelings. Gradually, and often without explicit realization, they allow themselves to trust the world rather than fearing it as fraught with danger. Hand-me-down ways of relating, copied automatically from others, are recognized as largely or totally unfitting. New ones emerge as men and women come to realize the forms and shapes of contact that are available and are required for dealings with new objects. Therapists help by explaining in the most convincing ways that they can find what responses and expectations do not fit the new object or the new situation, but are still injected into the new situation out of habit.

There is, however, a good deal more to the cure of the passions, the emotions, the ego, and the self, than advancing understanding of the inappropriate components in the old transferences. Individuals with problems not only have to be understood and accepted at whatever state of development they have been frozen stiff, but they have to be helped to bring about new conduct. Patients are given opportunities both for new kinds of relationships and for finally gratifying old needs and hungers which have hung on in the form of disgruntlement and resentment over their nonfulfillment. Under the situation is remedied through the repair experiences, they continue to cause emotional hangovers and specific repetitions of deformed ego and self functioning.

Patients thus come to grips with their old resentments over childhood longings to which they feel instinctively entitled but which were never gratified. Now at last they have the chance to make up for the former deprivations. Encouraged by the experimental climate in which psychotherapy proceeds, they let their emotions, their ego and self, now filled with fresh and invigorating currents which the belated fulfillments spark off, try out new functions and relationship modes. The essence of cure is that a new object relationship is formed with the therapist (Loewald, 1960). Within this relationship, the entire psyche achieves a bloom that was impossible during the childhood go-round with a non-facilitating and hence basically not benign environment.

Since we do know through the work of ego psychology that the healthy ego can only develop within an environmental setting that accepts and facilitates developmental needs, it is clear that verbal transactions alone will not suffice to bring the ego and self into possession of full bloom. *Relationship experiences* are the central salutary and transmuting factor. The therapist does not act out with the patient when such relationship experiences are permitted, but lends his existence and experience to catalyzing human growth processes which are as essential to the previously shortchanged psychological system as air, sun, and nutrition are to the healthy body. In therapy we not only discuss the neurotic distortions, but we actually take them away and prepare for pure and positive new forms by sharing with the patient the "human image which needs to be brought into its own" (Loewald, 1960). The idea that the therapist should become a new human object to the patient was proposed by Alexander and French (1946). Their idea met opposition because of the two clinicians' emphasis on *deliberately playing roles* in order to make clear the distinction between the old primary figure and the new objects. Actually, to be gradually perceived as a new object, the therapist does not need to stretch and twist himself nor exercise any theatricality. He or she merely needs to be mature, in tune with the patients' needs, as well as accepting and clear about the fact that progress means movement from one phase to the next higher level.

The unconscious or conscious need to repeat old, stale, yet familiar relationship patterns may be so strong that the patients' selection of their therapist is determined by resemblance to a parent; they hope that the similarity will allow them to coast along. Patients must be warned against choices that are prompted by the repetition compulsion. There are a number of enlightening discussions in the literature, not only about the pros and cons of repair experiences but also about contrasts or coincidences between a transference object and the real object (Blanck and Blanck, 1977; Dewald, 1976; Hoffer, 1956).

The first relationship stage with a new object is likely to follow certain rules, especially in the psychotherapeutic context. Frequently, if the working alliance is good, patients idealize their therapists and identify with them. Of course, these features inherent in the early relationship must be thoroughly understood and gradually altered. Initial identifications are bound to be global in the sense that the patient is not selective but idealizes and introjects everything (Jacobson, 1964). Such imitative identifications which are narcissistically tinged by idealization cannot be integrated properly with other features of the patient's biophysical-psychological self and are gradually eliminated through self-understanding and subsequent tries with other more congenial feelings and behaviors. These first identifications consist of actual "aping"; therefore, the term "modeling after" is not the most apt way to describe healthy development. Patients might begin by wearing the same kind of shoes or using the same vocabulary as the therapist. Gradually, however, the individual will be able to determine just what he or she truly wishes to emulate and how to fit feelings, functions, and certain attitudes about self into the system that represents the personality.

Of course, getting acquainted and working with a new human object has an impact on processes other than identification. As one becomes acquainted with the new object represented by the therapist, one learns in therapy to use perceptions more in the service of reality, gradually determining who that new person really is. One acquires optimism because the new object's gates for tolerance are most likely to be open much more widely than those of the non-facilitating parental environment. One learns gradually to evaluate the new object slowly once the birth of the first impetuous approach is recognized as the offspring of anxiety and the desire for narcissistic wish fulfillment.

DEVELOPMENT OF SPECIFIC FUNCTIONS: SELF-REPRESENTATION AND SELF-ESTEEM

Among the most difficult assignments for the therapist are the repair and, indeed, often the building "from scratch" of two pillars of existence: self-representation and self-esteem. It is my experience that these functions, once they have been stunted, do not unfold spontaneously when interchange with the environment improves and interest in and understanding of developmental needs are shown; enrichment demands systematic experimentation. Trying is essential.

SELF-REPRESENTATION

A person's self-representation (or self-image, to use a familiar term) is built gradually, affirmed, and continually revised from the early months of life, beginning with the body image. Mirroring on the part of the mother is one of the first steps, as she affectionately follows her child's movements with her eyes and exclaims at his or her body and the slowly acquired first skills (Kohut, 1977). All the well-known motherly attentions go towards laying the foundation of the self-image, such as maternal nuzzling and exclamations: "Oh, what a nice tummy Billy has!" "I love to rub those pretty pink feet." These and similar remarks lay down first layers of the self-representation through reflections in the parents' eyes and voice. When later the family applauds the teen-age son for fixing the car, for instance, then the growing boy starts perceiving himself as "somebody who knows his way about."

To possess a reliable self-representation means many other things as well: the ability to differentiate between what one *really* wants or merely *pretends* to want, awareness of one's liabilities *and* assets; developing a mental map of one's network of human relationships and correcting and expanding it as new experiences come along, and more.

Because the psyche, its functions and the intrapsychic representations develop largely through interaction with others—or, in terms of systems theory, because the human being is an open system which must be in contact with other systems in order to avoid entropy (Bertalanffy, 1968), we are dependent on *the ways in which others react to us*. This is true especially in the formative years. If a chief neighboring system with which we have contact and on which we depend for our self-representation and affirmation of our own reality is unresponsive, or highly idiosyncratic, this is one reason why our self-representation becomes fuzzy, incomplete, or entirely bizarre. The individual will function properly only if exposed to interaction with other normal, responsive, and informative systems which pay attention, show caring, and make corrections through exchanges of information. Only then does the self-representation become delineated because it bounces, so to speak, off others; only then does the skeletal form become rounded out, correspond to reality, and become stabilized until another period of regeneration occurs. The therapist and, in the case of group psychotherapy, the group members represent open and active systems from which a patient with a fragile or ill-fitted self-representation can expect shoring up and restructuring.

A man who was over six feet tall, bright, and capable was consistently humiliated by his ungenerous, very short father. He was 28 but felt like a child. When I asked him to tell quickly how tall he was, he instantly said not quite five feet, his height in mid-adolescence. This unrealistic body image, which was accompanied by a sense of being an irresponsible youngster, was gradually corrected when the patient was asked similar questions in individual and group therapy, encouraged to talk of accomplishments, and asked to articulate and revise constant negative comparisons with peers.

Another patient, Skip, 50 years old and the youngest of three brothers, was highly narcissistic, but did not possess a reasonably solid and broad self-representation or self-esteem. He relied entirely on the prestige derived from his status as an outstanding mathematician. As he put it, he could be anybody and was nobody. When Skip talked to a visitor from Britain, in a few minutes he had adopted the accent of an Oxford don, a position, incidentally, that he desired eagerly. When he had to make an appearance in a crowd, something he avoided as much as possible, Skip felt that he disappeared into thin air. Yet, he could not be alone. He needed the company of others, preferably as similar as possible to his own age, status, and articulateness, in order to get a fragile sense of self and a feeling of protection via identifications and contact. He referred to such companions as "they" and "them." Never did he call them friends. If Skip found himself alone unexpectedly, he either went straight to the telephone for two hours of quickly-forgotten conversation or soon went out to a bar or restaurant where he would overeat and drink too much.

It was pointed out to Skip that what made it so difficult to be alone was the absence of a self-image to keep him company, to refer to as an indelible structure, and to reaffirm his existence. Having no identity, he lacked a picture of who he was and any certainty that he existed at all (Lichtenstein, 1977). He missed the pleasant companion which the abstracted yet vivid "I" or "me" becomes via the self-image. Little children, for instance, often develop good self-relations through an imaginary companion to whom they make such remarks as: "Now if you sleep here, then you can come with me and play."

But Skip never had such an imaginary companion and forerunner of self-representation. As a little boy, feeling the watchful eyes of his stern mother always on him, he never undertook actions or showed feelings of any kind that could be censored. I interpreted to him that his phone conversations and bar visits were psychological Band-Aids that were needed in the absence of a closer companion, his own self-image. I explained that his practice of submission habitually placed emphasis on the person he tried to please rather than on his own self, which required strengthening and whose existence he needed to feel.

Eventually, this man achieved the first reflection of his own self through aggression directed at me. As he sat down one day, he took out a notebook and quoted two separate statements I had made which were contradictory. Then Skip explained: "When I am with you I make every effort to agree since assent is the keynote of my existence. When I am home alone, I cannot tell myself what I think since my existence becomes nebulous when I am by myself. But when you explained that disagreement might help me find me, I got this notebook. Before I get to your office, I buy a cup of coffee and make a note of my angers. When I get to your door, I feel I carry a bag of ammunition that will help separate me out." At this point, I asked the patient what he felt right then, and he replied promptly: "That I will defeat you. I feel great having said that. Oh, oh, now I feel terrible, ready to take it back." This exchange produced a building block that went into the making of self-representation.

Clashes with authority figures and outbursts of aggression against a person with whom the patient normally tends to merge out of fear of abandonment and separation are experiences which assist the formation of ego boundaries and delineate the self-representation (Fried, 1956). Aggression prepares the way for individuation. In short, it is one of the most essential processes leading to those changes and interchanges which have the ultimate purpose of all development—making individuals increasingly independent of the environment. As a result, they feel much safer and become more loving of the world. Thus, clashes with the therapist are important to therapy (Spotnitz and Meadow, 1969) since nearly every patient must learn how to terminate desires for symbiotic fusion and affirm independence.

While therapeutic soothing is often indicated as a reparatory experience when patients are restless and irritable because they have not outgrown unfinished symbiosis (Modell, 1976; Winnicott, 1965), there are other cases and occasions on which it is essential to make separation a familiar experience through accepting hostile stances. By contrast, absolute neutrality is easily and frequently construed as indifference (Dewald, 1976). Keeping in step with the patient's dynamics under the guidance of prudent psychoanalytic understanding promotes growth and health by affording opportunities to supplant dependence with a selfhood that is both proud and loving.

SELF-ESTEEM

To live, love, work, and play well, human beings need to rely on a fairly high level of self-esteem. This requires that patients learn to look to the self as the prime originator of their needs as well as the developer and curator of their resources, and that they consult their own opinions as the final arbitrator even though the ideas and convictions of others are studied and considered. In order to establish such self-esteem, it is essential to have experiences with unnarcissistic caretakers in childhood who consider the needs of the child and refrain from using the young organism as a means to fulfill their own satisfactions. However, if the child is exploited to satisfy the parent's needs for symbiotic reassurance, for a human target upon whom authority needs can be unleashed, or for adornment to gratify narcissistic needs, then the focus of self-esteem becomes the other person rather than the feelings, needs, and capacities of the self.

It remains for therapy to accomplish an all-important shift to the self as the center of the individual's psychological universe. Since the achievement of mutuality, affection, and loyalty is one of the major goals of progressive development, the shift to the self does not signify evasion of responsibility and concern for other people. On the contrary, the all-important turn from others to the self in terms of needs, feelings, and resources carries with it the very core from which giving and loving behavior springs. Only when the patients have acquired a "me" do they feel sufficiently free of anxiety, self-confident and autonomous enough to devote energy and feelings to others instead of manipulating the environment to sustain the shaky self.

> The 58-year-old patient, Friedrich, who was the victim of his mother's and grandmother's double-bind behavior (see Chapter 2), was expected to write as part of his academic life, but was usually paralyzed by severe writer's block. As soon as he started a sentence, he began to worry about what his retired teacher, now a national celebrity, would say about the idea just put down on paper. He tried to anticipate the reactions of two colleagues with a different viewpoint and gradually lost himself in speculation about how the world at large would accept his ideas and style. As a result, he endangered his position for he produced almost nothing except some translations. After all, one can translate without being responsible for the original text.
>
> After a lengthy course of treatment during which he gradually began to possess a self and developed a steadying self-representation, Friedrich risked putting down some of his ideas on paper. His prestige and professional security improved along with his self-esteem. Moreover, he was able to become more assertive with other people instead of depending on a polite and yielding manner which eventually drove away friends confused by his lack of direction. Relieved of anxiety, submission, and indecision, Friedrich was able to act frequently on behalf of his own family, where previously all efforts were bent on courting colleagues and students. His age was no barrier to these changes.

To enhance the autonomy of patients, therapists continuously encourage expression of the feelings, the hopes, and aspirations which patients often hide so as not to offend. Sometimes these have been buried so deeply and for so long that they have no form as yet. "What do *you* feel, think, desire," is the recurrent question that steers the patient to the own self with its resources and liabilities.

This does not dispense with the patient's need for praise or the therapist's willingness to extend it. But it does require that praise be extended with certain constraints. The emphasis on assets and accomplishment must be substantiated. Vain praise, so often the bribe through which the narcissistically demanding parent and their figurative successors obtain their ends, is strictly avoided. Indeed, patients learn in therapy to demand documentation and specification, an important growth experience for persons whose self-esteem was loosely anchored in some narcissistic schemata that exploitative authority figures dangled in front of a basically disrespected and carelessly used psyche. Dynamic psychotherapy does not become cold or rigid but actually more solid if patients insist on substantiation of either psychological or practical fact. Straight questions and straight answers are an inalienable right and contribute to sturdy self-esteem.

In addition to enabling persons who need strengthening of self-esteem to turn repeatedly to the own self and listen to its needs, fears, and unfolding pride, many measures have to be taken, all by way of relieving and eventually eliminating drains exerted on the self. Though in the limited context of these discussions steps in reforming the superego have not been discussed, one often successful form of superego mitigation will be taken up because it has a bearing on the importance of *action*. Mere contemplation and contained verbalization confined to the treatment session do not suffice to reinforce self-esteem. Action becomes an important ingredient.

To elevate self-esteem, individuals have to get rid of their bad introjects, whose perpetual murmur is heard by the inner ear, repeating ad nauseum: "You are bad. . . . I told you you will never amount to anything. . . . You are in the way. . . . Nobody would enjoy being around you." It is not only borderline cases and psychotics who are plagued by the effects of such voices. Many much less disturbed patients suffer humiliation, hurt, and perpetual setbacks of shy, budding self-esteem from such inner voices.

> Irma, who had been widowed four years earlier, hoped that psychotherapy would relieve her sleeplessness and many physical complaints which her doctors termed psychosomatic. She spoke of bad dreams in which her deceased husband, in real life a Don Juan and psychopath, appeared and hurled ac-

cusations at her. "You are a bad wife and I shall be back to punish you," he would say. With the help of psychotherapy, the patient recognized readily that many of the husband's reproaches were indeed an expression of her own self-censure, going back a long way to the insistent complaints of a chronically irritated father, an ever-suffering mother, and a domineering grandmother. As therapist, I encouraged her to rid herself of the accusations by others towards whom she was ambivalent. "Spit that stuff out," I would tell her. "Get rid of it. Talk back. Exorcise it."

A few nights after such therapeutic recommendations, when Irma began to have a bad dream of the recurrent kind, she ended it differently, a fact that greatly pleased her. The husband, while making his accusations, was unable to look at his wife. She, to her surprise, turned on him and said: "Go away. I was a good woman to you. Did I not mend enough socks, didn't I market prudently? I took good care, even though I did not love you." As Irma spoke these words, a door opened and the husband was gone. He had exited like a ghost, which indeed he had become, when his widow mustered sufficient strength to exorcise him. The patient *acted* in the dream, having gradually grasped that her feelings, thoughts, and behavior had ceased to justify the unwelcome intrusion of condemning voices. Her outcry in the dream was several cuts above mere self-understanding and musing within four quiet walls. It approached action; it woke her up, both literally and figuratively, for she awakened with a start after the words had been thrust forth; her self-criticisms waned and she felt much firmer and more content because her self-esteem had asserted itself.

To move beyond mere contemplation and the intellectual grasp of a problem, even where the emotions are involved, towards the dissolution of internalized structures such as the superego represents, real-life encounters in therapy and gradually outside are necessary. The parry, the refutation which is sparked off in interchanges between people in various settings, is the product of thought integrated with action. As long as action remains connected with thought, understanding, and anticipation, it has an important and thus far much neglected place in modern dynamic psychotherapy. It is not necessary to exclude all action for fear of encouraging destructive acting out, which is avoidable through the strict setting of limits and through vigilance. Decision therapy and some techniques of

Gestalt therapy represent interesting attempts to introduce some forms of behavior which are more definitive than verbalized thought. These deserve study and selective use. Much action is neither stereotyped nor the product of a compulsion to reproduce repetitively, nor does it derive from over-stimulation of the sense modalities. In short, it cannot be considered a form of destructive acting out but rather represents a final aggregate of courage.

In order to develop and sustain self-esteem, passivity, which is required in some situations, must be blended with activeness, for few states of existence are so prone to reduce self-esteem as a passive attitude which waits for what fate, coincidence, or the whims of others will hand out. The most extreme form of the kind of passivity that detracts from self-strength and pride is the lingering fear of abandonment. All patients need to realize that even though one or another person may decide to quit on them, opportunities for active creation of a social and personal world exist for every human being, certainly in Western culture. Active, initiating loving is forever open to those who exercise it. Where there is no awareness that loving is largely an active, mature process and can be acquired partly through self-awareness and partly through assuming initiative, often through interchanges in dynamic therapy the new awakening and practicing that take place literally create a function that had been sorely missing—that of engendering and maintaining a state of active loving (Fried, 1970). Thus, an all-important process on which self-esteem depends and which banishes the passive and deflating fear of abandonment is not so much reconstructed as constructed.

SHAME AND HOSTILITY OVER EGO DEFICITS

Hope is a great ally in psychotherapy, both for the patient and the therapist, and it is usually justified. Fortunately, the psyche, more alterable than the body, can belatedly grow the equivalents of new muscle power and even new organs. We need not rely on transplants to accomplish this; we need only remove obstacles, that is, defenses, resistances, and negative learning and building processes.

It has been assumed that to resolve conflicts one proceeds in just one way, namely by helping patients through interpretations to become aware in what ways they are covering up truth, facts, and longings. On the other hand, in cases of ego arrest, clinicians have been urged to interpret just what it is that patients are trying to accomplish. This distinction is useful, but in many disturbances conflicts and ego arrests are bound together and the therapist has to proceed in various directions. What is particularly striking is the regularity with which patients with ego arrests, who compensate for their deficits in ways which they themselves cannot understand and which often appear shameful and bizarre to the uninitiated, are embarrassed, frightened, and eager to hide their symptoms, even when they make great sacrifices to obtain treatment.

Combinations of conflicts, ego arrests, and attempts at hiding the most frightening and bizarre symptoms are easily observed in outpatient clinics, for instance among women who have just given birth. In the postpartum period they are often overcome by anxiety and phobias. The personnel who deal with such conditions are used to discovering that some of the new mothers are enraged by the advent of a baby they never wanted. Their conflict over whether to get rid of the baby or to protect the newborn and their own concern over weak ego controls generate anxiety and phobias. When these women are helped to discover what they want to ward off, namely their murderous rage, they sense some relief, but usually they still remain troubled. Merely to discover the warded-off rage and fear of harming the child is not enough. To complete such crisis interventions, it is usually necessary to give a boost to the mother's ego. She may be asked to move in with a neighbor so as to give the mother-child team a guardian, or told to make regular visits to the clinic (which implies check-up procedures of a sort) unless regular visits by a nursing aide are scheduled. Understanding what is warded off is combined with simple ego-building measures. These may be augmented later by ego work in outpatient groups in order to strengthen the mother's incomplete ego and thus enable her to deal more effectively with future hazards.

Not infrequently, other actions that seem to the patient reprehensible, disgraceful, and disturbing are actually the result of rather imaginative though roundabout attempts at self-cure. As long as the psyche, the ego, and self are in states of arrest, the patient, especially if he or she is resourceful, reaches for remedies that may not necessarily be as common as phobias, but are equally resourceful and yet subjectively shameful at the same time. Since the true nature of the deficit remains not so much unconscious as unknown, the psychological amateur's self-cure by way of random repetitions has to be applied so often that it assumes the character of a compulsion which frustrates and embarrasses the patient beyond words. When the ultimate purpose of the self-cure is understood and alternative solutions are adopted, relief from shame and anger sets in.

A young woman who came from a part of the country that was ruled by the strict ideas and regulations of a hard-working, hard-driving European immigrant group asked with great timidity for therapeutic help. Reared by parents who demanded unswerving obedience, she engaged much of the time in truculent, oppositional ideas and behavior but blamed herself sharply for her attempts at emancipation from parental authority. She regarded herself as insignificant, unattractive, unworthy of being noticed, and felt that if she entered a coffee shop or any public place all eyes converged on her with censure and disdain. The young woman perceived the eyes of others as disapproving of her rebelliousness and, as it gradually turned out, of her desires for sex without thought of marriage. After a number of meetings in which Arabel obviously struggled with the wish to disclose something especially shameful, she made what she considered a horrifying confession. She said she wanted to have sex with a man but could not pursue this because she knew that she was a Lesbian. With much encouragement, she told the story of sexual carryings on in her early teens. She would take off her clothes in the privacy of her small, all-white bedroom and look at the reflection of her own body, especially her breasts, in a fairly large mirror. Then she would move her hips in front of the mirror, watch her breasts move as she swayed to and fro, and draw circles around her nipples with a lipstick. Sometimes she also painted her face.

Arabel's previous statements indicated that her parents, emphasizing work and parsimony, condemned vanity in any form. They had, in short, permitted extremely little encouragement of healthy narcissistic growth when the patient and her sister and brother were very small. The young woman whose needs for narcissistic supplies in infancy in the form of being smiled at, looked at, and admired had been almost entirely thwarted, engaged in attempts at remedying the narcissistic damage. While she earned a living as an accountant, she wished to be a dancer whose beautiful body would be admired on the stage. She longed for frilly clothes and, in the course of treatment, started to buy some. Her "mirror games" were used in the service of repairing the narcissistic damage inflicted on her body image and her self-esteem. In addition, this lonely girl, whose siblings were considerably younger, discovered and cherished in her mirror image an imaginary partner of a narcissistic kind, somebody just like herself.

When Arabel was told that her teen-age games were inventive and constituted an attempt to befriend her own body and to enjoy its motions and attributes, she was speechless. She could gradually understand and absorb what was made clear to her, and felt relief and gratitude for being absolved of what to her was the true "witch" role of a Lesbian and exhibitionist. A competent and witty woman in many ways, although she had hidden her capacity for repartee, Arabel came out of her various shells and eventually married a man of her own age.

6

Backward Pulls and Forward Pushes

Change, as seen from the standpoint of modern dynamic psychotherapy, is change of the psychic structures. It is by means of their psychic structures, which in healthy persons are in a state of usually mild flux, that individuals find self-expression, discover and refine crude anger, develop and sustain relationships with others, and obtain wider vistas of the world. Psychic structures are never completed. Indeed, a certain degree of psychological zigzagging (which, if occurring in therapy, is sometimes unnecessarily considered as resistance whereas it results from healthy as well as pathological processes) is the rule rather than the exception.

The term psychic structure emerged when Freud began to view psychological life as the result of the balance between id, ego, and superego. The term has increasingly been used to emphasize the fact that psychological development is not linear and rational, though it is not irrational either. In fact, the dimension rational/irrational has significance here mainly in the sense that a mind which insists on an exclusively linear approach and, similarly, on linear language (Hall, 1977) cannot "cope" creatively with the world because neither human experiences nor the language expressing them are always neatly linear. The mind of the healthy person accepts the fact that experiences do not follow each other in a neat and "orderly" way. Rather what matters is that images, representations, perceptions, facts, and ideas be dealt with in a manner that establishes *significant* connections between them. Psychic structure, then, refers to the ability to take note of and to digest overlaps, incongruities, and contradictory facts, and to respond to them coherently.

The fact that many disturbed individuals, though hungering for a higher quality of life, are driven not towards positive and constructive relationships but instead towards fears of success can be explained only if it is assumed that they operate with psychic structures that are inadequate. In order to enable such personalities to permit themselves success, their psychic structures have to be realigned.

TURNING NEGATIVISM AROUND

The persistent and self-destructive use of negativism which many disturbed persons practice is their way of achieving various neurotic goals which are dictated by the confines of their pathological psychic structures. Therapeutically, one can proceed in two directions: uproot the pathology, and in so doing gradually help the patient to get rid of the negativism; or make the negativism a major focus and dislodge it, thus loosening the pathology.

Negativism is used to fend off stimulation. It serves as a tight screen to make the person impenetrable, that is, to render the ego boundaries rigid and immutable. By carefully sifting stimulation, one lessens the fear that among the incoming messages will be criticisms, derogatory comments, and attacks of other kinds. But this fear of being hurt which negativistic persons invariably harbor is not the only reason why they insist on their defensive negativism.

Another very important but less self-evident reason for keeping at a distance and rejecting other people's approaches, ideas, and even presence is connected with the ego boundaries. Although they are so often negativistic, persons whose ego boundaries are not sufficiently firm easily glide into union with others, even on a simple level of agreement too readily granted. They are the people who fuse so swiftly that their head begins to nod acceptance of the other's viewpoint without even thinking it over. They are not on safe ground but are all too often ready to allow inroads into their own self, their self-representations and psychological territory by giving in to primitive forms of identification. This exposes them to the danger of losing their convictions, originality, and creativity.

As a psychological barrier against this danger, they reach for negativism, for constant contradiction of others, for fortress-like boundaries. In this context, the borrowing of the term "boundaries" is quite descriptive. The inviolability of physical frontier lines is the constant concern of statesmen and the military. Yet we must realize that we are using a simile, a figure of speech. We must remind ourselves that a psychological "boundary" is not a physical line or a sturdy wall but the *capacity* acquired through psychological development to distinguish between self-representation and object representations. What we call boundary comes about through the clear and continuous awareness of our own body and our own self. The ego and self boundary draws on our ability to create sufficient distance from others to help review their demands and make conscious decisions as to which are acceptable.

People who have weak boundaries—paranoid individuals whose projections often show them to be conspicuously unable to distinguish between self and other—feel subjectively threatened by sudden ego boundary expansion. Above all, they relate to others either by accepting them too much (which afterwards makes them angry) or, in turn, by showing too much distrust, uncertainty, and criticism. In either case, confidence, affirmation, and affection are missing. Affirmation threatens to alienate them from their accustomed self-image. But there is much more at stake. If negativistic people were to let go before far-reaching alterations in the ego and self have taken place, for instance if they were to refrain from being obstreperous, isolated and detached, they would take risks that are much too grave. Their ego boundaries, which are shored up by hostility (Fried, 1956) would snap or sag dangerously. Stimulation, which pounds at the door of every individual, would not get sifted sufficiently and would overwhelm the person in the absence of more flexible and healthily protective barriers between the self and the world.

In speaking of ego boundaries we apply, of course, a meta-psychological term for something that cannot be observed, that we know only from subjective experiences and the accounts of patients, and that roughly feels, according to such sources, like a mental ego girdle. It seems to serve as an enclosure for the individual's personal experiences and ego capacities. People who venture beyond their ego boundaries, or whose boundaries are so fuzzy as to obscure where the self ends, report feelings of alienation and depersonalization. The ego boundaries make for a sense of safety by delineating the psychological territory over which one has some measure of control via acquired skills and well-entrenched powers. This territory provides a sense of familiarity.

The ego boundaries tell individuals how far they may extend themselves in terms of new ventures and how many emotional-mental tasks they can master. For instance, more people than is generally realized cannot travel as much as they would like and as much as they pretend, both to themselves and to others. If they move out of their accustomed environs, they cease to be safe in a psychological sense. They are compelled to stay within geographical limits because their perceptive powers, their adaptive skills, and their capacity for relating are limited; it becomes psychologically hazardous to venture too far. Somatic illness incurred during travel, episodes of homesickness, and general anxiety are results of a rupture of the psychological boundaries. The fuzzy boundaries of many disturbed personalities account in part for their inability to know how much or how little they can expect as their due, whether and when to insist on privileges and favors, and how to determine the extent and limits of their various responsibilities. The ego boundaries of negativistic personalities tend to be too narrow, and once attempts are made to widen them anxiety-provoking experiences result.

Speaking more generally about negativistic personalities, it must be repeated that they, appearances to the contrary, have never individuated sufficiently. They lack a sturdy sense of self and independence; in lieu of possessing a genuine and entrenched separateness, they clamor, sometimes obsessively, for their rights. Without solid individuality, they live ultimately in a human void (Lichtenstein, 1977). Because of their limited capacity for independence, they try to make sure that isolation will permit them to survive intact, even at the cost of a lonely and unsatisfied existence. The isolation that is combined with negativism protects such "unfinished" relators against the danger of being swallowed up. For, with their limited capacity for a calm and friendly independence, they actually incline too readily toward emotional surrender. Their conflict and hence their inability to change consist of being torn between the Scylla of defensive negativism, which spells loneliness, and the Charybdis of losing identity through emotional surrender (Freud, A., 1952).

Resistance to friendly relations with others and to a generally more cooperative philosophy will only be given up and a true parting with the negativistic orientation occur *after thorough ego changes have been accomplished.* In particular, defects in object relations have to be corrected. Symbiotic leanings are responsible for excessive submissiveness and for haste to conform and to merge with others, particularly with important personalities. It is against such temptations to give in to mergers that the negativism is defensively employed over and above its other functions. Negativistic patients benefit greatly, of course, from actively used insight into the functions fulfilled by their standoffish attitude and rebelliousness. In addition, they need a variety of reparatory experiences and many can be obtained in the therapeutic relationship. When, for example, their late arrivals, a frequent expression of negativism, are ignored or treated as necessary devices because to appear on time would be equivalent to merging and giving in, these patients begin to come on time. Their resistance is bypassed when their willingness to change is thus encouraged.

Concomitant with the relief these personalities experience when they can relax a bit because they are neither pushed nor coaxed, explanations and interpretations are very necessary. One has to explain why the person feels ready to part with old transferences and adopt new practices. Similarly, negativistic patients begin to change and to achieve new turning points when they are asked to observe just when and by means of what psychological engineering they reach their peaks of quick agreement. Small increments in psychic restructuring occur when they become aware of all kinds of mannerisms, such as their little endearing smiles or their willingness to stop in the middle of sentences that seem to arouse opposition. Often, they find out that the serious expression they observe on other people's faces does not signify disagreement but, quite to the contrary, interested attention. It is desirable to gradually extend the limits of their tolerance for praise and love which for negativistic persons accustomed to keeping a tight ring of restriction around themselves is difficult to bear. Starting to tolerate small doses of affection and success, they blush, become a bit tearful, and their faces twitch. In this regard, the willingness to endure small amounts of such softening in body and mind eventually helps to reduce negativism. The mental and physical preparations for a new expansiveness are of help in accomplishing eventual changes of major proportions. Repeatedly experiencing a gradually widening accessibility (looser ego boundaries) and friendlier, affirmative relations with others prepares the way for the lowering of barriers and the influx of emotional sunlight.

In the early phase of the struggle against negativism, and at times still in the middle stage, well-meant and quite objectively based support by therapist and group members proves unacceptable. No matter with what sincerity negativistic patients are told of their assets and capabilities, they shrug these assertions off because they are not prepared for the ego expansion which is the regular sequel to praise. But the situation changes after several important issues have been understood through active insight and small inroads have been made through revised behavior. The patient gains awareness of the fact that a lowly position may feel safe, both in terms of ego boundaries and in prevention of envy by others, but the fears are excessive and different forms of protection can be relied on without entailing so much self-sacrifice. For instance, by dwelling very factually on achieved successes and on reminders of the long preparations and waiting periods that finally led to them (in other words, by encouraging some leaps of optimism, small as they may seem), one can convince negativistic personalities that they can lower their basic distrust and still remain quite safe. By learning to appreciate a moderate success, they increase their tolerance for "good vibrations." Inch by inch, resistance decreases, and gradually they loosen up. The more this type of patient loosens up, the more positively will they cooperate in gradually removing the remaining slag of their negativism, and the better will be the chances for them to acquire that individuation whose lack was the main cause of their negativism.

FEARS OF SUCCESS AND HOW TO OVERCOME THEM

As the study of life histories shows, fear of failure is frequently matched or even outdone by fear of success. Indeed, it is an earmark of emotional disturbance that many problems which appear clear-cut and understood are not discarded but continue to be welcomed, or so at least it appears. Surprisingly, many people either continue to nurture difficulties they dislike and understand or substitute new ones when the old troubles disappear. Such persons do not find it easy to prolong and enjoy changes and spurts of growth, for which they have worked hard in treatment. Told by group members or acquaintances who have not seen them for a while that they have changed, the first reaction of such masochistic people may be one of happy surprise, after which discomfort settles in. Used to tension, crisis, failure, and psychological uneasiness, encouraging remarks of others may actually accentuate the conviction that something undeserved and precarious is happening. They have grown up with the unspoken philosophy that "having it difficult" is their fate and that, indeed, psychological discomfort is the natural state of mankind.

Periodic anxiety and panic and a chronic sense of worthlessness have become the customary setting in which these disturbed individuals go about their daily chores and experience their relationships. So habituated to trouble and defeat are many that if their lives go more smoothly and their inner strength accrues as a result of fortunate circumstances for which they could in measure take credit, or in the wake of treatment undertaken for the very purpose of dissolving such problems as anxiety attacks or depressions, they destroy their newly-found serenity.

A woman in her mid-forties underwent treatment because of a breakdown which followed a catastrophic love affair. Fairly soon her symptoms dissolved and she gradually became more capable of finding new friends, made a success of her work, and began to enjoy feelings of well-being. But then she noticed, to her surprise, that she committed small acts of awkwardness which were not her habit and which she connected with the upswing in her life: she would break some item she had rather liked, although never one that was very precious to her; she noted with amazement that she soiled some clothes, although usually not her special favorites; she spilled liquids on tablecloths and floors. Too ashamed to share these incidents with her therapist, she nevertheless decided on her own that they stemmed from a discomfort about her fast progress and represented an attempt to hold on to her good fortune by making small sacrifices in terms of a newly awkward behavior. This allowed her to remain in a state of quasi-transition between adolescence and adulthood and spared her the fear of assuming a clearly responsible position of success, until she finally decided to share her daily neglects with the therapist and to move on to a state of full success.

There exists in the negativistic person a reluctance to abandon the child-adolescent position that has been maintained into the mature years. It is often evidenced by whimsical or outright scurrilous mannerisms such as speaking with a false voice, committing childishly impulsive acts, or smiling ingratiatingly the way some fearful young people do. Quite clearly, there are hesitations and fears of assuming adult status, which is falsely equated with an obligation to stand and act alone without being befriended and protected. In actuality, and this must be made amply clear in treatment, adults need bonds in order to function. The all-important difference is that the bonds cease to be with parents or parent-substitute figures, but that instead the adult links up with friends, including, hopefully, members of the same sex (Du Plexis Gray, 1978). A deeply-rooted, unrecognized sense of guilt is responsible for the expectation that mental-emotional suffering must continue (Freud, 1961). Having grown up as the unwelcome children of people who did not fit readily into parental roles, many disturbed individuals live consciously or unconsciously in the shadow of and under the weight of doom which their rejecting parents prophesied for them: "You won't amount to anything . . . You are incompetent, evil." Such are the curses that used to be directed their way. No wonder they consider it their fate to remain ineffectual, to fail in their grades, to suffer, and to be monstrous in one way or another. As they approach the threshold of change and improvement, they hesitate to traverse it, assuming that the territory beyond the threshold is off limits for them.

Experienced therapists, well acquainted with the difficult and complex personal dynamics of success, have come to expect the hesitation, anxiety, and erratic lapses that occur when someone who is on the threshold of change, love, and success becomes anxious about moving ahead and halts his own progress. In such circumstances, it is indicated to wait for the shock to subside as patients, through the interpretations in therapy, first understand and then come to grips with the dangers they fear. To their surprise, they discover that these dangers are of an internal, intrapsychic nature and that only when the knots and fears are undone can they calmly await the next turn of forward movement. After all, what is involved is revolutionary. When the gears change, the old self-representation, self-image or ego identity, whichever term we choose, no longer fits the new emotional and cognitive conditions that are in the process of formation. Hence, an often far-reaching revision of self-representation must be undertaken by the patient. It will have new affective coloration and include awareness of the harbingers of cooperation, patience, integration, and hope. Negativism no longer fulfills its previously comprehensive role, and the newly emerging sense of power gets confused with omnipotence until the proper discriminations are made (Fried, 1954).

Positive changes are difficult to endure because, just as negativism narrows and tightens the ego boundaries, the positive changes widen them and make them permeable. When success, love, or any other positive change occurs, this literally expands the body and the mind. It is, for instance, not news that people in love feel that their chest expands, that their face acquires a new look, that they often stride more upright and take longer steps. Persons in the process of change get clear sensations that the narrow ego boundaries to which they have grown accustomed as if they were a corset are expanding until the prevailing feeling is one of being at liberty to move in a chosen direction and manner. This eventually joyous and energizing sensation of unaccustomed psychological-physiological freedom is initially accompanied by misgivings where one might leap now that the fetters have been dropped. To the everyday anxieties there has now been added the fear of freedom that comes with positive change and growth as dependencies are shed, as individuation is about to be established, and as ego and self become richer.

When the meaning of the newly emerging anxiety is interpreted, many persons are able to find confirmation in their dreams and body feelings. One dreamt she was dancing to a new rhythm, the unfamiliarity of which startled her; another that he took dangerous leaps over a clearing between two woods; a third that she was bursting the seams of a garment that had become too tight; a fourth that he was about to break into song at a vaguely identified place where silence was requested. When patients with awareness of and interest in their own body feelings as precursors of psychological change are apprised of what their rather unrestrained sensations signify, a good many feel relieved. Others remain puzzled and sense no parallel between what the body and the mind tell them. But reiterations of the fact that discomfort and some sense of strangeness have to be expected during the changeover from an arrested and depleted state to the stirrings of new beginnings is usually reassuring to both patients and therapists. One breathes more easily if one realizes that the general quickening of energy and pace is but the product of the storms of transition heralding growth of ego and self. The expectation that change for the better may well be accompanied by anxiety need not put the brakes on welcoming the sometimes sketchy and sometimes dramatic improvements that will follow. Forward steps can be hailed when the therapist shares with the patient the awareness that the onset of anxiety is a safeguard against going overboard; expecting and demanding initial improvements lead immediately to a broad highway of continually greater change.

The patient, Rachel, was brought up in the shadow of fear and poverty to which father and mother had become accustomed, although both parents had once enjoyed prosperity and social status. They were among the last people to escape the holocaust by fleeing from Europe to China, where the patient was born. Eventually, the family came to the United States. A relative bought them a small, dilapidated house in the South, and they ran a little candy and newpaper store which barely provided them with a living.

Rachel's mother had two psychotic episodes during the daughter's adolescence and never fully regained her emotional health. She was depressed and at times incoherent. She had been unable to prepare her daughter for adult life. In fact, she passed on to Rachel through explicit statements and implicit action a body of bizarre philosophical and behavioral beliefs. She taught Rachel that disheveled looks were to her advantage, that one need not pay attention to time, that all men were scoundrels, that to reach any goal one had to take circuitous routes lest one be caught and imprisoned.

Rachel, who was in her mid-thirties when she came to therapy, had had two previous treatment experiences. While she related to me in an interesting and personalized way, she evidently had little confidence that she could be helped. Indeed, she furtively confessed one day that she knew she would end up worse than her mother, that she had "no idea what improvement [for her] would look or feel like," and that she merely went through the motions of being a patient because she knew dimly, despite her disbelief in therapy, that there was nothing else which could rescue her from her miserable situation. When I pointed out that improvement was not a matter of being rescued but of actively rescuing herself this caught her attention. She remarked that she still felt tempted to pass over the "comedy" quickly. But she also had to admit that a few things had happened to give her a little hope, at least enough to dwell on them for a while. A few seconds later she turned restless and anxious. She then had an angry outburst and left. However, a few days later she came back.

After treatment continued for a certain period, I inquired whether Rachel allowed herself to face her fears and feelings fully. She seemed taken aback and said almost with a stammer that she had never revealed to anybody what she really thought. She became silent as soon as this confession was made. Asked whether she expected me to discontinue her treatment if she were really to open up, she answered in a near whisper, her eyes downcast: "I fear that I am insane and, especially, that the intensity of my continuous rage, if revealed, would make me unacceptable to any company of human beings." But thereafter she found the courage to expose to a considerable degree her envy, her desires to steal, and her violent fantasies when she was about to fall asleep. She feared she was insane because she thought often of murder and incest.

A few days later Rachel arrived with a book under her arm and placed it demonstratively on the table in front of me—evidently to get me to say something about it. I asked whether the book had anything to do with the fear that she could not possibly be understood or remain welcome as a patient if she were to reveal herself. She explained that the book was a novel and that one of its characters was the offspring of a mother available to her children only in conditions of crisis. Her misgivings came out of a conviction that she was not acceptable because she had been ruined by a mother continuously enveloped in fear of crisis. She was set apart from others. In essence, the message was that she was beyond rescue and that someone like myself, who was not jittery about her condition but on the contrary believed that she could be helped, could not possibly realize the extent of her disturbances. When I asked whether she was afraid I would be taken in by her brilliance and bluster, she nodded affirmatively. Yet, my reiterations that Rachel could help herself and that I had trust in her ability to extricate herself from her disturbed state and my gradually more piercing questions which kept me aware of her continued reluctance to open up, as well as many other interventions, eventually helped.

One morning Rachel arrived, unusually neat in appearance, and said she was preoccupied with a dream that was simultaneously reassuring and alarming. "I was undecided whether to let myself rejoice over it or get anxious and tight because everything was new. I am not used to becoming different, and it feels good one moment and frightening the next. I can't wait to tell you my dream, which helped me take my time to get dressed neatly. I wanted to mess everything up, but I got the upper hand and stayed neat. The dream has to do with your way of remaining calm and confident with me. It is more cheerful than my dreams usually are. Two thieves broke into my room while I was somewhere in my mother's messy kitchen, and they took my black address book. I almost caught them. I knew they would ransack the homes of my friends whose names are alphabetically listed in the book, and they were going to break into your home also. Then there was an interruption, and thereafter a second part to the dream. It started with a voice announcing, 'Everything is arranged,' and then some beautiful music followed, which I wanted to go on forever. I went to the phone and called you to warn you and then called everyone else. I said you must change your lock to protect yourself. When I got back, there was my address book, but it had turned into something sparkling and pink. I felt exhausted and fell asleep."

Rachel's dream had more meaning and called forth more remembered facts and associations than can be considered here. It suffices to point at her transformation that occurred between the two dream parts, and which is particularly revealing about her fear of success. The first part, in which her comprehensive pathology is acted out, resembles the first act of a drama. The subsequent part, starting with the announcement that "Everything is arranged," is reminiscent of a third act and the resolutions of conflict which the dramatist presents. Considering the enormous difficulties which Rachel had in letting go of her negativism and her stubborn defiance of the therapist, the conclusion is that she could change her psychic structure when she was "out of view" and not beleaguered by pressure coming either from herself or others, or ascribed to the therapist. Rachel had begun to change and to alter her psychic structures, and she made it clear in the dream that as far as she was concerned the rhythm of change, as the rhythm of the music to which she had listened with quiet rapture, had to be slow.

Rachel, although intrusive and impulsive herself, was irritated and pained by intrusiveness and felt that her psychopathic intentions needed to be controlled by some outside authority since she lacked sufficient self-control to keep herself in check. Her problem in therapy was that neither I nor the therapists before me could be seen and trusted in the two disparate roles of psychological policeman (helping put the brakes on her wish to steal) and source of hope (sustaining the belief that she could improve her inner life). In starting to go beyond the splits which she projected on other people, she had to start with herself. An attempt at unification and integration was made in the dream, where several parts of her self were temporarily joined together. The Rachel who tried to chase away the thieves was connected with the as yet emerging and still silent Rachel during the intermission and the rescuing and protecting Rachel of the second act. It was, incidentally, easy to note the identification of the bad, instrusive Rachel who stole with the thieves, for Rachel remembered and reported readily that two days prior to the dream she was tempted in a stationery store to steal a red wallet which was on display. In reality, she resisted her urge to put the wallet into her pocket because she did not like the shade of red which was crude and uninteresting.

The chief issue in this discussion is that the patient's reluctance to make a success of her life was related to such inner needs as clinging to a negative self-representation. The negative self-representation sustained the tie to the messy, deceptive, and rejecting real-life mother who, interestingly enough, appears at the beginning of the two-act dream in a kind of prologue. The prime therapeutic intervention consisted in offering a reparatory experience. The therapist, with this goal in mind, insisted on defining herself as a new female object, a woman who believed in the patient's restitutive powers. The perpetual endeavor was to extract from the patient responses to the new object and not to investigate at length the ties to the old, primary, and familial object.

This procedure is in keeping with one of the prime principles discussed throughout, namely the importance of assigning high priorities to new experiences. While emphasis on present-day figures, as well as on interactions and observations of change and growth, is not conceived as all-exclusive of the past, and while the exclusion of the past is in fact seen as damaging, the balance between past and present must be shifted. We can evolve a welcoming attitude towards success only if we alter the present psychic structures that have nurtured our fears.

The healthy psyche is a reasonably harmonious structure (Arlow, 1964). It is an organization or formation that consists of different processes which carry out divergent functions but have an impact on one another and upon the health or weakness of psychological functioning. The psyche is not a conglomerate of different substances or entities, and it does not work in linear fashion but is multidimensional. We can envisage its structure as similar to the formation of a tree, or we can compare it in some ways to a creatively written literary paragraph. It is not the mention of one item and then another that gives meaning to a written paragraph, but rather the connections that are made between thoughts, especially through the use of conjuctions such as "although," "but," "whereas," "despite." These little words make clear how ideas relate to one another and whether they clash, overlap, or are subordinated one to the other. Those persons whom we call disturbed suffer from character problems and other symptoms which stem from the shortcomings of the psychic structure. But although the patient comes ostensibly for help, he fights it and defeats himself in a variety of ways, as we well know. To assist persons in their struggle for a better psychological self, we need not only to establish a working alliance and make contact with their own highly idiosyncratic feeling and thought system, but also to become familiar with the broad range of circumstances that contribute to resistance.

With the ever-widening knowledge of human psychodynamics, we must give up the uniform theory that the prime reason why people resist their own progress in treatment is their insistence on keeping repressed wishes and thoughts under cover. Blocking is not the foremost reason patients do not or cannot accept the help extended to them. This was recognized many years ago by Fenichel (1954).

He noted that reluctance to change is often due to self-inflicted ego deformation which helps the individual get along as smoothly as possible with a noncooperative environment. In other words, it has been understood, though practically forgotten, that the ego undertakes twists, turns, and standstills so as to avoid clashes with the parental environment. But such instances where the ego halts its own growth and sidetracks its development must eventually backfire. An arrested or deformed ego might prevent clashes temporarily; however, in order to leave a shaky equilibrium undisturbed, it is eventually bound to resist desirable changes which its own insights recommend.

Another difficulty lies in the fact that the ego deformations and standstills have become so firmly entrenched that it takes unusual energy and many psychological detours to dislodge the cumbersome old behavior. In such cases, resistances are the result of psychological impoverishment and ossification rather than of unconscious forces such as repression. As a woman patient said in the second year of her treatment: "In my family I was only seen as real if I had problems and fretted. My parents paid me no attention if I was cheerful. So I have learned to equate misery and pessimism with being noticed, protected. I feel quite unreal when I am happy, like the last two weeks. I can't risk a hopeful outlook and I resist you when you anchor some joy in me."

Psychologically ossified and impoverished persons let go of their resistances for a brief time—which eventually can be extended—when they come face-to-face with a new level of living, a model of the world which differs from the parental one, and when they get a taste of the possibilities open to them.

I might add that, by contrast, some individuals who have not undergone transformations will sometimes take a risk when a disequilibrium is created in psychotherapy. As a 50-year-old patient of mine said when I made an intentionally provocative remark: "I doze off psychologically when everything remains safe. but when you take me by surprise, I wake up and rearrange myself psychologically. I dislike it and I love it, both at the same time." In this, as in other cases, a rigidified defense and resistance pattern was scuttled and thereafter reorganized. Since the realignment was repeated experientially as well as discussed, the effect of startle ex-

periences was not just temporary but had some permanent consequences.

EXPERIENCING A SENSE OF FUTURE, HOPE, AND PERSONAL IMPACT

Resistances of neurotic patients do not necessarily dwindle when
repressions are discarded and that which was warded off, say, an aggressive wish, is brought to awareness. However, positive experiences which elicit hope and affirm the personal impact of the individual make inroads in the patient's inaccessibility. For instance, I
have observed that persons become more cooperative in the process
of psychotherapy when their life space and reach are being altered to
stretch forward into the future and to encompass more psychological
territory. They can more calmly view the long history of self-
imposed restrictions on ego and self and mobilize a sense of urgency
to change if their sense of personal significance is enhanced. Interestingly enough, this occurs when their time sense is stretched
and the feeling takes hold that there is a future ahead. Even if individuals at first merely envisage that another half-hour lies ahead to
be utilized and then a day or a week, such widening of the time
perspective encourages cooperation and inner change.

Wishful thinking decreases and relaxation sets in ever so slightly
when the treasure of psychological time is discovered and relished
(Hartocollis, 1974). The feeling is: I count, I have access to activeness because I am discovering time. I want to acquire the ability
to make planful decisions (Jacobson, 1964). Among the three high
points of time—past, present, and future, the past has received most
of the attention in traditional psychoanalysis because of the interest
in the effects created by past traumas and past events that have been
forgotten or repressed. Since the advent of ego psychology, additional and comparable attention has been shown to the present
psychic structure as molded by the impact which parental figures exercised during the phases of past psychological development. By
contrast, the ways in which the future plays a role in the restructuring that goes on during dynamic psychotherapy have as yet to be examined.

The language of children gives us some clues to how the sense of
having an impact on the environment unfolds. At first, the child

refers to the objects which it perceives in a manner that suggests that the objects are thought of as separate things outside the child's realm of influence. There are no hints as yet of any relationship between things and child or of the child wishing to form such relationships. At first, then, "thing words" (nouns) are used when different items are noticed. The child says "dog" or "bottle" or "stick" without yet caring to express just what the relationship is to be between these objects and the child. There is no indication whether the bottle, for instance, is used to satisfy any need or what manner of relationship should be established, although the good mother guesses all this. Later on, this primitive method of speech, which makes no reference yet to what the child wants to do with the object or hopes the object will do for the child, is refined when "action words" (verbs) are introduced. Then communications emerge such as "I pat dog" or "I take bottle." When functioning is signaled, this means that psychologically a step forward has been taken. The child has got hold of the notion that he or she can have an effect on a thing, can make something happen, can create a situation.

Similarly, dynamic psychotherapy discovers that many steps can indeed be taken to get to know and influence the world around, inanimate and, especially, animate. Patients discover that they are not at the mercy of circumstances to the far-reaching degree they assumed. Instead they, themselves, can cause changes to occur to their own or to other persons' benefit. They have impact and power and can induce events. When disturbed personalities discover that they have chosen to be masochistic victims because of the neurotic gains this frame of mind gives them, but that they also have many possibilities to influence what happens to them, resistances are often dislodged on a broad scale. A reasonably accurate evaluation of the representational world is a prerequisite for psychological well-being and strength. Having an impact on the world is a basic process on which the sense of self and of identity rests. *Impact experiences,* as I shall call them, shape the backbone of psychological life. Human beings must discover the properties of the world and their own ability to manipulate them (Piaget, 1954). Especially valuable are the very simple impact experiences which every patient has vis-à-vis a therapist who is willing to affirm the patient's own reality rather than hold to the silent screen method which achieves neither the true objectivity for the sake of which it was designed nor meaningful exchanges between the two living systems of patient and therapist. These experiences introduce the hope of being understood and make the patient accessible rather than resistant to change.

When patients who guard their secrets like genuine possessions start to mention new objects, this signals that they are getting ready to take some psychological initiative. In dynamic psychotherapy, as in life, "getting hold" of new animate or inanimate objects, not simply through purchase or geographical proximity but by engaging in some interaction, precedes the readying of new functions. It is delightful to watch how patients disclose their readiness for new interests by proceeding quietly and as inconspicuously as possible. Indeed, often they "smuggle in" the good news by telling the therapist of the end results of some new psychological activity without ever having announced the beginnings. This is so because they do not wish to acknowledge that something is afoot, that resistances are melting away, and that they might have in the present the kind of impact which in the past a symbiotic mother resented and thwarted. Or they may not be turned on consciously to processes of their own growth. On the other hand, the tendency, at first, to "smuggle in" new developments, is salutary. In fact, sudden loud and proud announcements that a new leaf is being turned have in most cases to be taken with suspicion.

The patient, Norman, was shy and quiet. His original major complaints, namely excessive anxiety, tenseness, and stammering, were mentioned in passing. As these conditions improved—even the stammering became hardly noticeable—the patient spoke a good deal, and with a display of sadness, about his feelings of insignificance. He felt he had no impact on the small world in which he moved: his self-absorbed mother, his intemperate father, and the nice neighbors on the floor. He expected to be ignored or considered a lightweight, even only half a person.

As Norman improved, he was more and more aware of his sense of ineffectiveness, but began to recognize that his shadowy presence was of his own making. He counted the times somebody important looked at him when he spoke and was firm in his belief that VIP's never gave him a glance. According to Norman, after he made important points at office conferences, it was always others who later got credit for similar remarks. "I feel that I slide my statement across because I don't expect to be heard; as a result, I am not heard. When I say something in a way that I believe to be audible and important, I discover later that little of me came across."

It was because of this matrix that a small, hardly audible remark he made one day signaled new developments in the making. He mumbled something to the effect that he intended to get his own stockbroker.

When taken up on this, Norman gradually revealed that much self-search had preceded it, such as discovering his intense but largely repressed rages, his fear of giving up the reluctant symbiosis which he had with both parents for fear that he could not make it alone, his conflicts between submitting or rebelling. But the concrete and planful decision to employ a broker was for him a milestone, and it was essential to acknowledge its significance. The broker fulfilled a function similar to the one a child experiences when suddenly coming up with a new "thing word," because the real world has expanded. Norman, though referring to his broker by the merest allusions, was proud to focus attention on a new object, a means towards higher status. In his estimation, he had entered into the freshman class of the college of life. Every developmental step demands new objects with new channels and practices of implementation. The use of broker services and the announcement that they were being considered meant that the patient was moving ahead. The future was within reach, not only in the administration of money but, as it turned out, in many other forms as well. Norman married, bought a house, had his own and his wife's portrait painted, and six months after the wedding announced that "we are pregnant."

As Norman moved forward, he could understand retrospectively and overcome some fears that had previously upset him, but has been unable to pinpoint. Most of them, as is the case with many patients, focused around the fact that chronologically he was an adult and no longer a child, but he feared to let go of the parental strings; he had misgivings about letting himself use his powers out of apprehension that he would misuse them in some omnipotent and antisocial fashion and that they would arouse his father's competitiveness. He was not certain that he could claim maturity in an even and continuous way.

Norman's forward development was accelerated, it appeared, by shifting the attention from his fears about his future behavior to the imminence of new decisions. Being made aware that the allusion to a broker signaled the possible onset of mature behavior had a catalytic effect. It enabled him to make himself significant through the actions of adult financial planning he undertook.

FLEETING IMAGES SHOW NEW DIRECTIONS

The psychological raw material which exists at birth and from which mental life gradually evolves is inarticulate. In the beginning, the substance of the mind, which Freud called the id, is an unformed mass, existing in a kind of primordial condition. Yet, this substance or network of processes is and remains the soil out of which arise our emotions, our specific needs, intentions, and thoughts. Some measure of unshaped psychological substance seems to persist until the end of life. Gifted people seem to retain especially good connections with that primary psychic substance and to make contact with it easily, drawing sustenance from their creative work and their imaginative conduct of life (Kubie, 1958; Kris, 1952).

On the other hand, it signifies a cause and/or consequence of disturbed functioning if a person is either out of touch with this raw substance or totally overwhelmed by it, or is unable to draw a flexible separation between that substance and the organizing ego. In such cases, where bridges are missing between different structural processes, the problem is not necessarily that the organizing and rational ego is repressed, but that it has remained strictly outside, unconnected, and alien. In these instances, the id cannot tell the ego what it wants (Freud, 1961). If such all-important communcations have not been established or have been disrupted, then the person will have difficulties moving ahead and being adept in the art of living. He moves about without finely tuned steering. Deprived of the beam that shines from the id and illuminates new routes, such personalities remain stuck because they lack guidance toward selected destinations.

In such confining circumstances, therapeutic efforts may move in either of two directions. First, they might try interpreting the fears that separate patients from the urges and whisperings with which they cannot make contact. This approach is in harmony with a genetic view which unearths fears and desires that originated in the past. The other possibility is for the therapist to become, at well

chosen times, *the patient's agent of articulation*. This approach
necessarily implies that the therapist can approximate what the patient feels. The therapist's statements have to be well meant as well
as representative of "good" guesses. They come out of empathy, as
do interpretations. Patients must examine, discuss, and express
these articulations in their own language, and eventually they may
confirm them.

> From time to time the therapist's formulations and ideas
> seem to come from nowhere. They just pop up. I recall one day
> listening to a dream told by the patient, Strip, who never felt
> totally liberated from the observing and censoring eyes of his
> mother, whom he thoroughly resented, as he had come to see.
> In the dream he was a stowaway in a medium-sized ship that
> landed in Hong Kong. When he entered one of the smallest
> cabins to find his mother, who had supposedly died, he found
> her sitting up in her berth. She looked pink and pretty and had
> a smile on her face. Without thinking, the words that sprang
> into my head as this dream was told were *Pretty Baby*, the title of
> a current film that was set in a house of prostitution and involv-
> ed a young girl of about twelve. I jotted the two words down on
> a piece of paper and put it in the middle of the table. A few
> seconds later, Strip said: "I don't know what the dream means
> but it makes me think of the film, *Pretty Baby,* I saw two nights
> ago." I do not, in this context, want to mention other associa-
> tions to the dream, nor to describe how the dream was utilized,
> but wish merely to report the concurrence of the patient's and
> my own association because it illuminates occasional links be-
> tween a patient's and a therapist's system. On various previous
> occasions I had articulated something for Strip that helped him
> to mobilize himself and to express what was on his mind, not so
> much as an unconscious process but as a nebulous formation.
> But never had my thought content seemed so farfetched. I want
> to add that in his teens Strip had drawn several caricatures of
> his mother, showing her as a harlot. I saw these caricatures
> after the dream incident.

It is readily understandable that fledgling ideas and plans are
fleeting because fresh psychological processes are usually tentative.
They have as yet to become sturdy, clear, and significant through
inspection, through the act of being told, tested, and retested in
behavior. Clear definition derives from articulation, exchanges, and

debates with other people, as well as through the accumulation of memories that pile up when ideas are exposed to trial and error action. Fleeting images that happen when we are on the threshold of change resemble the tentative hypothesis, the shapes that emerge at dawn, the good guess.

Thoughts, feelings, and stirrings which are the harbingers of evolution trespass the territory of consciousness lightly and swiftly, often in the form of some idea captured by the words, "but things can be different." When ideas formulated in this or similar ways are heeded, we often step over the threshold of desirable change. The heeding of rebellious inklings and the digression from routines of thoughts and feelings signal the nearness and sometimes even the arrival of turning points. To accomplish change, regressive manifestations and arrestations must be linked to progressive steps (Zetzel, 1970).

> Mrs. Newman, a middle-aged woman who, with her husband, had gone for two weeks in the summer to an ocean resort, was asked by him to take two reclining chairs to the beach for sunbathing. She was about to put them into the car when she heard herself say these words: "Why not the black-eyed Susans?" Having recently come to the tentative conclusion that she wanted to change various aspects of her life, she stopped and reflected. She realized that she was referring to the bed of pretty gold and yellow flowers in the middle of the large and usually windswept area of grass in front of their cottage. It was *there* that she wished to lie in the sun. Suddenly it was clear to her that, while she loved the ocean and found swimming highly invigorating, she thoroughly disliked being on the beach in the sun and feeling the sand "creep up all over and invade my body." Next thing she not only refused politely to stay on the beach for any length of time but found that the fleeting idea, "No sun and sand, please," opened up an entire stream of associations.
>
> It became clear to her that she must bring to the foreground of her mind many things she truly wanted, instead of coping meekly with the exposures, situations, and relationships into which she had become immersed through habit and inertia. It was not a hornets' nest she had opened but rather an inviting package from which came forth a series of decisions that gradually amounted to a middle-aged emancipation and enhanced *joie de vivre*. She was en route to discovering her real

tastes in reading and living. Mrs. Newman acquired new
friends with whom she could be open and dropped the constraints that had previously burdened her. She became a peer to
her husband instead of remaining his domestic assistant; to her
surprise, she found that he became comfortable with and interested in this change of role. The woman's sense of humor
quickened and her energy mounted. The fleeting idea at the
beach cottage happened to be the beginning, but the willingness to listen and be open to innovation proved to be the
major boon.

THE DREAM AS PRELUDE TO CHANGE

Like the fleeting images which are subjected neither to the extensive daytime censorship of conscience nor to the procrustean
demands of completed rational thought, dreams have their own way
of stretching the imagination. They can alert us, for instance, to the
depth and extent of problems whose existence we minimize or even
ignore entirely. The dream can point at emotional as well as
cognitive resources of which we are not aware and which we
therefore neglect to use and expand. It can also confront us with in-
sincerities, with concocted pseudo-emotions, and with limitations we
hope to ignore. This self-confronting nature of the dream (Jung,
1945) is very valuable both for shedding pretenses and for
establishing just how far we can safely go and grow. Dreams are ignored at the risk of maintaining falsehoods and forfeiting emotional
honesty and the safety of life. While pointing at the nature and
wealth of as yet undiscovered resources and the novel directions that
are accessible, the dream also makes it clear where resources end—a
point beyond which we risk disaster. Viewed from such a vantage
point, the dream can indeed—with all due precaution—be a har-
binger of the future. It cannot be as reliable as, say, a barometer or a
seismograph, but it is an important means of emotional and
psychological guidance because it can indicate to the anxious individual who is cut off from familiarity with himself or herself, and
hence resistant, just how far certain steps might lead. Moreover, it
indicates to the therapist whether certain resistances should be
respected at critical points.

A psychopathic but creatively gifted man who authored

adventure stories came to treatment because he drank too much, spent his money gambling, and was unable to gain a safe human and economic foothold. After half a year of treatment, he decided for a variety of wrong reasons to marry a woman friend. The woman had, for instance, helped him in several serious financial pinches; under pressure from her, he wished to compensate her generosity by marrying her, minimizing the fact that he was not attracted sexually, was much too restless to settle down, and possessed only limited capacity for loyalty (object constancy). Like many personalities with neurotic-psychopathic inclinations, he focused only on getting rid of the pressure exerted by the woman, whose support he needed in various ways.

Before the wedding, the patient began suffering from insomnia or had deeply disturbing dreams in which he stood ready to jump onto an airplane or train which, however, took off without him as soon as he was found wavering. Ready to hop onto these various conveyances, he was usually dressed in pajamas, which embarrassed him because they made him feel he was not prepared to face the everyday world. He would always carry under his arm a yellow notepad like the ones he used in writing his stories, but the sheets were scattered by the wind, a sign that his productivity was diminishing.

I suggested that the dreams indicated his lack of preparedness for marriage and that he should seriously consider whether their "systematic" appearance implied his desire to postpone or cancel the marriage plans, which he invariably discussed in a depressed manner. I asked whether being restless, footloose, and inwardly reluctant to settle down to the suburban family life his wife-to-be planned was an indication of clash with his own plans for the immediate future. But the patient declared firmly that the dreams and forebodings were yet another temptation to give in to his irresponsible ways.

He decided to go through with his marriage and terminated treatment. Initially, everything seemed to go smoothly. He and his wife had three children and gave indications of domestic contentment. He accepted a position as a partner in a public relations firm where he did well. Yet, as it turned out, he functioned on the basis of pseudo-emotions and a basically untrue self. In the sixth year of marriage, shortly after arriving on a business trip in a foreign city, he slammed his typewriter against a wall and put a bullet through his head.

It would, of course, be an exaggeration to say that he could have avoided this fate had he "listened to his dreams." Nor were the dreams the only indicators of his still unresolved psychopathology. Yet, in the long run, this man failed because he refused to listen to warning signals, among which were his dreams, prior to his marriage.

Dreams deserve to be respected as forewarnings of either positive or negative events that are in the making and are waiting in the wings to make an appearance. When they are harbingers of future psychological events, this predictive quality does not derive from magic but from contact with clues which are so unexpected, minor, or fuzzy—they are the products of neurological and psychological processes not employed in the clarity of waking life—that they fall short of the standards we are accustomed to apply to the decisions of waking life; therefore, we disregard them.

But dreams do not only contain sound warnings; they also are a cause for rejoicing because they establish bridges between what is and what can be, alerting us to inner potentialities. Dreams may signal tensions, dangers, and crises, but they also highlight directions and resources of which the dreamer is not aware during the waking life. In this sense, the dream makes it less attractive to lie low and fallow, and invites self-confrontations and discoveries of unrealized potential leading the individual towards change and growth.

From extensive studies of dream episodes which occur during REM (Rapid Eye Movement) periods, it appears that such dreams are the product of more primitive brain structures than those which provide the neurological basis for waking life experiences. The substance on which REM dreams are based is different than that which nurtures more rational behavior. This neurological structure seems sensitive to the perceptions, experiences and content of what we call the id. It creates and understands symbolic representations in which the exact form of an object is less important than certain essential features which stand out and for which dramatic substitutions and comparisons can be made. Events are captured by dwelling on the aspects which stand out, the way the caricaturist captures a likeness by making a composite of outstanding features of which some are greatly accentuated. Yet, equally, the neurological substance which creates the dreams is highly sensitive to small clues which the moving rational eye is likely to neglect. Outfitted with such special abilities for perception, dreams capture possibilities and inclinations that are merely on the horizon of consciousness. For instance, during REM episodes the dream dwells on propensities and psychological novelties which the mind has not yet elaborated and which it is merely in the process of spawning.

For people who are ready and willing to register and utilize new perceptions—often by nature dim—rather than shunning them, the dream can become a prelude to new freedoms of action which are the privilege of human beings. Retaining contact with instinctual levels of behavior, yet going beyond them, the human race has the advantage of imagination, far-reaching exploration of new climates, tools and cultures, and immense flexibility. The more we open ourselves to new experiences, the more combinations of different levels of learning can we put together. We learn through repetition, through selective identification, through experience (Bion, 1962), through reframing of questions by placing a problem into an unfamiliar setting. We learn by postulating and then exploring opportunities which our imagination and dreams conjure up. Because of such multiple combinations of models for learning, human beings make up a species that can transcend its established habits (Perls, 1973). Human personality is never a finished product. We make situations new by dealing with them in new ways, some of which we envision by admitting and using fleeting images which are unwilled and spontaneous. Dreams are special treasures because they take us away from threadbare and frozen opposition to emotional explorations.

On the other hand, if some progressive steps have already been taken, or are about to be taken, dreams may tell us what the person's suppressed attitude towards them is. They alert us to fears of backsliding and tell a good deal about how the individual proposes to handle regressions that are feared or even expected. At times, in advancing progress, the dreamer appears as a liberal and encouraging self-regulator, at other times as the instigator of a new tyranny, not unlike the one just left behind through progressive forward thrusts. All is all, the dream lights up obscure corners of emotional life, thereby facilitating progress or caution.

Twenty-eight-year-old Gus described himself sometimes as

an arrogant elitist, an imposter, and a provocative snot. He wished to overcome his primarily homosexual orientation so that he could get married, have children, and lead what he called "the good hometown life." Early in therapy he had dreams in which appeared handsome young male figures: a prince, a musketeer, or a Vanderbilt, all, of course, impersonating himself. He cast most of his dreams in heroic and frequently medieval settings, with castles and fortresses, swords and luxurious costumes.

At the end of his second year of treatment, Gus began a love relationship with a young woman to whom he proposed in due course. Shortly thereafter, he dreamt that two men, both remarkably attractive and youthful, walked side by side dressed in sports suits of British tweed, each with a flowing navy blue cape with red lining slung over the left arm. The man on the right had an arrogant smile, and the one on the left wore the emblem of a Freemason. Passing them, Gus told his fiancee, "The one who does not get an erection is homosexual. He should be rejected."

Gus interpreted the dream as follows: "Both men are me. The sports suits mean that I am more in tune with real life, though the cape is a nostalgic reminder of romantic times for which I still hanker, especially when I get rejected. The red lining is the flamboyant side of me that has not yet quite given up. Of course, there are two of me, because I am still split as a person. My homosexual side needs to be exorcised, stoned. I keep wondering when the day will come when I shall divorce Diane [his fiancee], lose my children, and get back to the homosexual life. The homosexual relations help me hang on to my youthfulness and make sure I'll never get sick like grandfather or paralyzed like mother. Like the one man in the dream, they help me to sustain an exhilarating wickedness. The part of me that is plainly, but not struttingly, sexual makes me feel like a member of a persecuted minority group [the Freemasons]. It balances my feelings as they are today. I consider being a Freemason by far the healthier position. I miss my fortress dreams but I am glad to have gotten rid of them. I almost like being stripped of defenses and being more human. I used to hide my homosexuality, but now that that it is much more over, I want to warn people, and especially my fiancee, not to trust me. I am furious at you [the therapist] for not giving me more opposition. Guide me, force me, for goodness sake don't let me do it by myself."

So many of this dream's forward thrusts are clear through

the dream's simple imagery and the dreamer's comments that I shall only dwell on one important message. When discussing his dream, Gus demanded impatiently and somewhat arrogantly to be helped in his fight against his own homosexuality which threatened his aspirations to respectability and traditional family life. But in the dream the patient's own voice expresses the conviction that the "one without the erection should be rejected as a homosexual." Thus, when Gus urged me to push him in the more respectable and peaceful direction of heterosexuality, I countered that he could gather quite clearly from the dream that he was ready for the role of being his own sponsor. I had no intention of becoming the law-enforcing authority to whom responsibility could be attributed for his homosexual revolt. "Why not," I asked, "use some of your exhilarating wickedness to fight the battle against homosexuality which you want to win? It need not be a dull and childlike struggle. Put teeth into it." At these remarks, Gus was hilariously happy. "My," he remarked, "it is good to know that I can pick out from a dream the militant march to progress. It need not be goody-goody plodding."

7

Changing from Passivity to Activeness

The quest for activeness stems from basic needs of the human race. The mind avoids and, indeed, abhors a series of vacuums. It seeks out stimulation and responds joyously to chances for taking initiative, expanding its boundaries and experimenting with the world of human and inanimate objects. Recent observations show that unless a person is fatigued, ill, or poorly equipped to deal with the tasks before him or her, urges for activeness, emotional vivacity and efficacy outweigh any need to live in more or less perpetual equilibrium and pursue an untroubled existence. Indeed, unless living systems like the human being are exposed periodically to waves of disequilibrium, they atrophy and perish. To put it in terms of general systems theory, they become subject to entropy.

Therapeutically, this is of great significance because it coincides with observations that structure building in the psychological sense is never completed. As new life experiences appear on the psychological horizon, engendered by the mere fact that the body changes, that economic conditions vary, encounters with new persons bring on new impressions, the attempt to come to grips with these events calls forth emotional changes and many other realignments in the mental world of the individual. Unless a person has been overwhelmed by trauma, that is to say, suffered an excess of stimulation, the need to connect events, to scan and examine them in detail, thus continuing the structuring activity of the psyche, is subjectively enjoyable and objectively strengthening. To absorb and organize life experiences is not only a necessity, it is simultaneously one of life's chief pleasures.

The affirmative personality, which we consider the healthy and life-preserving model, has an impact on the world. It subjects itself to change and growth and even goes out of the way to locate conditions under which change becomes a necessity. It seeks out new ways of restructuring itself, expands the range of self-expression—Picasso was in his sixties when he began working with ceramics—discards clichés of thought and language, enjoys the exercise of the senses and the discoveries which searching thought rather than pensive doodling makes. In short, the affirmative personality is active, though not defensively hyperactive in order to cover up passivity. It relies on its own resources and strengths, a fact which eventually leads to higher forms of concern and love. As the truly active person draws on his own strength, he is able to take infinitely greater interest in the welfare of others. By being and remaining reasonably independent, we carry fewer grudges against others since they are no longer basic pillars on which our existence depends. Above all, we are free to love actively if we so wish because we no longer are enmeshed in desires to be praised and coddled nor steeped in acts of pacification and supplication. If we do someone a favor, it is done out of generosity, not in the hope of building up a credit account that will keep us in good standing and against which to borrow when the going gets difficult.

To be experienced as enriching, effective, and life-preserving, activeness must be *straight* and not *defensive*. Persons are active in the straight way when they deal with their emotions rather than hiding them. This means to articulate them privately or in public, and above all to respect and use them as psychological guides. Usually, emotions have urgency and call for a course of action. It is the individual's responsibility to decide whether the reaction is to be a mere reflective attitude towards the emotion or an immediate act. Such split-second decisions, together with the appropriate follow-up, represent an emotional activeness. Straight activeness is characterized by a preponderance of emotional openness, of ongoing mental probing and venturesomeness, with concomitant structualization and integration.

Activeness that is not straight goes into the elaboration and perfection of defensive strategies. While every person must rely, of course, on the availability of defenses and automatic reactions, an overinvestment in defensive psychological energy indicates that the active/passive balance is lopsided, that the emotions are likely to be unauthentic, and that the mind is too busy with mental bypasses to engage usefully and joyfully in the maintenance and expansion of the mental apparatus.

When human beings are introduced early to one of the most important principles of mental life, namely that human existence is often not pleasurable nor safe and the individual copes with this aspect of reality by developing psychological structures that are healthy, the chances of becoming lost in provocations and reproaches are slim. Anyone who has not only heard the thesis that omnipotence is not for those who are growing and becoming adult but has found the thesis acted on in life innumerable times is likely to incline towards straight activeness. By implication, this means that there will be a minimum of passivity in the form of sulking, withdrawal, provocations, and blaming, directed especially towards parents and parent surrogates who are perceived as unwilling to provide a painless existence rather than as unable to perform the functions of continuous rescue.

In order to be active at a certain time, the person need not engage in specific action. Indeed, far more frequently activeness is primarily a state of mind and emotions. The aim is simply not to remain or become a person who is primarily reactive. As a consequence of being primarily reactive and rarely active, patients locate the center of their own self in the other person and suffer from the subsequent fear that they will be abandoned should their life-giver(s) turn their attention away. Early in therapy, as the transference unfolds, the patient gives clear evidence of forfeiting the core self and limiting his participation to reactiveness; at this time the chances for starting to alter such dependency are excellent. It is then that the therapist has to be careful and make clear distinctions between situations. Regardless of the specific words to be used or a variety of psychotherapeutic rules, the message in answer to the patient's question has to be: "You don't need to ask me for my opinion and my approval. I help you most if I steer you back to the reservoir of your own resources. Now what answer do *you* decide to give to your question?"

It was this kind of clinical thinking that led Freud to demand that the therapist not answer the patient's questions. It was to prevent dependency from developing to unnecessary proportions that the recommendation was made to remain detached from the patients so that they might become the bestowers of their own approval. If one stays with the nature and aim of the therapeutic processes that were to be reinforced by technical regulations, one will use the "rules" in a flexible manner. For instance, one will, most likely, express one's acceptance to patients whose sense of deprivation and worthlessness keeps them in a state of emotional isolation. Where, on the other hand, the patient is tuned too much into an authority's judgment, good or bad, a therapist will try to encourage independence by leading the patient back to his own self.

All therapy has as one of its essential goals the restoration of activeness, which is the desired, healthy state of mind. Passivity, on the other hand, is a secondary and unsound condition resulting either from illness or from disharmony between the environment and the developing child (usually because the environment fails to offer the right kind of acceptance and does not supply a properly dosed series of frustrations that will puncture infantile beliefs in omnipotence). Patients frequently are not conscious of their passivity although they are burdened by its effects (such as depression, a sense of worthlessness, and general apathy). As they are gradually liberated from their passivity, they begin to thrive. They become subjectively much happier and their competence increases, if not by leaps and bounds then by small degrees. Their masochistic mishaps appear less and less attractive to them. Instead of self-failures, they note with astonishment an increase in popularity and success. Lusts and desires previously buried become palpable and keen, especially since the mind is getting busy figuring out new ways and means of satisfying the wants that have emerged. Even the oral appetite, the cravings of the stomach, ever-present yet undelineated during passivity, become more acute.

When Gus started therapy he was a hyperactive busybody whom nobody seemed to take seriously, according to his own reports. He was a graduate student at a small college, and it was quite obvious that fellow students avoided him, largely because of his lengthy and repetitive explanations of therapy. The teachers, despite or because of his fawning, had little esteem for his work. The hyperactivity was soon understood in psychotherapy to cover a general apathy and extremely low self-esteem. Gus slept away the larger part of weekends, was late turning in papers, and thought frequently of suicide. He fled to his small apartment for refuge, yet disliked being there at night because he was unconnected with anybody and felt sorry for himself for having to eat alone the same dreary evening meal: a large hamburger with relish and weak, tepid coffee bought at a fast-food store.

As this patient successfully moved away from his passivity and became more involved with others, especially with a young woman, his dissatisfactions and angers were openly expressed, the fawning disappeared, and a sense of humor and artistic sensibility revealed itself. Illustrating the change toward active behavior, he reported amongst several incidents the following little episode: "The other night when I was a bit hungry, wanting to put something into me, I noticed a difference. I used to feel like my Dad, not that I learned it from him so much as that he and I are similar people and I just drifted into things the way he did. Dad never explores any feelings; he leaves them in a murky muddle. He is rational—that's his forte. So, I also used the same pattern, would just go down and get a big hamburger to stuff into me. It is a quick way of eating, with feelings and tastes left out. But lately, and especially on that night, I really looked at my eating processes. I found out what I really *wanted* to eat. Nothing approximate about it any more. So I searched around and I discovered I wanted dark bread with sweet butter and a beer. I took the trouble to walk to another store and get just that. It was clear and determined, and I felt I was in charge."

In each of the various phases of development through which the young organism goes—the narcissistic and symbiotic state and, subsequently, separation/individuation and mutuality—passivity or activeness takes on its distinct look. This is especially true in the later stages of adolescence and adult life. Persons who want to grow need to be aware of this in order to spot passive behavior and dislodge it. But the form of passivity elaborated during any one phase of development leaves certain imprints on the character and remains attached to later forms unless corrections are especially deep. In this sense, passivity, like narcissism and hostility, is part of the basic core of human neurosis, part of a damaging fate that pursues man because of the prolonged human dependency which makes for both our particular loyalties and our frailties.

Passivity fulfills clear-cut functions which do not remain the same throughout childhood development and later life. To assist the all-important turn from passivity to activity, it is important to note just *what level* and especially *what function* of passivity the candidate for change deals with on particular occasions. For instance, to illustrate briefly what will be discussed later at greater length, the human organism, which is struggling to find its way out of the narcissistic cocoon but is not supported in this formidable effort, uses passive stances later on to guard omnipotent ideas about the world. In these instances, passivity is a strain left over from the narcissistic phase and is used later on to bolster a narcissistic, omnipotent behavior.

> The patient Gus, whose changes of appetite were discussed earlier and who was very narcissistic, often dreamt during the first year of therapy that he was a prince, a Viking king, or an irresistible American multimillionaire. Though he disclosed his dreams to his therapist and added to them his daytime fantasies (which were but modifications), he did not let on to anyone else what he thought and felt. Indeed, one of the reasons he bared his fantasies in treatment—he edited out many other less allur-ing stories—was that he hoped to entertain the therapist with his productions. Hiding his high ambitions, he dressed, spoke, and acted so often like a modest, socially conscious citizen that he would take his various roles seriously and became confused about his true identity. In the case of Gus, it was a slow process to make him aware of true fears or to help him cope realistically for even a few moments with thoughts or emotions about his frustrations and thus to broach activeness step by step.

As the person goes through the throes of individuation, passivity takes on special form and function. While the ultimate goal is to withdraw from the frustrations of life, people practice a silent rebellion when they render themselves passive during this phase. They appear amiable and cooperative enough, saying yes to re-quests made of them; however, they do not follow through in the end. This form of silent noncooperation is especially punitive as far as others are concerned because it is elusive, leaves no traces and makes concrete protests difficult. The passive offenders, whose transgressions appear in such innocent forms as forgetting certain promises, being habitually late, or making a seemingly harmless series of faux pas, use these methods of silent attack to guard their individuality. It is a big task to convince them that they use a special form of activeness which, for their own benefit, could be replaced by constructive, more direct forms of self-assertion.

MAKING A RELIABLE DIAGNOSIS

Because passivity seems to be an offense of omission rather than commission, it often goes unnoticed in ordinary life. In treatment, where the feelings (countertransferences) which the patient stirs up in the therapist and in other group members, if he or she is in a group, are utilized as a guide towards understanding what patients convey, their verbal assurances to the contrary, the rather tenacious passive condition becomes transparent. Generalized listlessness and depression are invariably signs that passivity has taken the upper hand, though we need to realize that other forms of non-functioning, too, contribute to these twin states. In the depressed state, patients complain that there is nothing they can do to help themselves because they usually feel that other people, not they, themselves, have tied their hands. Their conviction that the cause of their listlessness lies outside and cannot be influenced by them is not necessarily the result of projection, as has often been claimed. Rather, the patient is unable to make certain important distinctions which therapy, however, can eventually establish. In particular, it is difficult for depressed passive persons to realize that the concrete incident that frustrated them, while indeed beyond their influence, is different from the subsequent personal withdrawal which is definitely of their own doing.

A man of 49 came to treatment because he spent half of every day in bed, suffered from nearly total isolation, and was very depressed. He feared visits with his family, on whose good will he depended a great deal. They disapproved of his reluctance to find employment, to earn a living and give his life some direction. Early in treatment he was given certain concrete assignments, such as to memorize a poem, to call up one friend a day, to exchange small products that were the result of his personal interests like gardening and cooking. The purpose was to help him experience some concrete event as distinctive from the generalized and formless apathy in which he dwelled every day. The result was an experience of slight pleasure on the part of the patient. Until the assignments stirred up some feelings of both accomplishment and opposition in him, he underwent therapy with great misgivings because he feared that there was nothing to talk about since he experienced nothing. Eventually no hour was long enough to exhaust the many ideas and feelings he wanted to pour out.

In the fifth month of therapy, the patient, who within a span of five years had lost two jobs, dreamt that he entered one of his former offices from which all furniture and other objects had been removed. When he asked someone whether this meant that he was asked to vacate this particular work place or whether he was fired, he got the answer that it was not yet known what "he" was planning. The patient assumed that "he" was the boss of the publishing firm for which he had worked before it went out of business. Following this dream which occurred in the early morning, the patient, who had meanwhile gotten into the habit of rising at a reasonable hour, stayed once more in bed until the afternoon.

During the discussion of the dream I suggested that the patient was very angry at the boss referred to as "he" in the dream. He listened to this explanation with disbelief. He replied that his long unemployment, following the closing of the publishing firm, had to be blamed on fate, or God, as alluded to in the term "he." I told the depressed man that I recognized in him a confusion of causes. What had actually caused his depression? Fate or the patient himself? When he reiterated that fate was the cause, I answered: "Fate, if you want, caused your dismissal, but you are causing the depression. This is an absolutely crucial distinction. It is you who decided that the way to handle the disappointment that fate handed you was to go off in several funks. You resent the world, you have decided to turn your back on your friends, you have determined that there exists no other kind of work for you. You have caused your unhappiness, and you can make it go away." The patient, who was unusually eager to move on, understood what I meant. In further sessions, concrete examples of the non-participation in life which he engineered became apparent and he eventually initiated contacts and found interesting government employment.

One of the big steps that enabled this middle-aged man to restore his activeness, which had never been firmly entrenched and had been further shaken when he was dismissed from work though not "fired," was the belated awareness that any form of pessimism, hopelessness, depression, and listlessness that occurred after mishaps was strictly of his making even though outside forces control many aspects of life. For months on end he did not cease to be amazed at the ever-clearer distinction between what happened to him and what he, himself, had made out of it. He remarked: "When you first explained the difference to me, I sometimes considered this word-splitting. Now that I understand the enormous importance of my own responsibilities and actions, I feel really in charge of my world."

One of the ways in which this big change in experience was manifested was in the patient's frequent use of the words, "I have decided to. . . ." These words were quite literally the result of his new conviction that even though he was not in charge of most events proper, it was totally up to him to determine which way he would turn under given circumstances.

Just as constriction of affect, slowness, and a slackness of both mind and body characterize passivity, so does the active, affirmative personality possess vigor and snap. Unless passive personalities cover up their defects by hyperactivity, in which case they think and act impetuously, they usually react slowly and only to a portion or segment of a situation. They have difficulty perceiving the totality of another person and make their judgments on the basis of some partial perception. They are psychological stutterers, as it were, getting their thoughts out only bit by bit. Also, they prove to be usually erratic observers who, when some obvious fact turns up which they previously missed, exclaim: "Oh, who would have thought that this was so!" It should be added that the memory span of passive personalities tends to be short and that they have access only to indistinct and inaccurate recollections. Crucial events are leveled off, and few distinctions are made between peak events and in-between happenings.

One main reason for this complex of difficulties, which all amount to retardations of functioning but not a disturbance of brainpower, is the severe repression of aggression which goes hand in hand with passivity. Hemmed in on many sides by repressions, the patient does not dare risk making moves, as this might show what storms brew underneath the seemingly benign facade of passivity. Naturally, the repressions stifle not only the anger but other tributaries of the psychological flow: the speed of reactions, the rhythm and sequences of body movement, the courage to make searching and encompassing observations, the acuity of memory. Passive people usually come out from behind their withdrawal when they no longer feel they need to repress their anger so fully and they allow their hostilities, accusations, and criticisms to come out. Simultaneously, they become better observers, they begin to focus on and understand connections and structures, and their memory improves markedly.

    The previously mentioned patient, Gus, whose fawning manner and inhibition of feeling we have noted, was a strikingly poor observer of other people. This interfered not only with his daily life but also with his work, since graduate training was to prepare him for work in one of the helping professions where he would have to evaluate other people in order to help them make maximum use of their potential. Gus always worked merely with his head and not with his whole personality. Even on the intellectual level he had but a poor grasp of what another person was all about. He was usually unable to fit together the observations he reported in his timid, slow, piecemeal manner.

    His passive demeanor took a clear turn toward activeness when his attitude changed towards his mother, previously the prime recipient of his fawning manner. The patient, having gone to his parents' house for a vacation during which he planned to write a master's thesis, discovered with shock that he lay down on his mother's couch after each self-prepared meal, making a complete personality switch. He caught himself adopting his mother's arrogant and disinterested manner, for instance, when he picked up the telephone to answer it. Gone, on such occasions, was his usually timid and submissive manner, and instead his voice became sarcastic. Gus felt as if a different spirit had entered his body. He found himself fully, painfully, but also amazingly aware of the fact that identification with the maternal aggressor had taken place and that he was vicariously feeding off her strength in a manner that was eerie but that also familiarized him with the nature of power and overbearance. Gradually, this man, who, despite fits of arrogance, pressed himself into a humble role for all of his 29 years, got hold of and utilized his previously repressed anger, becoming a more outspoken, assertive, and active person. It was a veritable transformation; his gait became more assured,his voice deeper and stronger, and his arguments more cogent, daring, and challenging. Together with the therapist, Gus discovered specific measures and steps that helped him make the transition to strength on occasions when he had fallen prey, once more, to his subservient old ways. He helped himself to reach for strength by concentrating on a task ahead rather than wondering about how he offended the person he was with, especially his fiancee. He stopped the inappropriate friendly smiles, allowing himself to become somber, serious, and even grim-looking.

As former stringent repressions against anger were dissolved, as assertiveness came to be regarded not as a threat but as an ally, a noticeable enrichment of ego functions could be noted: his perceptions became much sharper and were expressed with wit. Gus grasped structures and connections in the world around him that previously had evaded him. For instance, highly interested as he was in international affairs, he realized that he had attributed too much significance to limited events; his previous picture of world events, a picture he now called "headline orientation," gradually changed. His memory improved and his people-preferences changed. Gus found, for example, that a female colleague whom he had disliked previously because her vivacity and strength rubbed him the wrong way was a staunch and reliable friend. The world made more sense to him and began to be seen in a different light. The ability to recapture anger which shores up the self-representation, which is part of the current that underlies human contacts and allows us to hold on to our own identity and boundaries during encounters with people of different persuasions, liberated the personality. It inspired fresh energy in the self and at the same time liberated it. The active Gus who emerged was not only strong, but better able to face and use his feelings, desires, and thoughts. This allowed him to follow his instincts and react to situations much more quickly and clearly than the Gus of the past was able to because he no longer needed to stop and check his every impetus or reaction.

Dramatic illuminations of the contrast between a passive way of being and an active one—and, for that matter, of other diametrically opposite states—need not remain a rarity nor be left to chance. They are more readily available than is generally assumed, although some preparations are necessary, especially in cases of individuals who have a certain control over their lives. Such preparations are furnished by repeated small encounters or mini-experiences (Kohut, 1977) which give the patient and the therapist a foretaste of the large conflicts, ego deficits, and looming structural problems that are responsible for the difficulties the patient is trying to solve. Before the major psychological flaws are perceived in their full size and total shape, small replicas in the form of microstructures become apparent. For instance, prior to facing the full extent and the deep function of his or her passivity, the person often merely reveals brief and mild passivity spells.

Passivity yields blunt and blurred affects; in the state of activeness, feelings become acute and clear and can be separated one from the other. When human beings, because of interferences with their development, are passive or have allowed themselves to turn passive later on (for example, by adopting broad-scale masochism in the effort to protect their narcissism), they do not have immediate knowledge of what they feel. Nor can they make reliable distinctions when an onrush of feelings occurs. Are they annoyed? Do they harbor curiosity or envy? Is suspicion their prime affect? When do they feel love? Lacking affective precision, they have to forego the guidance which feelings offer when the individual encounters the world. It is our emotions which give us that important knowledge we are accustomed to call instinctive. They furnish reliable signals on whether or not a specific situation or person is safe or warrants suspicion. Passive personalities lack these emotional directives and a general vagueness prevails. If the feelings surface at all, they do so belatedly and hence are *post hoc* facts.

Since the emotions are a source of psychological nourishment and refreshment, the passive person is and feels deprived. When patients complain, for instance, that little or nothing goes on in their lives, that they make no progress in any direction, and that their life is dull, it is well worthwhile to investigate whether such complaints arise from absence of their emotions or rather from the blurred mixture of emotions which passivity is liable to produce.

When persons regress from activeness to passivity and, by implication, permit the acuteness and distinctness of their emotions to slip away, often without noticing this, the basis for a most essential physiological-psychological communications system is rendered shaky. The emotions connect the outside world with the mental world of the individual. They also serve as connecting links between body and mind (Spitz, 1965, 1972). For instance, when the emotions are intact, then they alert and instruct the body how to participate in absorbing a trauma, a rise of pressure, or a newfound success. When the emotions are not accessible to the individual, as in a state of heightened passivity, then they do not carry out their assigned signaling functions; as a result the division of labor is topsy-turvy. In such cases the body often has to assume functions which the mind ought to take over, and vice versa.

The patient, Rachel, for instance, whom we mentioned previously, used to become dysfunctional when she faced an encounter with authority. Her pulse raced and a dull and deep pressure in her stomach practically paralyzed her. But her bright mind contributed nothing to reduce her misgivings. In other words, the body did much of the work the mind is supposed to do because the guidance of the emotions was missing. Eventually, as she regained activeness and with it emotional clarity, she became able to view and feel herself as a capable, responsive adult, small of stature but agile and quick on the uptake when she had to face encounters with authorities.

The characterizations given here of both the passive and the active form of existence will hopefully help both patients and therapists to evaluate the existence and intensity of either condition. Certain disturbances of ego functioning and of the affects will be seen as symptoms of broader disturbances along the passivity-activity continuum. Inevitably, the goal of therapy in such instances is to help the patient become a considerably more active and affirmative human being.

Let us not, however, overrate the value of such labeling. Useful as it is in pinpointing symptoms as the outwardly observable indications that there exist deeper roots than can be identified at first glance, the mere labeling of certain behavior as passive or insufficiently active does not make for dynamic changes. Although the old descriptive psychiatry and clinical psychology that were willing to settle for mere categorizing and labeling are on their way out, the tendency to settle for mere diagnosis can still be seen occasionally, especially with regard to passivity. Surprisingly enough, some masochistic tendencies in many patients prevail on them to be satisfied with the wrong questions. They keep asking, "What is wrong with me?" and fail to go ahead to the essential next questions: "What can I do about the fetter of my passivity? . . . How do I become a more active and initiating person? . . . Is there any homework I can do between sessions to stop the regression or to get out from under the psychological arrest that has paralyzed me long enough?" As it stands, homework is especially important in breaking through the encompassing, self-imposed harness of passivity.

WHEN THE FUNCTIONS OF PASSIVITY BECOME OBSOLETE, ACTIVENESS TAKES OVER

Passivity is the end result of repeated actions of withdrawal from people and situations that have proved painful. It is the end product of large-scale, sustained repressions of emotions, especially of anger, and of the refusal to be mentally involved, present, and responsible. Essentially, the passive individual's intent, though mostly unconscious, is to prevail on the surrounding world to make up for serious deprivations that occurred during the early developmental phases. Deprived in the past in various ways because necessary supports to complete developmental goals were frustrated, the hope of the passive person is to extract indemnity for the deformities and deficits of ego development with which the personality is stuck due to the mistakes of parents and their surrogates.

What form the passivity takes, what its specific functions are, and hence what treatment approaches are destined to put an end to the long passive haul and to make a person eventually active, responsible, and useful, have to be determined for the individual case. Above all, the treatment approach and goal have to dovetail with the passive condition in such a way that the specific functions and gains of passivity become superfluous because new dynamic constellations are created in treatment.

Towards this end it has to be established during which phases of development certain passive states were readied and integrated into the psychic structure. Patient and therapist have to find out what the specific ego deformations or arrests are for which passivity is to compensate and what functions specific forms of passivity serve. As we know, a person can be passive-dependent on one occasion and passive-hostile on another. Finally, patient and therapist have to discover what kinds of mental-emotional growth will prepare an individual to carry out necessary functions without the aid of the restrictive and noxious ways of primitive passivity. Only if certain psychological goals are either eliminated because the pathology changes and diminishes or carried out by other and healthier functions will a person let go of passivity and replace its benefits with activeness.

Steven, who came to treatment because of occasional homosexual affairs that he thought were sure to threaten his marriage, actually suffered much more deeply from the gnawing sense that he was a mere child whom well-meaning adults would occasionally pat on the back. He was almost continuously incensed over such imagined condescension, while at the same time courting it with flattery, shy smiles, and mincing gestures. It became ever-clearer that Steven remained stuck in such seemingly innocent dependent passivity and in the self-image of a child, partly because he had allowed himself to remain a most impractical man. He remarked, smilingly, that his only skill was writing checks.

Without going into the many deep roots of his childlike existence, it can be said that treatment, amongst many other goals, tried to awaken him to his nascent capabilities and encouraged him to hone and increase them. Gradually, there emerged a man who was able to say: "I found the other day that without hesitation I went with my wife to a carefully selected car dealer, asked what I was certain were all the appropriate technical questions, and within half an hour bought a new car. I find that I can play all the adult roles—I mean, really carry them out, without self-consciousness. It has all come together. I am a man, an adult, and I can envisage that one day I shall die, a terrifying thought previously. It is easy, clear, and immensely relieving that I am leaving the passive child role behind and entering into belated manhood.

ALIBI PASSIVITY/BARRIER PASSIVITY

In the narcissistic condition which predates other developmental stages and often reaches into adult life, it is a prime need of the organism that an outside power, the mother as a rule, be centrally attentive to and exclaim over the child's activities, and protect the young organism against all stress. If care is not proper and the body-mind entity registers its own fragility with alarm, the young child fantasizes—indeed, often hallucinates—a state of contentment. Many daydreams and fantasies have their origin in states of need which, when continued beyond a bearable expanse of time, are wished away. In such instances, either the fantasies or daydreams take over; otherwise, a high degree of insensitivity or apathy is developed. In either case, the organism abdicates from real life, either to overcome its frustrations by setting up a self-made dream world or by taking refuge in the nirvana of disinterest, disavowal, and insensitivity.

Patients who dream and fantasize instead of participating in life make the return to reality reluctantly and slowly. The therapist has to preserve and nurture every bit of interest in the world that is evidenced so as to keep alive the little flames that alert the patient to the fact that it is not total disillusionment but a self-erected, passive barrier that accounts for the withdrawal. The treatment sessions constitute probably the most effective incentive the patient has because the real-life contact with the genuinely interested therapist is appreciated, all protestations to the contrary. People who stay away from the bustle of the world and prefer their solitude relish the alibis of time and place which allow them to indulge in repetitions and elaborations of favorite fantasies and daydreams.

The alternately supercilious, passive patient, Gus, when frustrated by the real world, visited in actuality or fantasy a little cave he had discovered which he called "Green Tent." When he huddled in Green Tent, actually or in thought, he had the needed alibi to flee the world and develop delicious dreams and fantasies of finding hidden treasures, of discovering a tropical evergreen island off the coast, of sitting on the therapist's lap. He anticipated that towards dusk he would steal out of "Green Tent" and explore the woods and plants further away. I always asked him to tell me about these excursions. He did so, at first reluctantly and then with growing desire to share the exploits as well as his ideas about agricultural and political management, in which he was very interested. "When you voice your little interspersions, a question here or an occasional 'hmm' there," he remarked, "the realization that you listen and that I am not as totally shut off from the world as I pretend to want to be makes me feel real."

One night Gus dreamt that he was a small boy sitting on my lap until he felt the urge to slide down and chase rabbits in the garden. The dream signified that the patient was ready to give up his safe alibis and sanctuaries, such as Green Tent, his fantasies, and his fantasy refuge of sitting on my lap. Shortly after this, Gus started a relationship with a young woman who had also some fears of the world and a desire to withdraw, but less so than the patient. The new woman friend encouraged Gus to explore the city. One day I found a map of the town and gave it to Gus, who appreciated the gift and its meaning. "I think," he said, "that you assume my excursions into streets and various sections of the city represent progress, that they will open up a new chapter. I still hanker sometimes for the old escapes to Green Tent and the island of my fantasy, but I am making myself take new steps. The map you gave me is concrete and I cannot monkey around with it."

As this patient gradually, and at times by strong effort of will, ventured out into the real world and his "alibi" passivity diminished, strong positive feelings, especially towards the therapist, surfaced. But he was reluctant to let these feelings grow sturdy at this stage and to communicate them because of fears that they would make him more shaky inside than he could yet tolerate. When emotions, nevertheless, pressed forth at times, his eyes filled quickly with tears. He said on several occasions that while it was difficult for him to permit his emotions to take hold, the struggle with feelings felt like a relief, rarely permitted though it was, from his habitual quiet apathy.

A dangerous canoe trip which Gus undertook at the end of his second year of therapy showed that a counterphobic frame of mind, genuine activeness, and greater reliance on physical and inner strength were making an alignment. Significantly, the patient also began to put to practical use his interest in and skills of administration when he tried for, received, and carried out important committee appointments which required tangling with seniors and peers.

PLEA PASSIVITY

Many lives are marred because the experience of symbiosis had been either too short and unsatisfactory or too long and excessively gratifying. If too little is done for the infant and if, indeed, the mother rejects the psychologically unfinished organism's need for assistance and abrogates maternal care, the consequences will resemble those discussed as barrier passivity. Wounded, deprived, and continuously in a state of wanting but not getting, there occurs eventually a retreat behind apathy and a self-afflicted curtailment of wants. The more or less perpetually pained organism plays dead, so to speak, and does not express, indeed in some ways does not experience, wants anymore.

One patient who had grown up in Europe during the Second World War in an area where food was scarce and whose oral needs had been frustrated in other ways by an unloving mother, used from time to time to bend over in pain. The pangs, it turned out, were caused by hunger which, however, he did not register as such and hence failed to relieve with food. Gradually learning to detect and still his hunger, this patient eventually became a hearty eater who, in fact, had to watch his weight. This case is reported here not to illustrate plea passivity, but its exact opposite.

Plea passivity, as it is called here, contrary to barrier passivity, grows out of unnaturally prolonged symbiosis. This happens in many instances because the mother does not wish to separate from the offspring whom she regards as an extension of herself; therefore, she overindulges her offspring. Overindulged individuals need not take refuge in alibi passivity, fantasizing situations in which they feel soothed and noticed in fantasy only, bound of course to be disappointed many a time in the end. Rather than seek out alibi territory, the land of milk and honey which fancy creates and passive withdrawal sustains by protecting the person against sharp clashes with reality, the participants in extended symbiotic experiences set foot in the real world. However, they join the ranks of others not on an equal footing but as users of people whom they pressure, in their own subtle or dramatic ways, to take care of them. Remaining inert and using a show of masochistic helplessness and sadness, they mobilize on their behalf as much of the world as they can affect.

On first contact with passive personalities, others may not feel such pressures and may rally to their help, partly because the display of masochistic suffering makes them feel guilty and partly because the deep resentment of the passive person makes them fearful and they run towards a defensive solicitousness. The end result, however, will be irritation towards the individual who abuses the

passive pleas. Mates, children, and friends eventually comprehend
that the oblique requests the passive one directs towards them are
exploitations that warrant a sense of outrage. Frequently, in a marriage, one passive yet infinitely demanding mate proves to have been
the offspring of a doting mother while the other partner as a child
used to play parent to a parent. In such instances, both partners have
remained unaware of the roles they have assigned to themselves and
continue to play. They act their parts because they have remained
unfamiliar with the experience of genuine reciprocity, which they
may discover and eventually practice through therapy. As it is,
before therapy and in the state of unawareness, one partner, ad-
dicted to plea passivity, makes continuous aspersions, accusations,
and demands while the other, one-sidedly trained in parenting,
complies and serves. When the partner who acts as the caretaker and
parent becomes acquainted with the ways of reciprocity and begins
to balk at the claims made, the passive partner is indignant.

Beverly, an only daughter who had always mothered and
supported her widowed mother, catered to the demands of her
husband, Joshua, to a degree that made her overworked and
frequently ill. Joshua, the attractive oldest son of a doting
mother, wished his friends and even casual acquaintances to be
entertained in his home, but he never arrived in sufficient time
to help his wife with preparations. Indeed, at times he came
home a few minutes after the first guest had arrived. If Beverly
told her husband that money was short to run their household,
he would regularly ridicule her concerns and offhandedly say,
"There is nothing to it; just work a few extra Sundays and you
will have what is needed." Joshua, himself, was often behind
in his own work, failed to meet important deadlines, and usually blamed his employers for being rigid. He counted on the
charm which he, like other practitioners of plea passivity, could
readily mobilize to get him through the innumerable scrapes
which his lassitude created.

One evening the couple watched a television drama. Just
when Beverly became engrossed in it, as her serious face
showed, the big turnabout which was to affect Joshua greatly
began. Joshua had become bored and asked his wife to turn to
another station. The previously obliging wife answered calmly,
"You turn it off." This small yet unprecedented refusal shock-
ed the husband. He commented that he found rudeness abhor-
rent, turned his back on his wife, and fell asleep. During the

following months, such small occurrences multiplied, and Joshua often threatened to leave, objecting to the audacity implied in refusing his harmless requests. In essence, it was not love but the fear of functioning on his own and of loneliness that kept Joshua in this marriage, which improved only very slowly. Overprotected and overly exposed to the mother's presence as Joshua had been, he knew little about the process of building up and joining together internalized images or sets of representations of family members and other people who mattered to him. Rarely alone, he did not come to make ready use in solitude of even the sketchy images he had internalized; hence, he was not able to maintain a solid sense of self unless others, and especially a central mother person, addressed him or did something for him. Whenever the central person left, part of Joshua's sense of self dwindled, and he became anxious.

In the many instances where the symbiosis with the mother was extended too long, the organism did not perfect many of its own ego functions. Instead, the mother or mother-surrogate was permitted, often accompanied by unconscious hostility, to take over. As a result, the ego experience is tenuous, the ego functions are imprecisely carried out, and the individual whose ego did the leaning on a parental figure suffers lack of integration. After all, part of the ego experiences are self-developed and part are borrowed from another person. Inevitably, confusion, anxiety and pleas for assistance are the result of such lack of integration.

Of course, persons who allow themselves to fall back on plea passivity to overcome the hurdles of their life need to discover through the help of interpretations and confrontations how much they live on borrowed strengths and skills. Many are surprised to discover that the perpetual anxiety they feel derives from the fact that they are not the drivers of their own psychic vehicles but allow and, indeed, invite others to occupy the driver's seat. It is important not to answer many of the questions which such patients ask but to refer the questions back to the patient with emphasis on the fact that answers should be found through self-search, through investigation of the environment, and through practicing many neglected and fuzzy ego functions. If patients then wonder just what they should practice, it is well worthwhile to make mental maps together with them rather than to repeat that they lack skills and endurance.

Justin lost his well-to-do father when he was 35 and felt as though he were a little boy left alone. Aware of his dependency on the dead parent who had been not only father but also mother to him, he kept reiterating: "I know how lost I feel, how passive and awkward I am, but I don't know how to get out of it." With his father dead, older family members and acquaintances overwhelmed Justin with suggestions of how to conduct his financial and professional affairs, because his boyish behavior invited such advice. When Justin wondered in treatment whether a certain young woman loved him, I answered: "I am waiting to hear whether *you* love her." He replied with astonishment: "I never thought of that. I always want to know whether they [the others] love me." I suggested that he turn the question around and that he immediately line up questions about how he felt about the girl friend. I pointed out that in the transference he was always worried whether I liked *him,* and that it was time to confront precisely and clearly just what he liked or disliked about *me.* When Justin reported how kind somebody had been to him, I thereafter asked how he liked that person. The emphasis was on making his own feelings more delineated and helping him to overcome his fear of having dislikes and being punished for them and of taking the part of the adult and being called to task about that.

Sensing the tendency of these seemingly docile patients to find fault with the therapist and to look for substitutes when the favors they request are not granted, the therapist must watch out for countertransference feelings of too much caution and tolerance.

People with plea passivity will not improve unless challenged by others who genuinely want them to achieve maturity and self-sufficiency. What makes this sometimes difficult is the dependent and masochistic patient's occasional regression from plea passivity (that is, excessive demandingness) to barrier passivity (that is, injurious withdrawal). Such regressions may be genuine, in which case it becomes important to make clear that there exist only good will and care in therapy. Yet, at other times, they are a form of blackmail to test the therapist's strength and endurance, in which case it is important to remain firm in the demand that the patient help himself. Passive people want to take the easy way out. If we prepare them and encourage them to undertake steps that are difficult, they gain activeness.

HOSTILE PASSIVITY

When children are not permitted to individuate, to discover and try out their own ways, and thereby to establish the nuclei of their individuality and selfhood, they turn to rebellion. In the face of strong parental pressure and authoritarianism, the rebellion cannot be risked openly and goes underground. It takes on the form of passive resistance, sulking, reluctance to cooperate, and tenacious negativism that is not outspoken but appears in the form of doubts, inability to hear or understand, and general denseness. Behind a facade of bland quiescence, veritable vendettas are carried on through repeated "say nothing, do nothing, feel nothing" behavior. There is refusal to participate, to communicate.

Such forms of passivity represent punishment, a subversive and negative form of individuation, and often outlast the patience of even the most well-intentioned people. The distress which hostile passivity and the silent strike of "say nothing, do nothing, feel nothing" evokes is great and sensed though not readily identified by the very persons against whom the hostile passivity is brought to bear. Actually, passive-hostile behavior renders a social or work atmosphere inflexible and arrests humor and the quick exchange of ideas. Plans and initiative are easily brought to a standstill because the non-participation of the hostile-passive resister defeats teamwork in such subversive ways that those who are afflicted do not know what has happened to deflate their enthusiasm.

Another form of getting even with the environment through hostile passivity is sulking. Sulking is designed to deprive others of the psychological presence and the contributions which the angry sulker feels he or she is capable of making, but withholds in order to punish people who are seen in a role that denies individuation and independence. At the same time, persons who sulk and who usually assign a great deal of omnipotence to themselves, fear that were they to open up, their ideas would be deemed insignificant. Hence, this sullen passivity has two functions: to deprive the world, which is seen as withholding respect and denying the right of individuation, of the important contributions which the sulkers fancy they could make, and yet also to hide a feared ineffectiveness behind the cloud of silence.

Passive-hostile patients are helped when one allows them to carry out their vendettas without getting angry with them. If therapists understand that the patient's hostile-passive behavior originates in the wish for a reverse kind of independence and express, with or without words, that the defiance expressed does not disturb them, the patient eventually begins to cooperate. In this way, the biggest obstacle in these treatments is overcome, namely the conscious and stubborn resistance to accepting any communication or help. Patients recognize that, in the absence of objection to their self-assertion, they need sulk no longer by way of a more or less continuously negative and uncooperative attitude. Once the encompassing hostile passivity and noncooperation have been given up, at least temporarily in the treatment situation because patients have no opponent to punch but rather an ally who support the cause of their silent rebellion, therapy can proceed. Gradually, the long-term reasons that originally caused the hostile passivity and the ego deficiencies which require its continuation can be examined and understood, and corrections made. Indeed, to help a passive-hostile person to perk up and begin to work in therapy can be a most rewarding experience.

This chapter about passivity has been presented in order to illustrate how we can examine a particular form of pathology by proceeding along two tracks which always need to be followed in conjunction with one another. Track I pursues the various forms of malfunctioning for which passive tendencies are responsible. Specifically, it was shown how similar symptoms—the dependent, pleading, shy passivity, the hostile passivity, etc.—must be traced back to disturbances at different levels of development and that these passive stances, while outwardly looking fairly similar, fulfill divergent functions. Track II examines the angles of treatment, the specific emphasis in therapy that needs to be pursued in order to dislodge or, better yet, make superfluous the basically destructive functions which the various passive stances aim to accomplish.

Divergent forms of malfunctioning call for different emphasis and strategy in treatment if they are to be cured. Not only will the interpretations vary, as has always been assumed, but additional techniques, employed together with interpretations, will have to be brought into alignment with the problems that are being tackled. It is my contention that dynamic psychotherapy has been too exclusively preoccupied with psychodynamics and pathology and has neglected to ask questions and find answers as to how changes in psychic structure can be achieved so that healing occurs. As a result, we have come to know a great deal about how certain unhealthy conditions have come into being. The next wave of questions will have to deal with the all-important aspects of "working through," i.e., how to carve out alterations of and additions to the psychic structure. The great issue is what are the steps of cure and of creating better psychological futures for human beings.

8

The Personal
Contributions
of the Therapist

Many discoveries in the fields of ego psychology, developmental psychology, communications, and learning theory need to be amalgamated with the concepts and techniques which classical psychoanalysis has contributed. This amalgamation is happening right now and can be subsumed under the heading of a dynamic psychotherapy. The result is not as yet and may never become a unified approach. The essential thing is a comprehensive treatment, conducted by one therapist. Towards this goal the patient-therapist team views the different periods of life as intrinsically connected and strives for change and growth rather than settling for insight alone. Yet, within this comprehensive course of treatment certain disturbances might be singled out as calling for a special method of cure and various specialists who have particular experience may be called on by the principal therapist for interventions and help. I have found that within a comprehensive treatment process an exposure to, say, assertiveness training or to methods designed to deal with projective identification can have value.

Amalgams of different, but usually related concepts and different treatment procedures lack the elegance of the method that grows out of a single coherent system—but they do work. This is particularly true if the principal therapist is familiar with and has had personal exposure to classical psychoanalysis but is thoroughly acquainted with other philosophies of treatment. For example, anyone adopting the amalgam will ascribe at least as much importance to the impact which the pre-Oedipal years have on adult personality functioning as to the Oedipal years, stretching roughly from four to six or even seven. Indeed, an amalgam outlook will most likely claim that the manner in which the environment affected the earliest development of the baby and child—in other words, the impact of the pre-Oedipal years upon the personality—will in turn influence how the person deals with the Oedipal situation. The child handles sexual-genital, envy, and mutuality problems, as well as the relation with each parent, in a manner deeply affected by the baby years. A highly symbiotic child, for instance, conducts the new conflicts and the love relationship to either parent in more confused ways, remaining stuck in the poorly conceived delineation between self and mother, self and others.

As to techniques, we assume that insight into problems that have been repressed or have remained poorly delineated (they were never clearly conscious) is not enough, even when a good deal of elaboration has been accomplished. Only when *ego-building is combined more or less continuously with insight, sometimes preceding it, does change occur*. Ego-building refers, for instance, to the flexibility of the ego boundaries. Where these are primitively stiff, as though made of blocks of concrete, expressions of affection are difficult, and a negativistic stance is preferred. Affection makes the ego system soft and melting, a disagreeable condition for persons with brittle boundaries. They prefer to stay aloof. Another illustration may be seen in disturbed persons, even where we do not apply the diagnosis of borderline state, who use projection to some degree. They cannot get rid of their own criticisms of the self unless they steer the blame outward—to a spouse, an offspring, an employer. Whether we trace this problem back to a split between good and bad other, to the working of the defense mechanism of projection, or to the severity of the superego, insight will not "take" unless the projective situation is altered through some ego change. One type of solution is to assure persons about to project that they might be critical of *a variety of things, of human objects, of concrete situations, of possessions*. This can become a prelude for shedding the projective trend. It becomes clear that what matters is the distinction between inside and outside and not a special antagonist who has done one in. The ego polarity between the good inside and the bad outside becomes eventually a matter of ready acceptance instead of immediate and prolonged gravity. What I am emphasizing here is that the utilization of the most precious insights, the so-called "working through," can occur only if ego building proceeds simultaneously or even predates the collection and examination of insights.

Ego modifications are acquired through psychological learning and practice, especially in the arena of transference. If and when group psychotherapy is used, the scope of the new encounters and practices is greatly widened by the additional multiple transferences to the group members. The therapist is a new encounter figure, as are the group members. When this becomes quite clear, many old relationship habits that cloud new encounters are cleared up.

It appears in the light of many observations of dynamic psychotherapy that certain psychological problems can be eliminated through the use of processes particularly developed to cope with these conflicts, problems, ego arrests, and far-reaching confusions. This is done in the course of a comprehensive treatment program by focusing technically on more or less delineated problem areas. Among the varying brief courses for assertiveness training, some are highly effective if sufficiently based on the principles of deeper dynamics to constitute valuable contributions to a comprehensive dynamic psychotherapy.

I have found it effective to use several series of experiences that further the growth of self-esteem, interpolating them at various way stations of extended, dynamically oriented psychotherapy. For instance, in the case of a patient with serious self-esteem deficiencies, we discovered how strongly the self-doubts were related to a kind of cognitive omnipotence. The patient, a woman, could feel reasonably safe in her own esteem only if she was able to give evidence of mastering knowledge in whatever field was the subject of discussion. If she had lunch with friends who were art collectors, she lost her composure as soon as she had to concede to herself that her own familiarity with art history was limited. If she read a book in her own field, namely law, she got restless and put the book aside if a concept she had not mastered was discussed, for this made the book distasteful for her. As far as the forerunners of this cognitive omnipotence were concerned, suffice it to say that she had been disciplined early in every physical and intellectual way possible; as a result, she was alternately compulsive and impulsive, and had been forced into the role of a superior college student despite her own decided preferences for play and fun.

I urged this patient, who was placed eventually in combined group and individual therapy, to tell frankly of any gap in knowledge as soon as she spotted a whiff of ignorance. In this her eyelids helped, which during incidences of ignorance fluttered excessively. I urged the group members, on such occasions, to level with the young lawyer about the state of their own knowledge, embarrassment or ease. Such clearings of the decks were helpful. Depressions and rages connected with the discovery of cognitive defect did not assume a disproportionate size. The primitive urge to have power over everybody, which this patient tried to exercise by the ability to know everthing, was whittled down gradually as this clever and competitive lawyer exposed her need for cognitive omnipotence. Step by step, as she articulated the wish to be top dog in every situation and make that ambition safe by way of supreme knowledge, the dizzying size of both her urges and defenses was reduced. The patient discovered with relief that one need not make a secret of gigantic ambition and of equally large-sized defensive maneuvers. It became much more comfortable, less tenuous, and eventually relaxing to use as an outlet open expressiveness, playfulness, and games of exchange, for to let peers know how high one aspires can assume the nature of a special game.

THERAPEUTIC SKILL AND PERSONAL VERSATILITY

For the therapist who practices a dynamic form of treatment, some primary aims are to help mediate active insight; to contribute towards the taming and refinement of aggression (the term is used as an allusion to the process which converts the raw oil from the well into products that produce energy); to facilitate the building of self-esteem and the acquiring of psychological know-how. Practice plays as important a role as the achievement of the first glimpses of insight. Yet *no single form* of discovery and transformation plays *the exclusive role*.

In the assembly of therapeutic tools other than insight, the judgment of the therapist-in-charge plays an essential role. Patients who make their own assemblage run the risk of proceeding in wildly eclectic rather than prudently selective ways. A woman told a therapist who had helped her greatly that, wishing to proceed at an even faster rate, she was going to add certain methods of her own. When the patient came to one of her appointments three weeks later, she was exhausted, tearful, and highly anxious. It was apparent that she had overtaxed herself and exceeded a necessary level of resistance.

In keeping with the traditional ways, dynamic psychotherapy differentiates defensive strategies, often in the form of personality traits, from underlying problems which cannot be ameliorated unless the overlay of defenses is understood, softened, and in some measure altered. Among important goals of such dynamic psychotherapy is the achievement of spontaneity and capacities for creative, that is variable and renewable, forms of relating and living. These aims do not dispense with the need to make certain adjustments to existing external circumstances, as psychotherapists recommended excessively in the 1940s and 1950s. But they give more leeway to the individual in deciding which circumstances are going to be considered alterable and which not. Altogether, we have new ideas about a desirable proportion between defensive (which is partially adjusting) behavior and the expression of straight urges and self-needs and active and immediate psychological pursuits.

We demand that defensive structures be subordinated to or quantitatively less prominent than structures supporting straight, active, and immediate psychological pursuits which flow forward in a relatively unhampered manner and are part and parcel of the creative life. In modern dynamic psychotherapy, we are not satisfied to make the surface layer of the psyche, that is the symptoms, less oppressive. We aim for deeper changes which will alter the motivations for behavior, and the structures on which the person relies. The difficulties are seen to consist not only of conflicts but equally of ego and self arrests and deformations that linger on. Take a male who complains incessantly about the women he has chosen as lovers and who prove disappointing. Not only is this man viewed as torn by a conflict between love and hostility, but his dilemma is also evaluated from the point of view of ego psychology. He continually talks about his beloved one and complains because his ego and self have remained weak and dependent. He demands that the female lover play a caretaking role. The man cannot speak of his own self or rectify his self-needs because the self is so shadowy that it is not experienced as an independent structure. It is felt to be an appendix to a bigger and firmer other self. To get better, the unhappy lover has to become a much more defined, active, and individuated person whose self finds pleasure in satisfying his own and other people's needs and foregoes the help of mother figure protectors.

It is often appropriate for the therapist to inform patients what is wrong with some of the psychological structure, which relieves them of the painstaking effort of making their own diagnosis. This makes available important energies for the tasks of changing the dislocations responsible for their difficulties while still allowing for discoveries of important connections between related problems. Understanding what is wrong is usually an indispensable prerequisite for change, but it is not necessarily the responsibility of the patient. Many therapists articulate successfully the conflicts and especially the ego deficits that handicap feelings and behavior; then they go on to blueprint some of the corrections that will enable the ego to grow. As a rule, persons who suffer from ego deficits and distortions are glad to turn to suggested reparatory experiences and to flex and exercise unused psychic muscle. After all, one reason for earlier resistances, though not the only one, is the inability to have a coherent perception of what is wrong and to envision corrections.

Dynamic psychotherapy, as conceived here, agrees that problems which got the patient started on the twisted and abortive feelings, structures, and behavior had their beginnings in the past. But an equally essential assumption is that the prime reasons for erroneous and abortive attempts to get away from old crises, frictions, and failures are found in the legacy of injurious imprints upon the psyche. Though made in the past, these imprints are highly influential in the present in the form of ego and self arrests, malformations, and imbalances between the defensive and the straight structures. Also, there have survived erroneous assumptions about what constitute creative transactions between human beings, what are ultimately satisfying goals, and what is a valid psychological reality. Dynamic psychotherapy gives great attention to the present-day inner psychological reality. If some persons, for example, assume that the *only course of rescue* for them is forming an alliance with a powerful authority figure, while they alternate between idealizing and devaluing their own self, then what has to be changed are the images (representations) of others and self *as they interact right now*. That some grave disappointments in the past are responsible for current problems is important and worthwhile knowing about. But in itself, such understanding does not bring about a cure. The essential turnabout comes from giving up the ill-fated search for the protective and idealized parental figure and developing new forms of relating in the immediate transference with the therapist.

Another big step towards health and strength is taken when patients get rid of their confused self-images (the self-representations of which the abusive parent is a part) and base their inner life and henceforth their total conduct on structures that are in the making in the psychological laboratory which therapy offers. Dynamic psychotherapy is concerned with clearing the ground and getting rid of false foundations so that new structures may be built up gradually. The removal of the debris need not precede the formation of fresh processes. Often, individuals come to understand how useless their old fittings are when they have already begun to assemble new psychological outfits. Understanding and dismissal of old, erroneous ways are often prompted by looking back from the vantage point of newly accomplished ascensions.

When the notion is dismissed that injuries occasioned in the past by parents and parent surrogates are the present-day reason for disturbed behavior, anxieties and depressions from which individuals are suffering in the here-and-now (Perls, 1973), a reorientation takes place which demands a good deal of sturdiness from the therapist. As soon as the step to the immediate present is taken, many patients give up their habits of projecting their doubts and angers on the parents of yesteryear. From now on they project their dissatisfactions and frustrations on the persons with whom they have immediate dealings, amongst whom the therapist is conspicuous. Knowing that the therapist wishes to help the patients to acquire a well-functioning psyche, the patients find the experiences of the observing ego and of the neurotic ego to be at odds. The observing ego wishes to maintain the conviction that the therapist is an ally while the neurotic ego is ever ready to blame and reproach. The cure-bound therapist must be willing to receive a good deal of fault-finding and rage in order to give patients chances to discover that they can be angry without being punished, and that they can integrate and combine angry feelings which now take shape with their loving feelings, thus becoming broadened personalities. A healthy person creates transition between these two extreme emotions where a passive, narcissistic, and masochistic individual gets stuck in one or the other extreme. The sturdy therapist who is able and willing to be the recipient of anger will soon be rewarded by the friendly feelings that come not because patients are working with reaction formations or are compelled to pacify, but because they sense a relief that comes with being spontaneous and expressing everything. In the final event, the other reproaches recede into the background and relationships between patients and therapists became friendly, hopeful, and very open.

We do much to facilitate chances for patients to relate to therapists as new objects and thus to shed transferences, which are among the most noxious imprints of the past upon the personality of the present. It is not enough to stick to a review of false carry-over expectations, fears, grandiose expectations, and the like. It is considered important to facilitate innovative experiences. These patients become aware of the self-defeating, routine, and clumsy adaptations to which they have clung. They are also asked to try out in life itself new adaptations which are more creative, more gratifying and self-supporting, and which have been discovered in trial performances with the new objects. Not only, therefore, do they get a chance to recognize what their transference reactions are, but they are also led beyond them. They can move from rage to contact and affection (hence from inaccessibility to interaction), from prejudicial stances to open welcome of new situations, all this in an experiential form, that is to say *not by talking about possibilities and maybes* but by trying them on in the therapeutic situation proper. This demands a good deal of sturdiness from the therapist as well as an ability to be active and spontaneous rather than reactive. No matter what the patient confers on the therapist, the latter has to retain the initiative and behave spontaneously. Logic is not always, nor even usually, the required therapeutic contribution. Especially after the very first stage of treatment some non sequiturs stimulate and amuse patients who discover that their therapeutic partner has the strength to stay outside their influence, which is gradually discovered to be noxious.

Dynamic psychotherapy is concerned as much with actual, direct, psychological expansion and enrichment as with self-understanding. It is not primarily an interpretive discipline but above all a therapeutic one. The prime desire is growth, with clarification seen as an essential aspect of change (Turkle, 1978). In this sense, the dynamic psychotherapist is a pragmatist with the explicit goal of helping to change human behavior by altering internal psychological realities such as the balance between defenses and the immediate psychic structures, self-esteem, and readiness to entertain relations with other human objects. Self-understanding is an intermediate step but not the ultimate goal, which is equally the result of "working through" or psychic alteration.

When a patient who was reluctant to be alone was helped to understand that he was narcissistically empty and therefore needed continuous contact with others, this did not suffice to make aloneness more tolerable. He had to acquire in addition a vivid self-image and object ties through active loving. The self-image of a connection-seeking and connection-making person, buttressed by memories of past encounters and anticipation of future human encounters lent the tinge of aliveness to the experience of being alone. Aloneness no longer meant that the self faded away, or that the man lived in an objectless world.

Surprise interventions, surprise happenings, good-natured provocation, and, in general, a puncturing of the defensive structures are emphasized by dynamic therapy. This happens when the therapist or, in case group therapy is used, a group member makes an encounter startling, thereby making it clear to the patient how rigidified and nonsensical are his or her habitual ways. Through unexpected challenges, made not to ridicule a person with rigid adaptations but to shake up old, static, and hence maladaptive responses which cannot cope with life, habitual ways are brought to a halt. They are thrown into relief and examined rather than taken for granted; thereafter, they are often discarded. Again, one purpose is to intensify awareness that the individual deals in therapy with figures that are new and different from the old cast of characters.

Some of the remarks or actions designed to puncture defenses or long-standing assumptions and rituals are very simple. This happens, for instance, if a patient asks timidly whether the therapist would sign an insurance form. A blunt or funny reply is a useful eye-opener. I often say jokingly, "Of course not," as I reach for the pen. The patient understands the communication immediately and usually with relief. The signature is not a favor and the therapist is not some mighty authority figure to be approached cautiously. Indeed, such authority figures do not exist at all in adult life, and hence the notion that one must be ingratiating or careful stems from the way the cast of the past behaved; now a modernization in human relationships is due. Or, if a patient plagued by memories of all too vulnerable or inadequate parents asks cautious questions in order to establish whether I am tolerant, strong, or capable enough to deal with him, I remark: "It's okay to check me out."

On-the-spot innovative responses occurring within the therapeutic meeting take on special significance because they make the patient aware that he is dealing with someone new and different from the old figures. Thus, interactions between therapist and patient assume great importance and there exists not only a permission and tolerance for but indeed an encouragement of questions, expressed doubts, anger, and fears.

In the light of the discoveries made by ego psychology about human development during the earliest years of life, many severe and lingering disorders are viewed as deficit phenomena. They are the consequences of regressions or arrests undertaken because the environment did not encourage developmental steps forward. This happens when, on account of parental impatience or threats, exploratory behavior is arrested. As a result, clinging takes over once more, along with other forms of primitive attachment behavior that had already been in the decline (Bowlby, 1973). But the clinging is reversible when the accessibility of an essential figure is clearly demonstrated.

Other disorders are evident as the result of repetitive "forcing behavior" that the child uses intuitively in order either to fight for attention or to avoid the breakthrough of some urge perceived as dangerous, such as rage. Forcing behavior is in a line with the nature of obsession and consists of repeating certain muscle spasms, words, or motoric activity designed to make something happen or not happen. To give an illustration of forcing behavior, the child might sit by the entrance door of the home which the mother has left, hoping that the protracted act of waiting will "make her return." Many ego rigidities are the outgrowth of such forcing behavior.

This forcing behavior, the prototype of many forms of character rigidity and of obsessive-compulsive symptoms, can also be reversed. This happens in childhood if the mother becomes aware what the time limit of tolerating her absence is and shortens her absences. In the case of an older child, the mother helps if she designates on a clock the number which the hand will reach to announce her return home. In adult therapy, the gradual build-up of anticipation skills proves salutary. Many of the shortcomings of disturbed personalities, be they in the category of neurotic malfunctioning, borderline disorders, or psychotic afflictions, are the result of correctible ego and self-arrest caused not by occasional trauma but by continuous environmental failure to nurture psychological growth during the sensitive earliest years. In order to set in motion gradually progressing growth, the patient, together with the therapist, envisages intuitively and cognitively images of new formations that are to be attained. Both parties of the therapeutic team, the patient and the trainer-therapist, participate jointly to discover and practice the emotional-cognitive-psychological steps and sequences that initiate new developments.

A woman who suffered painfully from jealousy and fears that her husband, who was often away on business trips, might find someone else, said: "Gradually I realized that to concentrate on jealousies while he is away and forcing him to account for his moves when he returns is a form of collusion that we both practice. It is a collusion in the realm of fear and under the pressure of a form of 'forcing' I practice. Instead, I now train myself to ask him to express love when he feels it. I tell him not to let me inquisition him. I do not deny that he is away and that he might find another woman attractive. But then, instead of continuing my negative speculations, fears, and my 'forcing with muscles and thoughts,' instead of staying with him, I make a turn. I go outward and explore the world around. I try to discover a new food store or plant shop. And I make myself search out my own skills. This turn away from suspicions about *him* to outward explorations and to plans for lovemaking between him and *me,* this turn, that we discussed in therapy, really works. I learned something that is absolutely fundamental. If I shift from me, the victim, to me, the scout, I get grown up. 'Poor me' is hogwash, but me the doer, explorer, and arranger is good.''

The message that psychological potency is found when the person discovers and uses the "me," the "himself," or the "herself" leads easily to a form of confusion. If the "me generation" appears to pursue primarily selfish aims, it does so not because the turn to the "me" has been accomplished in the spirit of self-affirmation described here, but because the preoccupation is still with *other* people and *emotional supplies.* The dependency on them has not been overcome at all. On the contrary, the main idea is to exploit others in order for the "me" to float above deep waters. By contrast, people who make the right kind of shift to the self become less selfish, more independent, and more preoccupied with questions as to how increased powers of the self can be used on behalf of other people. Misunderstood, the message of self-discovery reads: I must get others to help poor me. Properly interpreted, the gist is: If I develop my true emotions and my psychological know-how, then I am no longer in danger and need not depend on others; instead I can love and cherish them.

A PROMISING APPROACH TO NARCISSISTIC INACCESSIBILITY

Young organisms whose need to progress from a state of enclosure in the narcissistic cocoon to contact with the world is ignored or even thwarted by the parents, especially by the mother, slide into a fallback position of inaccessibility and isolation. They are not energized, nor do they learn the know-how of moving on to the exploration of the world and to contact with other human objects. When a disinterested and self-involved mother fails to go through the seemingly small but highly important steps that establish and teach contact-making (Bowlby, 1970), the offspring intensifies the withdrawal from the world rather than beginning to approach, explore, and love it.

To reverse this narcissistic inaccessibility, the personal participation of the therapist is absolutely necessary. Specifically, the reparatory experiences which, of course, will be mingled with explanations and interpretations on specific occasions, consist of supplying attention to the psychological life of the patient and to the highly idiosyncratic ways in which each individual expresses emotional needs and responses. Inaccessible patients usually wish to watch the expressions on their therapist's face in order to check out whether signs of attention can be detected. Their query, "Are you listening?" is expressed in the many efforts made to capture especially the expression in the therapist's eyes. They are reassured when details of previous sessions are recalled by the therapist, when dreams told some time ago are referred to, and when their own contradictions are brought to their attention in a matter-of-fact way. They definitely need answers to many questions which they pose, usually with misgivings lest they be dismissed.

Relying frequently, as we shall see, on a false self, narcissistically inaccessible patients who are masters at pseudo-relationships are relieved, though also angered, when they encounter evidence that their therapists cannot be bribed or misled by false pretenses. Their trust and hope—the therapeutically most important emotions—grow as they become more convinced that their weak and fragmented self is recognized, and when they learn to make more spontaneous responses. While naturally clinging to defenses which rely heavily on charm, appearance and talent, assets vulnerable to the dents that passing time makes, they nevertheless give a sigh of relief if they discover that their fragility is also recognized.

The reparatory attention experiences which the therapist provides can be absorbed, integrated, and internalized only if they are repeated frequently over an extended period of time. At the beginning, the patients are inclined to confuse the reparatory processes, namely the repeated attentions extended to their idiosyncratically expressed emotional needs, with the personality of the therapist. What the patient mistakenly treasures and even idolizes is the person of the therapist who is the source of the newly-discovered and much craved emotional attention. In such often repeated instances, it is important to stress *it is what happens and not who makes it happen* that matters.

A very narcissistic woman, who needed isolation to a degree where she locked her lovely home to anyone who was not a member of her innermost family, became able to come out of her shell during the first seven months of treatment. Greatly encouraged, she sent a generous gift to the therapist who thanked her warmly but asked her to keep the present. The patient, insisting on acceptance of the gift, exclaimed: "When you have given life itself to me, why can I not give you something beautiful?" I told her that the process of change had given her the newly-found entrée to life. I remarked that she might decide to use this process forever, but not to confuse it with my person. She did understand.

By helping patients who are the victims of the deeply pathological narcissistic state to absorb or, as we say, incorporate the process of obtaining attention, relishing the experience, and seeking it out in the external world, therapists help to mitigate narcissistic strongholds. Though the majority of narcissistically isolated and inaccessible patients do not initially experience their cocoon condition as alien but come with complaints of depression and boredom, at best *they will bemoan the fact that they do not know what they want,* proclaiming thereby that theirs is a condition of all-consuming and yet not specified neediness. The reason is that the urges, curiosities, and sensitivities of the real self, which has remained underdeveloped and crippled, are buried and remain fragile under a mass of narcissistic defensive formations. Thus, the self of the narcissistic person registers as insignificant, worthless, and wounded, while the narcisissistic defenses, designed to hide the self-deficiencies, register flamboyantly as egotism, exhibitionism, vanity, and contempt of others. Invariably, it is the task of the therapist to distinguish between the wounds of the self and the narcissistic defenses so as to offer experiences which will strengthen the crippled self.

The emphasis belongs on the deepest layer of the narcissistic wounds and not the upper layer of the narcissistic defenses. Often, narcissistic patients have become so confused that they regard their defenses as the true self and have become alienated from the insignificant true self. Again, it is the emphasis which the therapist supplies that changes this unhealthy balance until the patients eventually recognize that it is their isolation and encompassing feeling of worthlessness that cause the comprehensive displeasure with life which often assumes suicidal proportions. As the afflicted individuals shift their attention from the narcissistic defenses of flamboyance and self-involvement to their loneliness and low self-esteem, the defenses gradually weaken and the self begins to emerge more fully. Since the defenses are particularly likely to alienate other persons while the patient's orphan status is likely to attract compassion, the reversal of emphasis from defenses to neglected self is likely to lead to a series of encouraging startles. The narcissistic patients discover that they are surrounded by well-wishers after all.

The mothers of persons who are narcissistically confined are themselves often narcissistic, while the fathers are often absentee figures. As a result, parental capacity or willingness to engage the child in simple, playful partnering is absent. This lack of the playful partnering that is a forerunner of later mutuality has even more significance than the failure of the child to experience sufficient empathy (Kohut, 1977). Partnering, initiated by the mother on behalf of her child, means that the two build up innocuous stimulus-response sequences which are repeated several times. This calls for a maternal patience which the mothers of narcissists don't have since they are only quasi-mothers with a good deal of reliance on automatic placation (pacifiers, rocking, sweet treats) to take the place of close attention to the child's idiosyncratic, unique expressions of inner physiological and emotional needs. To illustrate, a mother who initiates and herself enjoys partnering hands the child a doll. The child drops the doll, the mother picks it up and hands it to the child, who drops it again. The mother again picks the doll up and returns it to the child, who starts to smile, amused and reassured by the dependability of little exchanges which it now learns to anticipate. The little sequence is repeated again and again. Such interactions are important because they represent the first concretization of duality and the first willed interchanges with the environment. Moreover, they are the forerunners of anticipation.

Mothers incapable of emotional attention satisfy basic physiological needs but do little to initiate such forerunners of reciprocity. They ignore the idiosyncratic ways in which the child's psychological demands are expressed and fail to observe variations in the intensity and rhythm of behavior, though they may engage in indiscriminate joshing and hugging which is irritating rather than pleasurable.

This description aims to fill in some details of what Kohut describes as the need for empathic responsiveness (Kohut, 1977) which, if thwarted, survives as an encompassing hunger for attention later in life. A 38-year-old patient expressed her sentiments in these words: "I don't want more fantasies if I can get your attention. I want it all the time. I watch every muscle in your face to find out whether you are with me a hundred percent. If I don't get your attention, I feel insecure and tighten my muscles to force your attention in my direction. My fear is to be alone, adrift, a single, small, empty buoy on the sea." The fact that narcissistic patients are astounded and delighted when some insignificant detail they had reported is remembered later in therapy seems proof of their extraordinary need for emotional attention to idiosyncratically expressed needs. Conversely, even relatively small inattentions can cause gradual lapses into silence, withdrawal, and slight depression; they may present a problem for treatment unless these defenses are explored.

An arrest at the narcissistic level or retreat to it, and with that a considerable inaccessibility to many forms of contact, is also found amongst individuals who do get parental attention, but of a selfish kind. Such persons, often particularly attractive, talented, or otherwise exceptional, are fussed over by an early environment whose attention is self-seeking and given to expectation of vicarious returns. Such environmental courting has none of the selfless and enduring attention which young organisms urgently need. The mothers of child prodigies and their special children are illustrations of such teams of enchanters and enchanted; upon acquaintance one can often observe the emptiness, loneliness, and rage which are felt by the young. Often, the talented offspring use suicidal ideation to express the rage felt, the intent being to deprive the exploitative parent of the source of vicarious pride. It is not infrequent that the prodigy acts out the suicidal fantasy and sometimes succeeds in taking his own life.

If the therapist becomes impressed with the assets of specially talented patients who know how to impress people and ply their attention-seeking charms during treatment, then it is urgent to nip in the bud such interlockings of transference-countertransference reactions. Otherwise, patients remain stuck in the narcissistic deadlock which has caught them in a vicious cycle of seduction and exploitation. A serious working attitude on the part of the therapist is the prime personal contribution to be made. This helps the patient to believe in the half-welcome, half-painful truth that the basis for trust and stability is work rather than the counterfeit coin of charm and the admiration which it can garner. The reparatory experiences in these cases consist of the therapist's emphasis on earnest work in treatment and an immunity to charm, wit, and seduction.

The personality who is steeped in narcissistic self-involvement was considered for a long time to be as inaccessible to treatment as it was immune to other influences. This pessimistic viewpoint changed when it was discovered that anger and rage experiences make for bridges to reality. When therapists mobilize the patient's anger and rage in the transference (Spotnitz and Meadow, 1976) and patients discover that they are not punished for such supposed infringements, they can utilize their hostile feelings to puncture the cocoon that keeps them enclosed. It follows, then, that any therapist who wishes to make accessible to narcissistic patients the road of contact and communication must be willing to subject himself or herself to vehement outbursts.

A woman so isolated that she only leaves her spic and span little loft to go to work, upon coming home shuts the door against the world and then submerges herself in the stupor of television noises. During her yearly medical check-up, it was found that she had a growth on her breast. It took some time for a diagnosis to be made. She called me during the week-end and asked for an appointment, which I gave her at the first opportunity. When she came to the office, she started to scream that I, like the rest of the world, did not care whether she lived or died or else I would have given her the appointment a few hours after she called.

She threatened to walk out the door and never return, but finally sat down again. With tears streaming down her face and her chest heaving with the exhaustion of her violent accusations, she said, "I know I got heard now. The screams bring me back to life." No matter that this patient had not expressed her need for immediate and tangible attention much more clearly when she called in a rather nonchalant way. She had found a connection with life and me through the rage she launched at me. This was borne out in subsequent sessions.

Many reparatory interventions offer the patient opportunities to redirect, amplify, and strengthen inner structures by way of participating in human interchanges—in this case between analyst and analysand—which were not available and forthcoming when psychic development went through the first rounds of growth. In a way, it is like offering a plant that grew up without sufficient sunlight and nutrient soil the previously missed abundances of nature. As we know, if the dosing and care are good, many a plant catches up with its predestined growth even though the timetable is belated. To offer reparatory experiences such as putting up with patients' angers, paying attention to the idiosyncratic expression of emotional needs, not permitting oneself to be bribed by charm but insisting on disciplined mutual cooperation and making distinctions between psychic wounds and the defenses against them means that the therapist must use the diagnostic skills he learned, such as distinguishing between need and defense structures, a differentiation particularly important in the treatment of individuals with "tenuous self awareness" who readily confuse interpretation with attack (Nelson, 1968).

In offering reparatory experiences, therapists need not put on a role or twist themselves around artificially (Alexander and French, 1946). Rather, therapists who attribute great therapeutic value to *experience* need to be more or less continually aware of the processes that go on in the patient. This calls for brief identifications *which are used on behalf of the analysand.* It demands an honest and immediate admission of the feelings stirred up in the form of countertransferences and the willingness to use these sentiments as the basis for helping the analysand to reveal what he or she feels and to make corrections through the emerging interchanges.

During his or her working hours, the well-intentioned and trained therapist gets satisfaction from making his or her own personality available to the other person. This is no different from many other professions. The good teacher gets his satisfaction from selecting and molding his experiences in such a manner that they are of service to the student. The fine actor uses the instrument of his own personality on behalf of the role he has agreed to perform. The destination of therapists is to utilize their personality in the service of helping others to grow. We never think or say, "You should have done this or that." Instead, we indicate how this or that can be accomplished now and in the future.

DEPRESSION AND ENABLING

Low-level or middle-range depressions often elude the persons afflicted by them who merely feel a general malaise and sense of widespread disinterest. They blame this comprehensive discontent on some debilitating effects which environmental shortcomings have. Only when the condition deteriorates very drastically is there a sharp recognition both by the individual and the environment that the person's moods, level of activeness, and general psychological condition are pathological. No longer does the person turn up his nose at the world with a sense of vague displeasure, but instead there is a deep, painful, and distinctive sadness. The state of disinterest that previously prevailed and is often ascribed to unsatisfactory external conditions (such as exist in every life, of course) has clearly deteriorated into near total withdrawal. The patient is convinced that he or she is too shy, too worthless, and indeed incapable of making contacts.

When such a deterioration occurs to the point that it can be called a *depressive plunge,* certain therapeutic measures, combined with an attitude of firmness on the part of the therapist, can accomplish reversals that often appear miraculous. To pull the patient out of the apathy, the deep sadness, the despair, passivity, and masochism which in varying degrees are part processes of the depressive plunge, the *therapist must be willing and able to assume an active approach* and to postpone explorations of the past and the predecessors of depressive positions. On the contrary, the chief task is to mobilize the feelings, the self, and the ego, which requires both an adoption of activeness though not authoritarianism on the part of the therapist, mixed with special therapeutic techniques that will be described.

Therapists must be prepared and willing to draw on all their capacities for "enabling."* In their role as enablers, therapists draw on their own positive observations. They have taken note of the feelings, capacities, and valuable psychological processes that represent assets but are dismissed by patients because they are found too insignificant and worthless, or perhaps because they are associated with some family figure who was destructive or regarded as such. The therapists, in their genuinely affimative stances, are optimistic, acknowledging the patient's assets, aware that masochistic tendencies will depress self-esteem, and assured that life, while offering perpetual frustrations with which the healthy ego must deal, also offers opportunities. Through a capacity for calm affirmation which exists side by side with the capacity to recognize psychological liabilities and make ground for strength, therapists fulfill enabling functions. These, in turn, are processes which are internalized by the patient through observation, identification, and practice. In their enabling role, therapists steer patients towards the possibilities of the future and the gradual separation from the traumas and personal failures incurred in the past. Dynamic psychotherapy is decidedly future-oriented, with insistence that the person build a solid basis, not for future fantasies of escape but for future realities borne of true imagination and unfolding capacities of feelings, ego, and self.

One of the reasons why milder depressions frequently go unnoticed is that the deficit functioning which underlies depressions and which always involves loss, withholding, withdrawal, and passivity proceeds more gradually than defective functioning. The latter occurs in conflict situations and states of distinct ego deficiency, producing glaring failures. Deficit functioning resembles the gradual attrition of the musculature. Defective functioning bears a similarity to the circumstances that underlie an acute infection. The essential help, in the case of deficit functioning, comes from mobilizing the individual so that the psychological processes that constitute life will be resumed. The overt expression of aggression and the practice of every kind of physical activity, walking upright instead of languishing in the horizontal, swinging the arms forward, and the

---

*The word "enabling" as used here is defined in the context and differs fundamentally for the Alcoholics Anonymous use of the term.

like establish a bridge from morbid passivity to activeness. It is possible that for a while the display of deficit functioning represents a protection, a psychological "off limits" sign that warns the world to reduce its demands. But if it is such an individual "warning system" (Tiger, 1979), its functional durability is very limited.

Because all depressed people have experienced deprivation and loss, they feel helpless and hopeless at those points when their condition deteriorates into serious and dangerous inactiveness. It is important in these cases for therapists to evaluate in what measure the willingness to abdicate activeness is the result of losses and deprivations that have not yet been absorbed and countered by broader participation in life, which in many instances has to constitute a shift from the customary social milieu in which the deprivations occurred to new psychological territories. And to what degree is the hopelessness, helplessness, the lapse of participation, and the untamed anger that is harbored in many depressed patients (Glatzer, 1959) a way of rebelling against the inroads made on infantile illusions of omnipotence?

Of course, in many cases these two developments go hand in hand. In some measure, prolonged hopelessness is nearly always aimed at some secondary gains. Many persons attempt through oblique demonstrations of suffering and sadness to get even with the world and to blackmail it into compassion and love. This gets amalgamated with aggression, and the results are nonverbal provocations that not enough solace is offered. The access to passivity is a big gain because it permits a regression to a seemingly comfortable nirvana. The worst danger is that there lurks behind many depressions the idea and practice of "going for broke," which permits irresponsibility and revenge against the adults who demand that the injured individual stand up and be counted like everyone else.

When the entire condition deteriorates into what I have called the depressive plunge, the differentiation is essential between what are the "pure" streaks of sadness and helplessness and what aspects of immobilization stem primarily from narcissistic and masochistic streaks, such as described. Certainly, narcissistic and masochistic proclivities must be reflected back to the patients so that they may understand the nature of the secondary gains they wish to continue. And equally, all the currents which come together in depression, be they pure despair or planned pleas for love and indemnities, must be counteracted.

Whatever the causes, the symptoms are similar. The effectiveness of the senses is reduced to a degree where eventually only few perceptions, and fuzzy ones at that, are made. The sectors of interest are narrowed so that we note a person who used to read every section of the newspaper now skimming one or another segment. Instead of object relations, there appears more narcissistic self-preoccupation. Avoidances and fears of the world and of people increase to the point where persons in the depressive plunge begin to resemble the individual who approaches a psychotic break. Physical movement and the speaking voice cease to be directed outward towards the world.

Such deficit functioning, frequently indulged in when narcissistic and masochistic inclinations have the upper hand, can reach a danger point at which intervention becomes essential. When the condition threatens to go past the point of no return, that is to say when the self-destructiveness reaches such a degree of intensity and continuity that it appears to become irreversible, the therapist puts at the patient's service his or her own strength and enabling power. It is counterindicated to dwell on past precedents for depressive moods or depressions or, indeed, other historical data and reminiscences. Instead, processes which are far healthier than the multifaceted withdrawal and dormant aggression which the patients have fallen back on have to be resuscitated; the entire psyche and body have to be mobilized. A state of alert which gradually becomes permanent has to take the place of the apathy that has come to prevail. What patients need to hear (despite initial denials) are clearly articulated messages that address themselves to dormant capacities: "You can do it . . . You are able to . . . Start now, from this moment on . . . Use your strength . . . Fight and fight openly." These are some of the appropriate messages from the therapist.

Hanna, who had been left a number of times by her lover of seven years, who had promised to marry her, was deeply depressed when the man left her again, seemingly for good, after a year of therapy during which she had begun to comprehend her masochism, her narcissism, and the scope of her sense of defeat. Referring to a series of phone calls which her lover had made the night before, Hanna remarked reluctantly that she wanted him to see her tear-stained, agonized face. She was aware how much she wanted to make the man feel guilty, what a large role the implanting of guilt had played in her frequent resumptions of the relationship, and to what degree her sad and helpless feelings reflected her dependence on an obviously unstable man. Hanna had come to realize that a reliance on her own worth, sense of adventure, and self-respect needed to replace the depressive plunges which often rendered her unable to work properly for weeks and months. After listening for a while both to Hanna's pain and her wish to make the lover feel guilty, I said firmly: "The tears do not help you. You said he cannot commit himself to one woman, even you. But you can manage on your own. You can." The patient's face lit up under her tears when these references to her strength were made. "Tell me that again and again and again, that I can, that I am able," she said.

To halt and roll back the advance of passivity, masochistic self-draining and regression which are the forerunners and companions of depression, many kinds of cognitive-emotional activeness are encouraged. Patients are asked to express rather than hold back specific and pointed questions that refer to things, events, or people. These questions are answered, a practice designed to keep interest in the world flowing and draw attention to the psychological life of others and to outside reality. The movement is away from the fantasies and avoidances that were and are being used to sustain a passive state. It is pointed out that the person is not as weak as he or she feels and that the ego can take self-protective measures. In other words, a philosophy of self-help is implicit in many of the therapeutic communications which spell out the notion: "You can do for yourself; you can give up the passive longing to be taken care of; you can part with passive processes."

Nora, a woman who was depressed off and on throughout her life, began to recognize the existence and causes of her depressive condition, previously glamorized as unwilled, determined by fate, and infinitely sad, like the leitmotif of a Russian novel. She also had come to understand how her own masochism, namely her wish to blame and destroy her critical mother, had accelerated a process for which she was in no way responsible at first, since Nora was born into a pathological and poverty-stricken environment. The patient put it like this: "I have allowed all this stuff to come over me. I make myself feel as though it was legionnaire's disease penetrating every pore of my body in its quiet way. It is not that way at all. I am just lazy and reluctant to fight my depressions, especially since they have got better with therapy. But I am not 28 anymore, and no one loves my 'Lady of the Camellias' nor wants to pull me out of the day-in, day-out lows. You say I can stand up, I can find my strength, I can take aim and reach a goal. Of course, I can reach out for new ways of functioning and I will. I suspect that, like my own mother, I spread this depressive atmosphere around me without other people knowing it. I was just about to do it again and tell you that you don't have to treat such a burden as I am. But that is a lie. I know you don't plan to give up, and I won't feed my disaster spirit."

Another woman, Priscilla, who was in combined individual and group therapy, had been encouraged to stretch and try for straight activeness and remain aware that there is always some process that can be mobilized to counter despair and helplessness. One evening, just before her group was to start, she grabbed her chair and moved away from a male group member, giving him a dirty look as she sat down at a distance. She remarked: "I need to sit six feet away from Lou or *I will catch it,*" referring to his depression and passivity. "I have discovered how susceptible I am and that I must find my own direction, starting with where I sit or walk. I hate to do this to Lou, but I have a stake in climbing out of the slump. I pick my classical music records more carefully; I don't just put anything on the turntable that comes handy. I will be more deliberate until I can afford to be more spontaneous." A little later Priscilla suggested to Lou, who had stopped talking when interrupted, that he stop sulking and despairing. "It will catch up with you before you know it," she remarked, "and you will sink again into the slump in which you were a month ago. You better watch out for every inch you give in."

Instead of giving in to the depressive plunge, patients may engage in active self-assertion once they become aware of its forerunners, namely feelings of sadness and weakness which gradually become flatter. People can fight back at unjust persons and acts and against internalized images and voices that are critical, accusatory, and domineering. They can search for and use processes other than

passivity, submission, reproach, and self-pity. Searching for and expressing an opinion that diverges from the majority on even such
minimal issues as how to dress for bad weather or what plans to
make for free time, making efforts at perceptual reliability rather
than giving way to fantasy, initiating contacts, however brief, and
the deliberate uncovering and use of aggression, all these processes
are preferable to passivity.

In attemping to alert individuals to the all-important turn from
submission to overt expression of self-assertion or aggression, I seize
every possible opportunity to encourage patients to challenge me in
the therapeutic situation. At times I illustrate the nature of the essential turn from submission to assertion with the following small
episode which concerns a little girl. She was the youngest child in a
vociferous family to whom she gave in too often. One time too many
the grandmother said to the little girl who stood in front of the win-
dow, "Go away." The child, about to obey the command, stopped
herself in the middle of the body turn she was about to make, wrin-
kled her forehead, and replied, "*You* dow away [go away]." Nearly
everyone likes this little incident because it well illustrates the turn
away from all that ends eventually in sulking, slump, passivity,
pain, and plunge into depression. Turning about, fighting back, expressing the unconventional, no matter how tiny are the doses, can
be enormously effective. Such actions need not make for corpses
strewn alongside the road to health, after aggression has been tamed
and converted into energy.

When they have allowed themselves to be pulled into the
depressive slump from which they do not know how to escape, patients profit from the therapeutic reminder that the ego and the body
form a partnership (Lowen, 1969) and that as the ego influences the
body, so the body can have an impact on the ego. If the body recap-
tures a state of physical alertness, then this will carry over to the ego.
For therapists, this means being attuned to the language of the body,
namely the significance and emotional consequences of body
postures and movements. It can be pointed out what movements
assist and which ones decrease the depression-oriented use of the
body and which promote alertness. The two-way principle always
holds: If the individual acquires practical, physical capacities, they
have a positive influence on internal psychological power, which, in

turn, benefits the practical, physical skills. Indeed, it is often necessary to require that patients adopt the postures which favor alertness and the return of strength. Sitting, especially sitting tall, promotes alertness; lying down gives more leeway to depression. Walking, forward swings of the arms, and laughter move the person towards alertness.

Certain physiological changes which help to reestablish the alert condition, interestingly enough, resemble the somatic transformations occurring when anger is expressed overtly rather than remaining repressed. The blood vessels expand, the pupils dilate, facilitating better lateral vision and thus a wider view, more adrenalin pours into the system, and breathing becomes deeper (Burn, 1963). Such changes in the direction of activeness come about because emotional, cognitive, and physical attitudes are encouraged to resuscitate patients and make them amenable, once more, to the therapeutic dialogue and interaction. The stances that are called forth are not artificial, though they are summoned selectively and actively by the therapist.

The language used to describe depression calls forth visions of water, waves, overwhelming currents, and *drowning*. The words that spring to mind to characterize rescue from depression connect with successful fight against going under. One speaks of waves of depression coming over a person and of drowning in misery; by contrast, one keeps one's head above water, stays on top, doesn't go under. The images used to describe depressive moods and rescue from depression illuminate what is happening to a patient and show that the prototype for ego loss, which is prevalent in depression, is the fear of drowning. Against such images we can mobilize images of motion, kicking, and pushing away the water with the arms so that one may move forward, which in psychological terms means to leave behind the past and the primitive processes identified with it. One now works on summoning new processes and looking towards the future. To aid the fight against depression, therapists wear two hats: one as the object of old transferences, in the form of reproaches and accusations, and the other as an active member of the two-member fighting team—the patient and the therapist—that goes for confrontation, fighting back, and self-assertion instead of masochistic self-weakening.

THE THERAPIST AS A NEW HUMAN OBJECT

The many ways in which personality development is influenced by the object relations established with the parents (especially the mother) and other family figures highlight the fact that the individual person is not a closed system but in large measure the product of interchanges between self and environment from the earliest age. This leads to the premise that distortions, arrests, or gaps are correctible and subject to change, provided we can discover and utilize the proper parameters.

One principle of change is the idea that the previously malformed, arrested, incomplete, and weak ego becomes ready for new growth through exposure to nonintrusive, encouraging, and indeed ego-nourishing new objects. New objects—and new situations and challenges as well—are capable of setting off interaction processes that spur the ego on to discover heretofore hidden emotions and psychological capacities, to turn the individual around so that he or she moves toward the world instead of withdrawing from it, and to try out new forms of psychological integration. Having made a reacquaintance with the person as an open system—after all, such openness was taken for granted when Freud spoke of external overstimulation as the prototype of trauma—the importance of novel objects is recognized and the importance of the therapist as a primary new object is understood. As has been said, "The resumption of ego development is contingent on the relationship with a new object, the analyst" (Loewald, 1960).

The therapist does not remain a neutral figure, but makes himself or herself available for the gradual development of a new object relationship, notwithstanding the patient's attempts to convert the new interactions into facsimiles of old ones (in other words, transferences). In order to keep the relationship with the patient on a forward path, therapists adhere to various principles. To support the patient during treatment which is painful as well as exhilarating, the therapist forms the so-called working or therapeutic alliance (Zetzel, 1970; Greenson, 1967) with the observing, reasonable, recovery-bound part of the patient's ego. This makes it ever clearer that patient and therapist are collaborators in the work to be accomplished. Thus it becomes more difficult for patients to regard the therapist transferentially as an authoritarian figure, to forget that it is they who have hired the therapist to help them grow, to fall back on the idea that the therapist is a parental figure who will throw them out or otherwise punish them should they express disagreement and anger in the new relationship, which has been described to them as one in which they are free to tell what is on their mind.

We need to be aware of many past experiences patients have had in order to comprehend certain present-day motivations and the essence of seemingly unwarranted but self-perpetuating fears, and the special significance that certain dangers hold. While one individual, for instance, fears success because it signifies the likelihood of friction with a formerly envious and competitive parent, other persons might shun the limelight because, remembering how easily they could capture attention, they believe that they can win but never hold on to conspicuous status since theirs is a win-fast strategy which has only a brief life-span. But essentially, while therapists rely on some detailed information about the past, they are really mediators of a more fulfilled and happier future. The familiarity with the past, which need by no means occupy the extensive role assigned to it by traditional psychoanalysis, does not in itself make for a remedial impact but constitutes merely a means to understand the flaws in the present-day psychological machinery which the patient not only uses but will continue to use unless profound corrections are made.

It is remarkable how readily disturbed persons make new situations into old ones by means of the transferences and how much they are welded to the past. It is this past which has created pain and unhappiness, since psychological disturbance is defined as the result of destructive interactions between an individual and his or her early environment. Patients act as though it is the way of the world to perpetuate old pains. This happens only too often in psychotherapy after a honeymoon during which the patient considered the therapist as a miracle worker who could fix the world, and during which manic, unrealistic feelings of hope predominated. One could say that the more intense the honeymoon interlude and the supra-good feelings, the deeper the slide into feelings of despair, fear, and the sense of personal captivity. Of course, the close correlation between such elation and despair is expectable if we consider that the rescue which the patient has envisaged has been based entirely on the notion that the problems of living would disappear if only the right person came along. The truth, as has to be pointed out to every patient, is that the only way to lighten the problems is to accept them as part of human existence and to raise the psyche to a level where it deals with them more effectively.

Therapists help a great deal if, through interpretations and behavior, they avoid becoming overestimated and idealized persons or accepting other old roles. Rather they are helping patients see them as new objects. This means not only to interpret the shape which the false connections, that is to say the transferences, take but also to highlight occasions on which new situations can be planned or envisaged and new object relations can be undertaken with someone who will not get lost in the obscurities of the past. Transferences are essentially false connections (Freud, 1959a) made between present events and a present figure and old events and old figures. Such false connections make life dull, since little that is new happens, at least not in the important realm of human interactions. False connections and carryovers prevent the imagination from taking over and lead to pessimism.

The disturbed individual who makes the false connections acts as though he had old agenda on his mind that need to be repeatedly gone over. What is more, the old agenda often consists of grievances that could have been put aside. As it is, the person acts as though old wars had to be fought again and with antiquated weapons at that. One is reminded of the French and their Maginot Line, built after the First World War. By relying on the Maginot Line, which was designed to win the lost artillery attacks of the First World War, the French remained blind to the possibilities of the next armed clash fought with new airborne weapons and tactics against which the Maginot Line was useless. The old circumstances had been reviewed too much and too exclusively while the new ones were not considered and evaluated.

Indeed, the Maginot Line comparison leads to another point. False connections between past and present not only lead to a special kind of blinding, but they also prepare the individual too frequently for the eventuality of war rather than peace. Disturbed people, in paying too much attention to the past and keeping it foremost in their minds, gravitate to the expectation of frustrations which, after all, were regular occurrences in their misguided youth. They do not show themselves sufficiently receptive to understanding, facilitation, accomplishment, and fulfillment. By focusing on the object relations of the past and perpetuating them, no matter what opportunities the present may offer, the person sets up the circumstances before him in such a way that habitual failures will recur; there will never be a bare table, ready to be set for new feasts. In the midst of false connections and preoccupations with transferences, the therapist must remember that primary growth comes about when patients discover repeatedly that the therapist is a new object who calls for new ways of relating and is willing to give the patient chances to be himself or herself in more spontaneous ways than before. One means of conveying the newness is spontaneous and accepting behavior on the part of the therapist.

When Hilda came to treatment, upon the advice of a supervisor whom she partly admired for her competence and partly feared and envied, she tended to speak of the affection felt for the therapist. This was during the honeymoon period. "I like to wait in your office," the patient remarked, "because your plants and paintings give me a sense of peace and the noises in my head stop." When I suggested, prior to the summer holidays which were going to be particularly long, that Hilda come for an extra session, she missed the next meeting, calling to say that she had mistakenly set her clock to wake her up at the wrong time. When she did arrive the next time, she avoided looking at me and said she was angry. "It seems you forced me to come, just as mother always forced and manipulated me," she said. When I nodded agreement, the patient's demeanor cleared up like a spring day. "Thanks for not defending yourself," she stated. "I knew I was laying something on you. I want to change and move along, and yet I want to hang on to my 'beloved misperceptions.' If I close my eyes just a bit I can see how tempted I am to go the old ways."

In this case, the patient, more aware than many other people who claim that they wish to change, got hold of a glimpse of transference insistence and resistance. She also made an interesting discovery, namely that she wished to perceive the therapist in the old image of the mother so as to allow herself to continue in the climate of her beloved misperceptions.

To dissolve transferences and with them the false connections between the old objects and a new one, we can use, among other methods, two lines of questioning. One revolves around the question *why*, though "why" queries can take any number of forms, not necessarily introduced by the actual word "why." When we ask patients why they perceive us as relatively unaltered editions of former parental or familial figures, they tend first of all to come up with historical answers which are not among the most dynamic data. Secondly, they are inclined, usually in quite unconscious ways, to reinforce the idea that something is the way it is by casting about for explanations for the "why." This works against wellness, which in this connection means newness, rather than working for wellness. The results are quite different when we ask the question, *"Why not?"* Such "why not" queries start individuals on fresh routes. When people wonder why they do not initiate courses of action that are entirely different from the ones usually pursued, their imagination begins to work and they envisage and begin to explore possibilities that had been ignored.

Ormond, a bright, artistic and educated man in his late forties, had been told by his late father that he was a playboy and ne'er-do-well who did not know the value or ways of hard work and would undoubtedly end up in the gutter after the father's death. This prediction, which was more like a curse uttered by a father considerably less talented and attractive than the son, never left the patient's mind. It reduced his occupational successes inasmuch as he quickly despaired and gave up on some initiative or idea which, as it turned out later, did well in the hands of others in whom he had confided. The father's dire prediction also colored business relationships because this man quickly became evasive, unsure, or else too overbearing when he detected disapproval of a paternal kind on the faces of senior members of the business community in which he worked.

In the course of treating Ormond, who appeared talented and had economic and financial expertise, I often introduced the question, "Why not," which was both startling and encouraging to him. Once when he mentioned that he contemplated working as a singing waiter in a California restaurant, I remarked: "That could be an interesting and new experience for a few months. But as to a special restaurant, why not start and own one yourself? You've been interested for a long time." Ormond replied to my surprise: "Exactly. Why not? I am a hard worker and have many ideas, you know." And several weeks later the patient remarked: "I have thought about your why not inquiries. They make sense. There is no reason why I can't hack it."

A number of therapists, and group therapists in particular, believe in "therapist transparency," that is, a readiness on the part of the therapist to disclose, emphasize, and highlight the person he or she is (Yalom, 1975). This direct method of achieving the status of new object certainly deserves to be considered by all those who do not believe that a transference neurosis, induced by the therapist who insists on remaining a silent screen, makes an essential contribution to recovery.

A good relationship on the part of the therapist overlaps partly with the therapeutic or working alliance but goes beyond it. It consists of acceptance, a term used frequently in this connection, and especially of *flexible* acceptance, which is a form of therapeutic love. It differs from detachment, criticism, and rejection and contrasts sharply with indiscriminate, sentimental, indulgent protectionism, which does not deserve to be called love, either in daily life or in psychotherapy. Therapeutic and flexible acceptance offers discriminating understanding through both intuition and cognition of the respective patient's developmental needs. The accepting therapist grasps that the person still enclosed in narcissistic inaccessibility needs to find his or her idiosyncratically expressed needs to be recognized and requires a certain form of emotional partnering, as described earlier in this chapter. Therapeutic acceptance offers a certain soothing to individuals who have been deprived of completed symbiosis; it supports even as it interprets the rebelliousness of patients who have not completed their individuation; and it furnishes outer controls to those who have none until they have grasped how to exercise various forms of self-control. In no way does acceptance mean indulgence. Rather, it signifies a temporary willingness to fill ego gaps while patients prepare to discover the ways and means of completing their own ego structures.

Some people have a particular skill to "enable" other persons. They know, through a combination of empathy and thoughtfulness, just what words and ideas will help others to get into stronger, clearer, more optimistic frames of mind. They exhibit a directedness, clarity, and integratedness which, through varying processes of identification, seep into their human surroundings and enable them to muster greater stamina. There emanate from them energies that help those who are in touch with them to pursue the very routes leading to the goals on which they have their sights set. To call these "enabling" personalities charismatic does not do justice to the endowment they have, for many a charismatic leader actually inspires other people to pursue the ends which the leader has in mind and thus to forego evolving their own identity. One can find this ability to "enable" in certain parents who successfully encourage their own and other people's children to "keep trying." Therapists who lend patients energies until the latter can find their own resources make personal contributions to recovery without becoming intrusive.

REACTIVE FLEXIBILITY CREATES A CLIMATE OF GROWTH

Dynamically-oriented therapists usually do not *act* on the needs that are repressed or articulated but convey in a simple yet convincing manner that the directions of belated satisfaction and growth for which patients struggle as adults, albeit in defensive and roundabout ways, are understood. Therapists are willing to aid growth, not through palpable deeds but through appropriate reactions, interactions, and interchanges. Relations with patients are handled in such ways that the feelings, thoughts, and interactions conveyed become nutrients (Piaget, 1952) of emotional-cognitive and even physical structures and functions which had been stunted during the original dealings between the young organisms and parental environment. The therapist does not belatedly become a replacement for a mother, father, or sibling. Rather it is possible, indeed imperative, to become a friendly, steadfast, and at times insistent agent of growth. Conflicts are solved and development is completed belatedly because of access to a growth-promoting climate.

As described earlier in this chapter, persons still stuck within the confines of the narcissistic cocoon need the emotional attention which helps them venture into explorations of mutuality. Somewhat similarly, people who were deprived of adequate symbiosis and whose unstilled hunger produces tension, displeasure, and restlessness require the experience of a soothing therapeutic climate in order to summon sufficient energy to alter primitive structures (Winnicott, 1965). Those who were symbiotically overindulged learn, by contrast, to acquire self-disciplining functions and firm up the boundaries separating self from environment if their masochistic complaints and reproaches are countered with therapeutic firmness. In order for change processes to succeed, the emotional and personal participation of the therapist is a sine qua non. To offer the participation that will have a healing effect on pathology, therapists need not (and must not) play artificial roles, apply stage directions in their offices, or make themselves over for different patients. Quite to the contrary, the chief requirements have to do with human qualities that are associated with high levels of personal maturity: an unnarcissistic ability to listen to the other person (Langs, 1977), an absence of defensiveness and presence of spontaneity, assertiveness rather than primitive aggression, a genuine self, an ability to love, and other humanistic assets which are achieved or reinforced through successful personal psychotherapy.

Therapist and patient in effective treatment become a working team which understands how to weave the reparatory reactions of the therapist and the sound growth and behavior of the patient into the whole cloth of health. The therapist's participation in the treatment process, though unforced and genuine, is undertaken on behalf of patients and their longstanding developmental and present needs with which the therapist interlaces. This does not call for unvarying gratification but for a wide range of interactions, offered so as to make more convincing the case that it is safe to keep the system open and to interact with the environment. Though chance encounters, especially with everyday peers, often make similar realizations possible, they do not necessarily have a therapeutic effect. They tend to be seen as the result of special arrangements with a select peer segment or as the result of chance circumstances; they are not included in a systematic and long-range reexamination and reevaluation of the world, as is the case in therapy.

To give an example of a therapeutic reaction borne of intuitive understanding and of dynamic knowledge on the part of the therapist, let us look at passive hostility or excessive rebelliousness, two attitudes that are due to incomplete separation-individuation processes. Therapists who wish to convey understanding and believe that their own responses serve this purpose will communicate through their behavior that it is safe for the patients to express opposition directly rather than through channels of subversive nonaction, that is, passive hostility or protracted non-participation. The patients, in turn, realize that incessant negativism is unnecessary since their refusals as well as demands have a chance to be understood in the treatment situation as an expression of a need for independence. Interpretations given after such reparative and understanding responses have occurred a number of times have an excellent chance of clicking since resistance has been practically removed.

Fritz, a man in his mid-thirties, was a failure in virtually all respects, largely on account of the hostile passivity that held him back on many fronts. A teacher in a private school, he did not get student evaluations in on time. A procrastinator par excellence, his mail remained unanswered in a heap atop the kitchen table; bills were not paid on time. Of course, he was always late for his dates and, once he started therapy, for his sessions. I countered the regular latenesses of Fritz with reaction flexibility, that is to say, I responded in a way that lightened his pathology and eventually made it superfluous vis-à-vis me and others. With whatever delay Fritz arrived, I greeted him in a friendly way and did not inquire as to what made him late. Nevertheless, he always apologized, to which I responded that it was not necessary to give an explanation or excuse since I was aware that it was important for him to pick his own time without a sense of pressure and "shoulds." This was not said facetiously but because I realized how much this man, the son of a disciplinarian German father and a puritanical New England mother, had been subjected to outside "musts," "ought tos," and punishments for any infringement. I assumed that given the conviction that in personal matters he could indeed make decisions according to his own preferences, the grip of the only form of rebellion and self-assertion he knew, namely hostile passivity, would lessen. Reactions of this reparatory kind did indeed make the patient amenable to the idea that he could make various choices. They allowed Fritz to listen receptively to interpretations which are by necessity more abstract but drew his attention to alternative internal psychological solutions as far as asserting his will was concerned.

THE NEED FOR VALIDATION

Treatment offers an excellent opportunity to liberate people from the confusion and restlessness which the environment, particularly the early environment, caused whenever the perceptions of the offspring conflicted with the subjective needs of parents. Many persons are thrust into self-doubt and feel compelled to repress or make a secret of perceptions and emotions because from early on these were censored either by the external world or by inner loyalties towards primary figures whose shortcomings the child perceived. When the personal reactions and statements of the therapist acknowledge and in one way or another confirm intrapsychic processes which the patient has been compelled to pursue although validation was not forthcoming, considerable relief sets in. The division is finally laid to rest between those emotions, perceptions, and thoughts the patient registers intrapsychically and the ones which the external world confirms as actually occurring. Few conflicts are as severe as the cleft between what and how the individual feels and thinks and what and how the world demands that he feel and think.

The breach between the occurring inner processes and the outwardly acknowledged and/or demanded processes is among the most severe causes of psychological stress and constitutes the severe pains resulting from double-bind situations (Berger, 1978). It is the most current schizophrenic-like experience which neurotic people can commonly have. Whenever the dilemma between inner reality and outer validation takes place, disturbed personalities who function relatively well lose the ability to make decisions, feel dizzy, deeply dejected, and have experiences of unreality much as schizophrenics undergo regularly.

The patient, Lewis, who underwent psychotherapy when his youngest son was put on probation for sociopathic behavior, was devastated when the young woman he hoped to make his third wife rejected him. Before she left, she told Lewis that he did to her what he did to himself. He would spend hours trying to argue her out of her feelings. Lewis, wiping away his tears, stated: "I do to her what my narcissistic mother always did to me. She could not conceive of any feelings other than her own. I want to hit my head to get it straight that if people have a feeling, I've got to let them feel their feelings. Here in therapy I am learning to be affectionate about my own point of view, at least to start that way, before I make the corrections. People don't have to talk about their feelings if they don't want to, but I have to allow them to know what they feel. If I can be affectionate about my own stuff, that is a place to start accepting others. Any official truth is nonsense. I minded being told what I think and feel. I am getting fiercely territorial about that. So let others be that way."

Understanding what it is that patients experience, grasping the idiosyncratic forms and makings of their perceptions, and following their own causal connections offer prime reparatory experiences. The task of making these possible precedes and supersedes other therapeutic tasks such as, for instance, interpretations. Only by being understood and recognized do we obtain affirmation of the solidity and truth of our existence. Only when analysands have become convinced that their emotional life is understood, albeit with their own help by reporting feelings, doubts, fantasies, can they profit from interpretations. First and foremost, the full understanding by the therapist, gradual though it may be, is of primary importance.

The therapist's understanding, when interpretations are eventually made, differs from the immediate world's capacity to acknowledge an experience. The therapist needs to react with full awareness of the special secret place which many desires occupy in the emotional register of the patient. Many fantasies are the present-day remnants of primitive world models (Bion, 1962) formed in childhood to understand the world in terms of the child's own experience. Thus, unrealistic, so-called irrational behavior and assumptions are necessary until the fantasies become shared.

The patient, Francesca, desired her boyfriend sexually but had many fights with him—much against her will, so it seemed. She was critical of his ideas, distrusted his ability to make a living, and humiliated him frequently on social occasions. After having listened to various accounts of her quarrels with her boyfriend and her guilt about them, I asked Francesca whether, though she found her male friend sexually attractive, she had low regard for his brains and even his common sense. With great relief, the patient readily stated that she considered Robert inferior to her intellectually and that she kept this thought to herself. She then recalled how terrifying her experiences with her father had been, who was an uneducated, severely neurotic man who acted dumb either for these reasons or because his intelligence was indeed limited.

Francesca had been a precocious little girl and disagreed with her father regularly at the dinner table. She had been unable at that time to comprehend why she was smacked in the face several times at every meal. My question as to how she felt about the boyfriend's intelligence had suddenly illuminated for her an obscure picture and furnished the connections. Francesca's father, so the patient put it, had been unable to take the continuous disagreements which stemmed from the little girl's superior wits. Ever since, it had been essential for her to achieve validation of the accuracy of her own observations by showing up any man who was more or less intelligent than she. While the boyfriend had superior qualities as a human being—for he was courageous, kind, and extremely humorous—she had felt compelled to validate her observation that he was intellectually inferior to her in the incessant quarrels.

After Francesca had told her story, I asked her whether my own obvious belief that she possessed superior intelligence could fulfill her need for intellectual validation and help her dispense with competitive quarrels. She felt that the chances for more conciliatory relations were good, and this, indeed, turned out to be true. Francesca was being validated by the therapist, of whose intelligence she also had occasional doubts, and thus a conflict that had alienated her from many persons came to rest.

Because the lives of many disturbed persons are characterized by a lack of exchange with the world, so that the person lives as a closed rather than an open system, treatment must help to articulate urges and even the forerunners of urges that have not congealed into definite form and are not being expressed. Such needs must be recognized by the mother during the early years and in the case of treatment the therapist becomes not only a mediator but an articulator as well. Many narcissistic persons need such articulation, particularly since they live in a state of isolation.

A spectacularly narcissistic and needful person, Alex, well into the second year of treatment, did not know when he was hungry. Often, he walked about with intense stomach pains as a result of hunger feelings that remained unidentified. When it was recognized in therapy that, contrary to his usual custom, he began to say "no" to questions and suggestions, it was apparent that such feelings of intense negativism followed on the heels of oral hunger that remained totally unconscious. Alex was awed by the discovery that the state of hunger could be understood intuitively and also be deduced from his behavior, yet bitter that nobody had previously been aware of his want for food. Subsequently, Alex was willing to identify situations in which he either did or did not want something. It was through the experience of being understood plus a deductive kind of reasoning that he, himself, gradually consented to become the custodian of his own urges.

Persons whose ego and self have been stunted and twisted by developmental lag and who built defensive structures to conceal their psychological shortcomings and pains take their defenses rather than their self and their basic needs to be the nucleus of their existence. When the therapist similarly fails to distinguish between needs and wounds on the one hand and defenses on the other, the treatment results are negative. Many interactions between patient and therapist become fruitful when the therapist, distinguishing between defensive structures and need structures, makes it clear that he or she is the ally of the need structures. At crucial points where acknowledgment of the needs is lacking and the defenses are given primary weight or else mistaken for the real self, a confusion that occurs only too readily, the treatment is defeated from the very beginning.

A mild-mannered, seemingly shy patient reproached the therapist for paying too little attention to his timidity. Whenever it was pointed out that he had fierce emotional undercurrents that testified to his high energy level, he ignored such statements. But when, on one occasion, the therapist made the error of listening too long to the man's pitiful account of his childlike feelings, the patient bristled: "You are making an error if you take my childish side seriously. I do not need you for compassion. My modesty is a put on. What is the matter with you today?"

Every change in structure and functioning is the result of combinations between interventions made on behalf of the deepest needs and other interventions designed to unseat the defensive strategies which we consider as a rule less deep, though they are an integral part of the personality. When therapists attempt to alter the defense structure, they are readily experienced as intruders. When reactions to the needs, the desires, and the deepest energies are articulated, the picture of the therapist as an ally becomes strengthened. A treatment that does not loosen defenses is considered by the analysand as ineffective; one that focuses only on the needs is seen as sentimental. The optimal approach is one in which alternately and in some rhythm dictated by the pathology both pedals are worked in a harmony that permits progress. The threat of undergoing wrenching change which eventually unites analysands with their deepest potential and the "power of their inner truth" (Mahrer, 1978) is rendered less frightening when defenses are reduced through exposure to the therapist's reactive flexibility. At the same time such reactive flexibility broadens vistas so that analysands may see the many potential ways in which their needs and their true self can be expressed.

References

Abrams, Samuel. The Teaching and Learning of Psychoanalytic Developmental Psychology. *Journal of the American Psychoanalytic Association,* 26(2):387-406, 1978.

Alexander, F. and French, T. *Psychoanalytic Psychotherapy.* New York: Ronald Press, 1946.

Alport, A. and Bernstein, I. Reversability of Pathological Fixation Associated with Maternal Deprivation in Infancy. *The Psychoanalytic Study of the Child,* 14:169-185. New York: International Universities Press, 1959.

Angyal, Andras. *Neurosis and Treatment, A Holistic Theory.* New York: The Viking Press, 1973.

Arieti, Silvano. *On Schizophrenia, Phobias, Depression, Psychotherapy and the Farther Shores of Psychiatry.* New York: Brunner/Mazel, 1978.

Arlow, Jacob A. and Brenner, Charles. *Psychoanalytic Concepts and Structural Theory.* New York: International Universities Press, 1964.

Bateson, Gregory. *Naven.* Palo Alto: Stanford University Press, 1958.

Bateson, Gregory. *Steps to an Ecology of the Mind.* New York: Ballantine Publications, 1972.

Bateson, Gregory. The Birth of a Matrix or Double Bind and Epistemology. In: *Beyond the Double Bind,* Milton M. Berger, ed. New York: Brunner/Mazel, 1978.

Berger, Milton M., ed. *Beyond The Double Bind.* New York: Brunner/Mazel, 1978.

Bertalanffy, Ludwig von. *General Systems Theory.* New York: Braziller, 1968.

Bibring, E. Symposium on the Theory of the Therapeutic Results of Psychoanalysis. *International Journal of Psychoanalysis,* 18(2):170-189, 1937.

Bion, W.R. *Learning from Experience.* New York: Basic Books, 1962.

Bion, W.R. *Transformations.* London: William Heineman, Ltd., 1965.

Blanck, G. and Blanck, R. Transference Object and Real Object. *International Journal of Psychoanalysis,* 58:33-43, 1977.

Bowlby, John. The Making and Breaking of Affectionate Bonds. *British Journal of Psychiatry,* 1970, p. 130 ff.

Bowlby, John. *Separation: Anxiety and Anger*. London: Hogarth Press, 1973.

Brenner, Charles, *Psychoanalytic Technic and Psychic Conflict*. New York: International Universities Press, 1976.

Burn, Harold J. *The Automatic Nervous System*. Oxford: Blackwell, 1963.

Dewald, P.A. Transference Regression and Real Experience. *Psychoanalytic Quarterly*, 45:213-230, 1976.

Du Plexis Gray, Francine. A New Kind of Freedom for Women. *Vogue Magazine*, August, 1978.

Fairbairn, Ronald D.W. *Psychoanalytic Studies of the Personality*. London: A Tavistock Publication, 1952.

Farber, Leslie. *The Ways of the Will*. New York: Basic Books, 1966.

Fenichel, Otto. Early Stages of Ego Development. *Collected Papers*, Vol. II. New York: W.W. Norton & Co., 1954, pp. 25-49.

Fenichel, Otto. Psychoanalysis of Character. *The Collected Papers of Otto Fenichel*, Series II. New York: W.W. Norton & Co., 1954, pp. 198-215.

Fenichel, Otto. *Collected Papers*, No. 2. London: Routledge & Kegan Paul, 1955.

Freud, Anna. A Connection Between the States of Negativism and of Emotional Surrender. Abstract. *International Journal of Psychoanalysis*, 33:265, 1952.

Freud, Sigmund. The Aetiology of Hysteria. *Collected Papers*, Vol. I. New York: Basic Books, Inc., 1959a.

Freud, Sigmund. The Dynamics of the Transference. *Collected Papers*, Vol. II. New York: Basic Books, Inc., 1959b.

Freud, S. Further Recommendations in the Technique of Psychoanalysis. Recollection, Repetition and Working Through, 1914. *Collected Papers*, Vol. II. New York: Basic Books, Inc., 1959c.

Freud, Sigmund. A Case of Paranoia. *Collected Papers*, Vol. III. New York: Basic Books, Inc., 1959d.

Freud, Sigmund. On Narcissism, An Introduction, 1914. *Collected Papers*, Vol. IV. New York: Basic Books, Inc., 1959e.

Freud, S. The Ego and The Id, *The Complete Psychological Works of Sigmund Freud*, Vol. I. London: Hogarth Press, 1961.

Freud, Sigmund. *Three Essays on the Theory of Sexuality*, rev. ed. London: Hogarth Press, 1962.

Freud, S. with Breuer, Joseph. On the Psychical Mechanism of Hysterical Phenomena. *Collected Papers*, Vol. 1. New York: Basic Books, Inc., 1959.

Fried, Edrita. Rate and Circumstances of Change in Psychotherapy. *American Journal of Psychotherapy*, 6(2):279-293, 1952.

Fried, Edrita. Self-Induced Failure, a Mechanism of Defense. *Psychoanalytic Review*, 41(4):330-339, 1954.

Fried, Edrita. Ego Functions and Techniques of Ego Strengthening. *American Journal of Psychotherapy*, 9(3):407-429, 1955.

Fried, Edrita. Ego-Strengthening Aspects of Hostility. *American Journal of Orthopsychiatry*, 26(1):179-197, 1956.

Fried, Edrita. *The Ego in Love and Sexuality*. Chapter V: Narcissistic Isolation, Quest for Similarity and Self-Repetition. New York: Grune & Stratton, 1960.

Fried, Edrita. Techniques of Psychotherapy Going Beyond Insight. *International Journal of Group Psychotherapy*, 11(3):297-304, 1961.

Fried, Edrita. Some Aspects of Group Dynamics and the Analysis of Transference and Defenses. *International Journal of Group Psychotherapy*, 15(1):44-56, 1965.

Fried, Edrita. *Active/Passive, the Crucial Psychological Dimension*. New York: Grune & Stratton, 1970.

Glatzer, Henriette. Clinical Aspects of Adult Therapy, Notes on the Preoedipal Fantasy. *American Journal of Orthopsychiatry*, 29(2):383-390, 1959.

Goulding, Robert and Goulding, Mary. *Changing Lives through Redecision Therapy*. New York: Brunner/Mazel, 1979.

Greenson, Ralph R. *The Technique and Practice of Psychoanalysis*. New York: International Universities Press, 1967.

Guntrip, Harry. Clinical Studies. In: *Psychiatry*, H.S. Terry, M.L. Gavel, and M. Gibbon, eds. New York: W.W. Norton, 1956.

Guntrip, Harry. *Schizoid Phenomena, Object Relations and the Self*. New York: International Universities Press, 1969.

Hall, Edward T. *Beyond Culture*. Garden City, N.Y.: Anchor Press, 1977.

Hartocollis, Peter. Origins of Time. *Psychoanalytic Quarterly*, 43(2):243-261, 1974.

Hartmann, Heinz. *Ego Psychology and The Problem of Adaptation*. New York: International Universities Press, Inc., 1958.

Hoffer, W. Transference and Transference Neurosis. *International Journal of Psychoanalysis*, 37:377, 1956.

Horney, Karen. *New Ways in Psychoanalysis*. New York: W.W. Norton & Co., 1939.

Howard, Jane. *Families*. New York: Simon & Schuster, 1978.

Jacobson, Edith. *The Self and The Object World*. New York: International Universities Press, 1964.

Jung, Carl G. On the Nature of Dreams. *The Collected Works of C.G. Jung*. London: Routledge and Kegan Paul, Ltd., 1945.

Kauff, Priscilla. The Relationship Between Theoretical Concepts and Technique. *International Journal of Group Psychotherapy*, 29(1):51-65, 1979.

Kernberg, Otto. *Borderline Conditions and Pathological Narcissism*. New York: Jason Aronson, 1976.

Knopf, Olga. *Successful Aging*. Boston: G.K. Hall, 1977.

Kohut, Heinz. *The Restoration of the Self*. New York: International Universities Press, 1977.

Kris, Ernst. *Psychoanalytic Explorations in Art*. New York: International Universities Press, 1952.

Kris, Ernst. The Recovery of Childhood Memories in Psychoanalysis. *The Psychoanalytic Study of the Child*, 11. New York: International Universities Press, 1956.

Kubie, Lawrence. *Neurotic Distortion of the Creative Process*. New York: Noonday, 1958.

Lachman, Frank and Stolorow, Robert. *The Treatment of Developmental Arrest*. New York: International Universities Press, in press.

Langs, Robert. *The Therapeutic Interaction*. New York: Jason Aronson, 1977.

Levenson, Edgar. Psychoanalysis: Cure or Persuasion. *Contemporary Psychoanalysis*, 14(1):1-17, 1978.

Lichtenstein, Heinz. *The Dilemma of Human Identity*. New York: Jason Aronson, 1977.

Lowen, Alexander. *The Betrayal of the Body*. New York: Macmillan Publishing Co., 1969.

Loewald, Hans W. On the Therapeutic Action of Psychoanalysis. *International Journal of Psychoanalysis*, 41:16-33, 1960.

Mahrer, Alvin R. *Experiencing, A Humanistic Theory of Psychology and Psychiatry*. New York: Brunner/Mazel, 1978.

Mahler, Margaret S. *On Human Symbiosis and the Vicissitudes of Individuation*. New York: International Universities Press, 1968.

Martin, Alexander Reid. The Dynamics of Insight. *American Journal of Psychoanalysis*, 12:24-38, 1952.

Masterson, James F. *Psychotherapy of the Borderline Adult*. New York: Brunner/Mazel, 1976.

May, Rollo. *Man's Search for Himself*. New York: W.W. Norton & Co., 1953.

May, Rollo. *Love and Will*. New York: W.W. Norton & Co., 1969.

Menninger, Karl. Hope. *American Journal of Psychiatry*, 116(6):481-491, 1959.

Modell, Arnold. The Holding Environment and the Therapeutic Action of Psychoanalysis *Journal of the American Psychoanalytic Association*, 24(2), 1976.

Nelson, Marie C. Effects of Paradigmatic Technique on the Psychic Economy of the Borderline Patient. *Psychiatry*, 25(2):1962.

Nelson, Marie Coleman et al. *Roles and Paradigms in Psychotherapy*. New York: Grune and Stratton, 1968.

Perls, Fritz. *The Gestalt Approach and Eye Witness to Therapy*. Palo Alto: Science and Behavior Books, 1973.

Piaget, Jean. *The Language and Thought of the Child*. New York: International Universities Press, 1952.

Piaget, Jean. *The Origins of Intelligence in Children*. New York: International Universities Press, 1952.

Piaget, Jean. *The Construction of Reality in the Child*. New York: Basic Books, 1954.

Piaget, Jean. Explanation in Psychology and Psychophysiological Parallelism. In: *Experimental Psychology*, Vol. 1, P. Fraisse and J. Piaget, eds. New York: Basic Books, 1963.

Piaget, Jean. *Structuralism*. New York: Basic Books, Inc., 1970.

Polster, Erving and Polster, Miriam. *Gestalt Therapy Integrated*. New York: Brunner/Mazel, 1973.

Rangell, Leo. Similarities and Differences between Psychoanalysis and Dynamic Psychotherapy. *Journal of the American Psychoanalytic Association*, 2:734-744, 1954.

Rapaport, David. *Collected Papers*, Merton M. Gill, ed. New York: Basic Books, 1967.

Ricoeur, P. *Freedom and Nature: The Voluntary and the Involuntary*. Chicago: Northwestern University Press, 1966.

Riess, Bernard. Family Therapy as Seen by a Group Therapist. *International Journal of Group Psychotherapy*, 26(3):301-310, 1976.

Ritvo, Samuel. Margaret S. Mahler, Scientist, Psychoanalyst, Teacher. In: *Separation and Individuation*, John B. McDevitt and Calvin F. Setlage, eds. New York: International Universities Press, 1971.

Sandler, J., Dare, C. and Holder, A. *The Patient and the Analyst*. New York: International Universities Press, 1973.

Sartre, Jean-Paul. *Existential Analysis*. New York: Philosophical Library, 1953.

Schachtel, Ernst. *Metamorphosis: On the Development of Affect, Perception, Attention, and Memory*. New York: Basic Books, Inc., 1959.

Schafer, Roy. *A New Language for Psychoanalysis*. New Haven: Yale University Press, 1976.

Schafer, Roy. The Interpretation of Transference and the Conditions for Loving. *Journal of the American Psychoanalytic Association*, 25(2):335-362, 1977a.

Schafer, Roy. The Role of Appreciation in the Analytic Attitude: Technical and Theoretical Implications. Presented at the Postgraduate Center for Mental Health, New York City, December 2, 1977b.

Selye, Hans. *Stress Without Distress*. Philadephia: Lippincott, 1974.

Smith, Joseph H. Understanding Human Freedom. *Journal of the American Psychoanalytic Association*, 26(1):1978.

Spitz, Rene. *The First Year of Life*. New York: International Universities Press, 1965.

Spitz, Rene A. Bridges: On Anticipation, Duration and Meaning. *Journal of the American Psychoanalytic Association*, 20:721-735, 1972.

Spotnitz, Hyman. The Need for Insulation in the Schizophrenic Personality. *Psychoanalytic Review*, 49(3):3-25, 1962.

Spotnitz, H. and Meadow, P. *Modern Psychoanalysis of the Schizophrenic Patient*. New York: Grune & Stratton, Inc., 1969.

Spotnitz, Hyman and Meadow, Phyllis W. *Treatment of the Narcissistic Neuroses*. New York: The Manhattan Center for Advanced Psychoanalytic Studies, 1976.

Stolorow, Robert D. The Concept of Psychic Structure: Its Metaphysical and Clinical Psychoanalytic Meanings. *International Review of Psychoanalysis*, 1978.

Sullivan, Harry Stack. *The Contributions of Harry Stack Sullivan*, Patrick Mullahy, ed. New York: Hermitage House, 1952.

Tiger, Lionel. *The Biological Foundation of Hope*. New York: Simon and Schuster, 1979.

Turkle, Sherry. *Freud's French Revolution.* New York: Basic Books, Inc., 1978.

Watzlawick, Paul, Beavin, J.H. and Jackson, Don D. *Pragmatics of Human Communica-tions.* New York: W.W. Norton, 1967.

Winnicott, D.W. *Maturational Process and the Facilitating Environment.* London: Hogarth Press, 1965.

Wolberg, Lewis R. *The Technique of Psychotherapy,* Part II. New York: Grune & Strat-ton, 1967.

Wolpe, Joseph. Behavior Therapy Techniques, in *A Guide to the Treatment of Neuroses* by Joseph Wolpe and Arnold A. Lazarus. New York: Pergamon Press, 1966.

Yalom, Irvin D. *The Theory and Practice of Group Psychotherapy.* New York: Basic Books, Inc., 1975.

Zetzel, Elizabeth. *The Capacity for Emotional Growth.* New York: International Univer-sities Press, 1970.

Index

237